It's Not the Bricks, It's the Mortar

It's Not the
BRICKS,
It's the MORTAR

Optimize Your RETAIL BUSINESS for LASTING SUCCESS

Mike Cosentino

BROWN BOOKS
PUBLISHING GROUP

It's Not the Bricks, It's the Mortar
Optimize Your Retail Business for Lasting Success

Brown Books Publishing Group
Dallas, TX / New York, NY
www.BrownBooks.com
(972) 381-0009

A New Era in Publishing®

Publisher's Cataloging-In-Publication Data

Names: Cosentino, Mike, author.
Title: It's not the bricks, it's the mortar : optimize your retail business for lasting success / Mike Cosentino.
Description: Dallas, TX ; New York, NY : Brown Books Publishing Group, [2025]
Identifiers: ISBN: 978-1-61254-680-3 | LCCN: 2024951095
Subjects: LCSH: Stores, Retail--Management. | Small business--Management. | Success in business. | Leadership. | Customer services. | Teams in the workplace. | BISAC: BUSINESS & ECONOMICS / Small Business. | BUSINESS & ECONOMICS / Leadership.
Classification: LCC: HF5429 .C67 2025 | DDC: 658.87--dc23

ISBN 978-1-61254-680-3
LCCN 2024951095

Printed in Canada
10 9 8 7 6 5 4 3 2 1

For more information or to contact the author, please go to www.ItsTheMortar.com.

For Inge.

You are my Sunshine! The timeless principles you exemplify for me AND the proven plans you administer for our family are my inspiration. I love you more than my actions ever likely convey or that words could ever adequately express.

For Campbell & Monica.

Of all the lessons I've learned, the ones you have both inspired and taught are those that are most valuable and for which I'm most grateful. As you both know, you're my favorite. I love you, I love you! So much, so much!

Above all else, for His glory.

The master in the art of living makes little distinction between his work and his play, his labor and his leisure, his mind and his body, his information and his recreation, his love and his religion. He hardly knows which is which. He simply pursues his vision of excellence in whatever he does, leaving others to decide whether he is working or playing. To him, he's always doing both.

—JAMES MICHENER

Contents

Preface

If I'm honest, even I would ask myself this question: Has not enough been written about brick-and-mortar retail and the imperatives necessary for such bold and benevolent enterprises to thrive? To me, it seems the volume of content is already overwhelming. From bestselling books to barely read blogs, this is a theme drowning in commentary.

Equally intimidating, there are regular cold splashes of reality that reinforce concern. In 2021, the retail industry soberly endured the permanent closure of ten thousand doors while overall consumer spending grew at a booming 8 percent. More recently, UBS (a top-20 bank in global assets) shared its belief that it will be lights-out for another forty to fifty thousand stores in the United States by 2026. Whether confirmed or prospective, these types of casualty rates leave a scar on both Main Street and Wall Street—but the dismal headlines no longer seem to surprise either consumers or investors.

Yes, I'm certain I could find a less crowded topic with more momentum to study and editorialize on . . .

Nonetheless, I'm bothered. More specifically, it bothers me that everything I've recently and regularly heard or read in this critical service sector is perspective and guidance from people who likely mean well, *but*—they're not actually doing it. They are not doing retail. They are not tangibly tied to the daily operations of the more than four million brick-and-mortar retail establishments in the United States. They are not fully immersed in on-site or online selling. They are not directly dependent upon their own provision of hospitality. Or customer service. Or procurement. Or anything that is observably linked to the business of providing these *real* services that *really* matter.

Simply put, they are *not* in the arena.

"It is not the critic who counts; not the man who points out how the strong man stumbles or where the doer of deeds could have done better. The credit belongs to the man who is actually in the arena, whose face is marred by dust and sweat and blood; who strives valiantly; who errs and comes up short again and again, because there is no effort without error or shortcoming; but who does actually strive to do the deeds; who knows the great enthusiasms, the great devotions; who spends himself in a worthy cause; who at the best knows in the end the triumph of high achievement, and who at the worst, if he fails, at least fails while daring greatly, so that his place shall never be with those cold and timid souls who knew neither victory nor defeat."

—THEODORE ROOSEVELT, FROM SPEECH AT
THE SORBONNE, PARIS, APRIL 23, 1910

The irresistible resolve in this presidential quote presents an opposing side to my dilemma. Its spirit inherently defies popular speculation and can be invoked to dismiss the notion that content promoting retail-related prosperity is either dated or saturated. Even better, it is on this side where we find those who already represent an industry that perpetually proves it is greatly resilient and generationally relevant. Standing together, it is all of us who consciously choose pursuits that result in honest commerce, beautifully illustrated through our personally connected service propositions. Every day. We are living it. Breathing it. Betting on it. And betting so much on ourselves.

And, man, so many of us are doing it, oh, so well! We know the retail industry can be a dazzling storefront window into the societal importance we assign to service and serving others. It is legacy work that deserves to be preserved, sustained, continued, and consistently improved.

Despite the naysayers and the negative prospects frequently associated with retail as a discipline or an industry, I've resolved my hesitation as to whether more should be published about this profession . . . I guess you could say I care too much to share too little.

But! Hear this, too: The consequences of our decisions and actions are our constant companions. And there are times when we want or even need to step away from our occupational role. In chapter 1, I share how these lessons unfolded for me. Through the most uncertain season of my life, I learned it is only when we reduce or even unfasten our involvement that our example, our delegation, our training curriculum, and our operational processes are materially tested. The success of our enterprise—and the sum of our previous efforts—becomes fully dependent upon how well we have intentionally prepared others for what we may have initially felt only we could do.

It is this hard-realized awareness that guides this manuscript. As researcher and university professor Brené Brown assertively suggests, "Regret is a fair, but tough, teacher."[1] I too have found this to be true. In fact, it was this otherwise icky condition that influenced me to greatly adjust my approach to leadership in my retail business. I will refer to this specific adjustment on the pages that follow as "Uninvolved Optimization." Like much that is difficult at the onset, it has led to an upgraded version of myself and an improved future for others.

Just as importantly, this approach has a prerequisite: "Involved Maximization." Both concepts underlie a syllabus that goes far beyond basic business survival tactics. Let's formally define them, remembering that the process of Involved Maximization precedes that of Uninvolved Optimization as a critical frontload:

Involved Maximization (Task-Oriented): The conscious decision and concerted effort of a leader to approach a project, department or enterprise in a manner that combines the pursuit of results with an intent to transition future iterations of the effort to others.

Uninvolved Optimization (Target-Focused): The condition in which a project, department or enterprise is operating effectively without direct involvement or instruction from a senior leader and/or key predecessor in the effort.

To be direct, this should be the pervasive approach for motivated leaders with meaningful targets. Whether pursuing new-and-improved products, ambitious goals, undeveloped possibilities or enduring contributions, the ever-shifting demands of change and growth mandate leaders to be on the move without stagnation, lethargy or collapse in their wake. The earned latitude with Uninvolved Optimization is *not* a systematic hack or shortcut to less work or responsibility. If anything, it is the opposite, as the pursuit of potential is perpetual—and consequential. For top performers, seasons of personal-time poverty are necessary with Involved Maximization to ensure a target-rich future through Uninvolved Optimization. The continuous transition from IM to UO requires the best retail leaders to achieve mastery of both. They consciously remain devoted to Uninvolved Optimization while strategically—and visibly—engaging in Involved Maximization.

So let us delay no longer. The bricks have arrived—and the mortar is being mixed. We will start with a foundation that ensures peak performance in the most critical aspects of our craft and close only when we have a level of confidence that matches the potential impact of our passionate endeavors.

—July 11, 2024 (Blue Ridge, GA)

Prologue

It was a Sunday evening in London, gloomy, close, and stale. Maddening church bells of all degrees of dissonance, sharp and flat, cracked and clear, fast and slow, made the brick-and-mortar echoes hideous. Melancholy streets, in a penitential garb of soot, steeped the souls of the people who were condemned to look at them out of windows in dire despondency. In every thoroughfare, up almost every alley, and down almost every turning, some doleful bell was throbbing, jerking, tolling, as if the Plague were in the city and the dead-carts were going round. Everything was bolted and barred that could by possibility furnish relief to an overworked people.
—CHARLES DICKENS, *LITTLE DORRIT*

It is in this depressing passage from Dickens's late-career satirical novel that we first see the term "brick-and-mortar." Like today, it was used to identify workspaces dedicated to the resale of tangible goods. Of course, the practice of retail-related disciplines long preceded the 1857 publish date of *Little Dorrit* or the resulting popularity of this term. Archaeologists have presented evidence from the fourth and fifth centuries of merchants selling their products in the Athenian agora. Products were likely presented on mats in temporary stalls, including fruits, clothes, pottery, wreaths, ribbons, purple dye, perfume, incense, and other luxury and religious goods. Merchants would produce or secure these goods nearby for easy transport on market days. Later, the Roman forum (500 BC) arguably became the earliest example of a permanent retail shop front.[1]

As basic building components, bricks and mortar themselves also have a long history. Even older than those ancient storefronts, remnants of mud bricks, shaped from clay and earth—and dried by the sun—have been disinterred in both the Middle East and South Asia. By 3500 BC, there was the advanced use of fired bricks, much like those found and deployed today.[2] The dimensions of such a building block from the earliest structures remain very similar to those used in modern construction. As for mortar, both basic and more sophisticated masonry utilized a malleable adhesive as far back as 6500 BC.[3] The earliest confirmed uses featured only locally available ingredients as the bonding material. This included sand, lime, gypsum, and volcanic ash.

But even with the long legacies of both retailing and bricklaying, it is only in the twentieth century "brick-and-mortar" begins to refer to an operation that showcases its means from a material location. This popular expression now serves to distinguish such businesses from retailers that operate online or through virtual or digital mediums. Even more recently, the idiom has become more all-encompassing. Today it is no longer only the traditional merchant referenced as brick-and-mortar. It includes the coffee shop, the web services agency, the franchised financial planning firm, and the dental office, to name merely a few. In short, "brick-and-mortar" currently represents both products *and* services that connect an available offering to a specific physical space.

In the end, contemporary usage of the term can be exactly what it references. And in those instances when it is not quite as precise—like a commercial building alternatively made from concrete, steel or stone—it is close enough. Brick-and-mortar is now a widely understood concept with an impressive history of storekeeping and personalized service . . .

But it also comes replete these days with an increasingly voiced concern about its future as an industry altogether.

Bricks. Mortar. As functional materials and as marketplace slang, they are found together. Always, it seems. Where there is one, there is also the other. They are fittingly and solidly inseparable.

It's Not the Bricks

Even though we might suggest Bricks and Mortar are the perfect power couple, one of these elements is first among perceived equals in this reference to retail businesses. The title of this book identifies which is most important. More notably, we come to understand why Mortar is our foremost ingredient as we take the continual journey from "Involved Maximization" to "Uninvolved Optimization."

For the sake of our analogy, let's start with a primer and a preview.

Whether for a building or a business, we likely notice the bricks. Both visually and metaphorically, they are so unmistakable! In my retail business that proudly presents the latest and greatest in performance athletic footwear, my "bricks" include carbon-plated, nitrogen-infused, gel-packed, air-bagged, and maximally cushioned midsoles found in running shoes made for athletes of every ability. My bricks also include leases in the best shopping centers with greatly desirable anchor tenants. These mostly brick-built properties sit on congested corners with desirably high traffic counts. My award-winning fit process has its own bricks, as it features depth cameras, gold-plated sensors, high-speed video capture, and 3-D foot-scanning technology. And my marketing budget? Oh, let me count the bricks! They encompass sponsorship agreements for the biggest events and paid partnerships with numerous local teams.

The visibility of these elements is undeniable and important. Along with many other long-standing assets, they represent a *whole* lot of bricks. At the same time, it is mistakenly presumed that success or failure has almost everything to do with these very specific items. As the most observable markers of our businesses and organizations, they are the equivalent of our own personal Tate Modern!

Tate Modern, Modern & Contemporary Art Gallery, London, England.
Reprinted with permission by Flickr user brewbooks.

But, really, *it's not the bricks*.

Said differently, with *just* the bricks, we are just not enough. We are, instead, an organization destined to be undistinguished, as we underdeliver on our own potential. And as time passes, the odds for continual success decrease—and it becomes the opportunity costs that start to stack. Figuratively speaking, bricks alone will not sustain even our best-laid plans. As false assurances, they obscure responsibilities associated with Involved Maximization . . . and often weigh us down when we pursue Uninvolved Optimization.

In essence, if we wish to soar, we must add more.

It's the Mortar

"Mortar is a workable paste that hardens to bind building blocks such as stones, bricks, and concrete masonry units, to fill and seal the irregular gaps between them, spread the weight evenly, and sometimes add decorative colors or patterns."[4]

This is how Wikipedia describes mortar. Even those who are not particularly talented with "hardscape" will find this definition without cracks. Most importantly for our analogy, we can agree mortar is a cornerstone of effective and long-lasting masonry work.

The same is equally true in organizations and businesses founded and grounded in the service of others. "Brick-and-mortar" is not just a widely adopted expression to refer to the retail industry. As a metaphor, it also suggests the perfect foundation on which to build something that lasts.

The marketplace "bricks" we acquire will be supremely useful only when put in place with a less conspicuous element that strengthens any organization. Needless to say, this is our metaphorical mortar. And as with mortar for construction, the various ingredients in the mix work together to "fill and seal the irregular gaps." They also keep our work interesting and appealing, as we "add decorative colors or patterns."

Uninvolved Optimization itself is paramount to ensuring the integrity of our mortar. It is the proven way to "spread the weight evenly." The challenge, of course, is to sustain this condition! And it is not easy. In fact, it is darned hard, as it simultaneously requires us to tap soundly into the "soft skills" of communicating effectively and the "hard skills" found in the practical application of our training.

To go even further, we cannot allow ourselves to become imbalanced with one over the other. After all, there are days when the schedule calls for conscientious empathy in the morning and formulaic arithmetic after lunch. There are also seasons of leading others in the discovery of individual purpose alongside the lonely, ongoing oversight of organizational policy. As leaders, our mortar is poured into the gaps of an enduring brick road we frequently travel with our Team* between what is definitively objective and that which is admittedly subjective.

Fortunately, the weighty work of setting bricks is worth it. With reward

---

* Throughout this manuscript, you will see the term "Team" (and its variations) is capitalized. When I realized Uninvolved Optimization was unattainable without others on my Team—and that the most meaningful accomplishments only transpire when a Team comes together—I decided to write my own rules for capitalization. The names of organizations and companies are capitalized; so are job titles when placed on résumés, business cards, and electronic signatures. And of course, our names and all proper nouns are, too. But my belief is that a Team intrinsically makes some of these entities whose names we capitalize possible—and makes most of them *better*. So in order to give a Team the credit it deserves, I start with giving it the capital "T" I believe it should have always had.

now outpacing regret in my own retailing endeavors, I can testify how the mortar truly matters most in this industry. This is the substance that girds the very structure of our aspirations and enables us to withstand the inevitable tests faced by all who are involved with service-centered organizations—

So let's get ready to build! As a final preview of our mix for the bricks, here are the ingredients for a well-bonded and future-ready retail environment.

SOFT SKILLS	HARD SKILLS
Great Service (the Retail Experience)	The Only Ways to Increase Sales
Fueling a Favorable Message	Strategic Planning
Your Leadership Characteristics	Value-Creation Methodologies
Preservation of Team Unity	Procurement Principles
Core Values and a Sticky Culture	The Prioritization of Profitability

Section I

Soft Skills
What Feels Good Is Really Hard . . .

With customers and colleagues top-of-mind, we will start with content likely categorized by academics as "soft skills." The peculiarity of that term is not lost because you already know interpersonal disciplines are hard. Organizational life is messy. Even products perceived as perfect have people behind them who are not . . .

To be sure, the work specifically designed to make others feel good is really hard.

Fortunately, there is ample reward for the difficulty. We embrace the inherent challenges connected to our service proposition, personal growth, and Team empowerment because our work is meaningful and matters to others. Our desire to get better is not a selfish ambition.

In his book *Talent Magnet*, leadership expert Mark Miller rightly notes what it is that every Team Member wants from their leader: a Better Boss, a Brighter Future, and a Bigger Vision.[1] To follow the strategic simplicity in this ground truth, Section I will be straightforward. In fact, you may find this section's highlighted concepts of service culture and employee satisfaction to be surprisingly intuitive. Even better, there is no need for complicated

11

formulas to elucidate these qualitative disciplines. Rest assured, this material will not require a scientific calculator, external hard drive or graph paper!

At the same time, the concepts into which we'll be diving should challenge you and enlighten you to new opportunities. The suggested methods ahead do indeed require incremental effort, collaboration with others, and constant coordination. There may even be material that stirs up discontent or opens a workplace wound that will never fully heal without applying additional procedures. A willingness to confront—and a resolve to conquer—some formidable foes will be necessary to reach your potential. These oppressors may include current trends, the absence of corporate momentum, and some otherwise likable persons who oppose your commitment to an upgraded future. The chief concerns in this initial installment are unpopular to wrestle. It is even to be assumed that the daily demands of any enterprise already offer innumerable challenges. And now we will be covering demanding topics that come alongside all you already have to do and currently hold dear.

Again, this material is challenging. And the timing is not perfect.

But despite these realties, YOU are poised to make a difference. And the timing is seemingly good enough. Otherwise, you would not be here . . .

And I'm so glad you are.

Onward!

CHAPTER 1

The Uninvolved Optimization Epiphany

Introducing the Opportunity—and the Obligation

For most of us leading a retail or service-centered business, the amount of cumulative authority we have provided to others is insufficient. It is rare for us to set a priority that is not directly affected by—or, perhaps, even completely dependent upon—our own input. Even more worrisome in the organizations I have studied, there is no visible momentum for this tide to change.

But we innately know this pattern of behavior is suboptimal. Even dangerous.

And we are right.

On January 12, 2021, I received a text at work from a friend where I live. I include "where I live" because my primary residence is not proximate to where I work. The two locales are more than one hundred miles apart. This distance and detail will directly serve the concepts in the pages that follow . . .

But back to the text message I received.

The text read, "Call me. Your son has been in an accident."

My friend, Adam, had my attention. Kind of. He had called first while I was amid correspondence of my own on my laptop. I let his initial attempt go to voicemail.

Even after digesting the text, I assumed it was a benign incident. My son, Campbell, had put in time conditioning my unanxious interpretation of those words . . . It was barely six months prior when my wife called me at the same workspace (I did elect to take her call . . .) on the backside of my 6:30 a.m. workout—and before the start of a solidly packed day. She indicated she was on the way to an accident site, where Campbell had just been involved in a single-vehicle mishap that rendered both his truck and a luckless power pole unusable . . . Without hesitation, I grabbed my keys and headed for the interstate. I spent the drive from Atlanta to Blue Ridge, Georgia, rearranging my schedule and issuing apologies for my late notice of cancellation.

My arrival home a few hours later yielded a mangled Ford F-150 in our driveway and my offspring already gone again. Most thankfully, he was fine—and was now carrying about his day in my wife's car. Despite the disturbing condition of his vehicle, it was a dreadful scenario averted.

Coincidentally enough, Adam had also been previously entangled in somewhat similar circumstances with me. Two years prior, his own son collaborated with Campbell to render my Jeep Wrangler undrivable after a forceful maneuver of the manual shifter into reverse at thirty miles per hour (in a completely failed effort to find the third gear). Adam was gracious enough to call me from where my transmission had been obliterated when sensing Campbell's understandable reticence to share the news with me himself. With no answer and some reliable intuition I was out of town, he left me a voicemail.

In that episode, Adam did *not* feel obligated to send a follow-up text to ensure my immediate awareness. For those who know me, this is critically sensible behavior in an emergency or with a time-sensitive message. I rarely listen to my voicemail. As I eventually mentioned to Adam, I did not actually retrieve his voicemail until the following month. Campbell ended up having to be the first to dispense the details to me, after all . . .

So, for sure, it was the existence of Adam's text message this time—even more than the content contained therein—that compelled me to consider a return call and acknowledge his communication. While noticeably sensing my own frustration with this recurring theme, I made my way to the index of recent calls. I applied meaningful pressure to the screen where his name was below . . .

"Hey, buddy, Campbell's been in an accident."

"Yeah, I got your text," I responded. "Is everything all right?"

Adam was truthful. "I don't know. James's girlfriend somehow came across it. It happened on the highway. It sounds like they've got the highway shut down now. That's all I know. But I do have the number of someone who called me because they knew we knew each other. Let me give you his number."

Even now, it is emotionally challenging to recall the series of conversations and actions I took after concluding the next call. In short, it is true: life changes in an instant.

In the numbness of the first few days that followed, I created a CaringBridge page to offset our inability to provide worthwhile updates to the overwhelming number of friends and family who so greatly supported us. This was my opening entry:

Earlier this week, our son, Campbell, was a backseat passenger in a highway collision near our home in Blue Ridge, GA. Due to visible injuries to his skull by first responders, it was determined on the scene that LifeFlight to a specific care unit would provide the best opportunity for his survival. Medical personnel was awaiting his arrival a short time later at the Trauma Center at Northeast Georgia Medical Center in Gainesville, GA.

As this first update is two (2) days after the accident, I'll refrain from sharing the details of notification, travel to the hospital, the impact of COVID-19 protocols disabling the ability to see patients or medical personnel and viewing your child unconscious amidst an entanglement of hospital equipment. To say that a series of events like this is rightfully toward the top of any list a parent might have of "a nightmare scenario" is accurate. And for those parents who have experienced even worse, I still cannot imagine . . .

I'll also indicate that I will fully respect the other students, passengers and families involved in this accident by not mentioning specific names. At the same time, there were two friends of my son also in the car who need your prayers, love and support. We live in a small community. Even outside of the friendship our son enjoys with these kids, the families involved are people with whom we already go to church and high school games, ask favors, share meals and have a meaningful relationship and genuine concern. When this accident occurred—AND at the onset of this journey—there were no strangers involved. There was no occasion when families were meeting others or hearing names for the first time. There are only families who would have come together in any circumstance, anyway. My heart breaks, too, for the pain they are also experiencing.

As of this morning, one of the students has been discharged from the hospital. Even though such is good news, I know there is still much recovery and healing for this individual to occur. Although I'm so grateful for that family now being able to come together outside of the hospital setting, our prayers and involvement with them will be no less. For Campbell and the other passenger, they remain in critical condition with Traumatic Brain Injury, among other injuries sustained in the crash. My son also has a fractured skull, fractured sternum and numerous lacerations that have seemingly been fully addressed.

The depth of prayer, amount of support, indications of concern and expressions of love for our son have been humbling, overwhelming and truly life-changing for me, my wife and our daughter. Our prayers each morning now include the opportunity to someday cry with our son in a way that he'll be able to understand how deep and far the love for him and our family has already gone during this incident. As a parent, it's also been hugely gratifying to learn how many ways Campbell has impacted others in this community—other students and adults alike. If you think you're proud of your kids for what you know they do, rest assured there is much that will make you even more proud that you likely have no idea . . . But as so many of you have assumed with your indications of "no need to respond," it has become challenging for our family to keep everyone apprised and express our true level of appreciation for the prayers, notes, positive vibes and outlook for healing and recovery. We hope this website will assist our efforts of being better with updates . . . and communicate with you in a way that adequately expresses our love for your involvement with our family (and this unfolding story that WILL have a purpose).

(If you wish to learn more about CaringBridge, visit www.CaringBridge.org. Donations are always welcome.)

More Persons Impacting More Priorities More Quickly

At the onset of my own retailing endeavors, I, too, was uncommitted to sharing or passing along functions core to the business or central to the operations. There were only occasional instances when organizational development or process enhancement were even blinking lights on my radar. And any actual consistent institutional commitment to empowering others was altogether absent. Heck, I met with an advisor about an employee stock ownership program before I had any purposeful discussion with key team members about a proper *sense of ownership* with vital processes and our biggest projects. Only when I had my back against a wall did I realize I needed more leverage along that wall if we were going to successfully push back—*and* push ahead—with any measure of meaningful strength.

Of course, that meant I needed more people impacting more priorities more quickly.

Still, this is not just another hard-charging reinforcement of why you should develop workable ways to share your organizational and marketplace influence with a greater number of qualified persons. Yes, I'm very much for it. BIG time! But I'm a retailer—not a researcher. And there is already plenty of very convincing material in full support of sharing our workload, extending our authority, and embracing collaborative innovation. I'm confident any such coaching on these matters that passes through your own discernment will attach capably to the content that follows. Candidly, the best methodologies for delegation also inspire optimism that can be otherwise hard to find in the Human Resources department of most retail industry entities.

But also remember this: optimism is just a state of *mind*. To be sustainable and successful in our most meaningful pursuits, we equally need a proven state of *existence*. The hero's journey for a retailer is along the pathway that takes us from optimism to optimized! And consistent with our previously agreed-upon definition of "mortar," a truly realized state of optimization is when the most irregular of gaps have been filled and the weight of our work has been spread evenly.

The Rest of the Story

My son was an unrestrained passenger in the backseat of a car that turned left on a state highway from a still position. It did so in front of a diesel truck carrying one-thousand-plus pounds of paving stone that was traveling almost sixty miles per hour. The first responders only discovered my son as an occupant when they opened the hatch to affix the hydraulic apparatus necessary to free the front-seat passenger. This passenger succumbed to her injuries, while the driver was, ultimately, charged with vehicular manslaughter for his brief and tragic lapse in judgment. As friends of our family, these results brought ineffable pain. It was in these losses, as well as in Campbell's initial prognosis as "unlikely to survive," that I resolved to be at his side in any prospective effort toward rehabilitation. Even a slim chance for recovery was a blessing unbeatable in its power to set priorities.

I soon announced to my Team and other constituents that I would be decidedly uninvolved in any professional matters for however long was necessary. My role as a parent was paramount. There was no other option. There would be an understandable and total dependency on others for the objective health of my retail business, maturing brand, and growing organization.

Importantly, this declaration had years of advanced planning standing behind it—even though the announcement itself was never planned. The words of spiritual teacher Anthony de Mello in his last book, *The Way To Love*, could not have felt more true, as I stepped away . . .

"You must cultivate activities that you love. You must discover work that you do, not for its utility, but for itself . . . whether it succeeds or not, whether you are praised for it or not, whether you are loved and rewarded for it or not, whether people know about it and are grateful to you for it or not. How many activities can you count in your life that you engage in simply because they delight you and grip your soul? Find them out, cultivate them, for they are your passport to freedom and love."[2]

To the best degree I could really analyze this notion in the moments I made this decision to fully trust others with the work that tangibly gripped me, I genuinely believed I had dedicatedly cultivated our organization in the last fifteen years. It was not always easy. In many instances, it was very imperfect. But there was ample evidence that it was a conscious approach and a constant effort.

And true to de Mello's words, such cultivation was now, indeed, my literal and emotional passport to the freedom and love I needed in this season—and was fully necessary for me to lead and support my family properly.

The Case for "Uninvolved Optimization" and "Involved Maximization"

Yes, it is possible my motivation for leaning into the merits of what I will refer to as "Uninvolved Optimization" may be more dramatic than yours. But without knowing you, I know something about you: as magnificent as you are at what you do, there is something—many things, perhaps—that would compel you to re-prioritize your efforts and attention . . . Think about it. What is it for you? I hope you think of something spectacular. And special. Even more so, I hope you never encounter a situation where dire circumstances necessitate a rapid reorganization of your priorities.

But regardless of whether you're prompted by delightful or grueling circumstances, my greatest desire is that you arrive at this prospect with confidence and equanimity. When these days come (and they will!), your efforts and preparation should shield you from worry or delay. Such is the shrouded bounty of Uninvolved Optimization!

Even so, take heed that any accomplishment involving legitimate Uninvolved Optimization is only preceded by a period of intentional, critical work. As difference-makers, entrepreneurs, and leaders, we must first commit to the pursuit and routine of Involved Maximization. We are not unlike the athlete who intensifies her training in the off-season, confident the evidence of her discipline will emerge when it matters most. And it is, indeed, in this initial work that this book aims to add to your ever-expanding roster of resources.

Before going further, let's review and reconsider the formal definitions for Uninvolved Optimization and Involved Maximization:

Uninvolved Optimization: The condition in which a project, department or enterprise is operating effectively without direct involvement or instruction from a senior leader and/or key predecessor in the effort.

Involved Maximization: The conscious decision and concerted effort of a leader to approach a project, department or enterprise in a manner that combines the pursuit of results with a specific intent to transition future iterations of the effort to others.

With a focus on the latter definition as the means to the former, Involved Maximization Imperatives are provided at the end of each forthcoming chapter. Whether a seasoned service provider or a newly appointed leader, we instinctively know wherever there is direct control, there is *not* Uninvolved Optimization. My recommendations tangibly connect to crucial elements of a retail operation that can be purposefully prepared for relocation away from you. Such "imperatives" will also serve as quick and reliable references for ensuring clarity between you and the people you are empowering . . . In essence, the stated imperatives become the "mortar" to be expertly mixed for use with your "bricks."

The architectural plans are ready. Let's get to building!

CHAPTER 2:

Another Analogy ... and a Handful of Enemies

You *Must* Leave First Base

Whether you are a fan of America's Pastime or not, you likely know the role of the pitcher. Throw strikes. Keep the bases empty. Limit the number of runs scored. As casual observers or as coaches, we scrutinize those in this role for accuracy, versatility, and command. And when observing a thrower on the mound or in the bullpen, most spectators watch this player just long enough to see the release of each pitch.

Wonderfully enough, our journey to Uninvolved Optimization starts at the ballpark. Popcorn, anyone? The game is about to begin.

On the first pitch of the game, the batter hits a ground ball. We're barely in our seats. But just like each time contact is made, players and spectators alike immediately look at both the ball *and* its likely destination. In this instance, the ball is authoritatively smacked onto the ground toward the untended space between where the first baseman and second baseman positioned themselves when the pitch was hurled. Neither of those players hesitates. Both players instinctively head in the direction of the ball, knowing success is dependent upon getting the ball to first base before the hitter arrives at the same place. For most groundballs, this scenario plays out with a throw to the first baseman from another infielder. In this particular sequence, however, such is an impossibility—after all, the first baseman has moved *away* from the base. He may even be shouldering the burden of fielding the ball now. Regardless, the initial action is a significant distance from the same base he was assigned to monitor—*and* that is also the required destination for the ball to arrive in advance of the opponent!

Our first baseman makes this intuitive effort to field the ball because he knows such will not be in vain; the objective to ensure the ball reaches the base before the runner arrives remains unchanged. For it is literally from the crack of the bat that our pitcher—whom we have otherwise stopped watching—sees the trajectory of the ball. It is as equally innate for him that the next responsibility for this position is to cover the base that is perennially abandoned when such a sequence unfolds. As the first baseman adeptly fields the ground ball, he is assured his Teammate, our pitcher, is ready to receive the required throw at the base. The first baseman, simply, knows there are times when he must "leave first base" to make the play and move the objective forward.

It is also when he knows he must confidently count on others to do what he is most known for doing.

Washington Nationals first baseman Riley Adams making a toss to a relief pitcher who was covering first base during the 8th inning in a game against the San Francisco Giants at Nationals Park in Washington D.C., April 24, 2022. Reprinted with permission by All-Pro Reels.

For a service-based business, the same is true for the proprietor, the principals, and the primary influences *if* the service proposition itself is going to transition from dependency on an individual to others capable of such important contributions.

You *must* leave first base.

To reach your business's—and your own—potential, there is work away from the "base" that needs to be done . . . and there are key plays away from the base that only you can make. Having the confidence that someone will not only be standing on the bag but also ready to receive the ball when you do make those plays is critical for long-standing viability.

Easier Said Than Done?

So, go ahead and say it. I know what you are thinking: *Easier said than done.*

And for the record, I agree. Instances when staffing shortages, training deficiencies, and fire drills kept key personnel tethered to "first base" were common and frequent for me, too. I'll admit we tried various shortcuts to cheat the distance and the time away from the bag. Our failed ideas included the construction of mezzanine offices inside our stockrooms and policies mandating that vendor meetings take place only at our stores. These efforts (and plenty of others) were not inherently bad or immediately burdensome . . . They just nipped our potential in the bud. And the ability to form meaningful, rich relationships was curbed.

So let's start here. This is the inconvenient truth: we cannot get the same amount of ancillary work done—*nor* can we steward the critical variety of work that needs to be accomplished—in the same place where our primary retail services are delivered. In a post-COVID scenario, there are likely industries that need to bring their workforce back to the offices. Many businesses are still trying to find the proper balance, while others have already determined a remote workforce is best for their organization. But for brick-and-mortar retailers (even with online capabilities and an increasingly automated service proposition), operating in an entirely remote manner is not yet an option. *However*, working at the site of service for a retail professional is ineffective *unless* you are directly involved in the sales process itself. The interruptions are incessant—and usually unplanned. The distractions are abundant and deceptively demanding.

Most unfortunate of all, Uninvolved Optimization is thereby doomed.

To be clear, I am not all-out assailing conventional workspace practices. There are times when specific meeting objectives make our place of service the ideal location. If a meeting participant benefits from witnessing how a product is manufactured or presented—whether in a factory, accounting firm, church sanctuary, cafeteria kitchen, hardware store or pawn shop—there is no better way to exhibit such processes than through on-site, in-person visits. To witness how personalized service is prepared and delivered is undoubtedly magical!

But in most instances, meetings (in-person or via videoconference) that take place near the retail sales floor occur in that location because it is convenient. Or required under the umbrella of "office politics." Or because we want to see what is transpiring in our service environment while simultaneously conducting other business . . .

It is not because we believe that setting is optimal.

When I detailed my son's accident, I indicated I lived over a hundred miles from where my businesses are located. Many years ago, this self-induced geographic disparity was my "burn the boats" effort to practice what I am now preaching. It embodied my dramatic commitment to embrace my need for "first base" to be fine without me standing on (in?) it. When I am more than two hours from the daily requisites of keystone service elements, such cannot be dependent upon me. Conversely, and just as importantly, when I am in our stores, I am truly *in* our stores. I am fully present. My smartphone is only out of my pocket to take a note or a picture. My laptop is left untouched in my bag or in the car. No calls. No messages. No meetings. No administrative duties or strategic plans moved ahead. I am disciplined toward a dual purpose for these occasions: to serve and to observe. That's it. I am on-site to serve our Guests and the Team in a manner that is eagerly and joyfully unrestrained. And while doing so, my senses are tuned in like a tracking dog in the forest or an eagle flying high above its meadow. Through the interactions we're sharing and witnessing in this immediate environment, there is just so much to take in!

As a reward for practicing such well-intentioned in-store immersion, previously unknown details about our stores' operations and their offerings are revealed! On-site observations and conversations broaden perspective like no other means. Of course, these special discoveries can be either encouraging or concerning. And when the latter transpires, our store may unquestionably be the most appropriate place to convene for a meeting.

But, again, this is the exception.

In the end, we instinctively know our work should be located where it can be done most expertly and comprehensively. In most instances, this is *not* our primary point of service. Whether an individual or group effort, we must train ourselves to leave first base when productivity is estimated or demonstrated to be higher elsewhere. We should, in fact, *only* lock ourselves onto first base when the objective truly demands it. Just like in baseball, leaving first base contributes to better results. On the shortlist, these include better concentration, an increased yield from meetings, and staff empowerment.

Best of all, Uninvolved Optimization is ushered forth.

The Other "U" Word

It is easy to find enthusiasm among colleagues for remaining unaffixed to processes that work reliably without them. Even masterful micromanagers can find other work to do when results suggest there is no danger associated with detachment. For good reason, there is little debate that Uninvolved Optimization is a worthy pursuit. Our noble and unselfish aim to be the confident first baseman who never delays in making the most consequential plays is a freedom-filled advantage in any enterprise!

Nonetheless, every leader intuitively knows the mere attainment of such latitude does not ensure its continuity. Frustration is predictably magnified when specific involvement in a task, though dutifully delegated, returns like a boomerang to that same person who worked so hard to give it a successful send-off. To avoid such disappointment, there is a special mixture of mortar that must be incorporated to support the plans for Uninvolved Optimization. This mixture will enable our ability to leave first base and appropriately migrate our attention to other priorities. Without hyperbole, it is a master key for unlocking the full potential of our Team. And conveniently enough as a memory aid, like "Uninvolved," it is another word that begins with "U" . . .

UNITY.

If one were to do a broad online search for the conditions that create Team unity, they would come away with a paraphrase along the lines of "the alignment of all team members toward a shared purpose."

Regrettably, "unity" is more easily defined than it is performed. I have found this to be especially true for those who lead retail-centric organizations. There is a natural drift that separates those based inside the stores and in sales operations from those who are working most hours away from the registers and the sales totals. It is unimaginative to insert the theme of Unity into a keynote speech or suggest it as a required condition in a Team meeting. On the other hand, the consistent presence of such in your organization, though a weighty undertaking and ever-fragile condition, is an enormous achievement.

So where do we begin?

Although the alphabetical proximity that the word *Unity* has with *Uninvolved* would be lost, I'm only half-joking when I contend that it is more appropriately spelled *Younity*. After all, this minor adjustment in its appearance would suitably remind leaders that both the concept—and its sustainment—start with YOU.

Because it does. And whether you have a Team of two or two thousand, unity is a requisite in organizations where leaders aspire to get *and* regularly stay uninvolved in key aspects of the enterprise.

Common Purpose, Supportive Structure

Many discussions I've heard about organizational unity include an honest admission of its general absence followed by an expression of genuine desire for its reliable presence. As no surprise, enduring commitment is an undeniable advantage in working toward this objective. And in a timeless 2011 article in the Harvard Business Review, three management experts concisely outline the task necessary for us to instill unity, furnishing their requirement for a collaborative community: "Marrying a sense of common purpose to a supportive structure."[1]

'Til death do those elements part, indeed! Common purpose. Supportive structure. These are well-paired bedfellows, for sure. And leaders who know how to make them everlasting, as they faithfully construct and conserve unity, are the ones who are never looking for work. They also smartly anticipate that the very unity they've established will be relentlessly under attack. They know an organization composed of people who sincerely care about reaching their potential and exceeding expectations never embrace moratoriums on strong opinions. They know when the pace is fast and the progress is impressive, there is always the opportunity for division. To be sure, the headlines will continue to showcase those who initiate immediate growth and make aggressive decisions that prove notably gainful in the near term. But for those leaders who intend to make the biggest impact in the same organization over an extended period, they must combine their strategic maneuvers with a tireless preservation of organizational unity.

Friends, set your sentries at their posts and stay awake at the castle gates . . . Unity is forever under attack!

The Four Fiercest Foes of Unity

Most people are justifiably irritated by the overused expressions "Teamwork makes the dream work!" and "There is no I in TEAM!"—let alone the insistence that TEAM is an apt acronym for Together Everyone Achieves More. These colloquialisms are nonetheless popular because they rightfully reflect that the most robust results are effectuated when self-interests are deferred in service to the greater objective.

But this is not a natural posture for most individuals. Self-preservation *and* self-promotion are seemingly hardwired into our genetic code. Despite seven of every eight persons in the United States having been recently reported as having their basic needs met (see: food security),[2] neurobiologists and psychologists still group such considerations as "survival instincts."

But let's be honest: organizational life is *not* an episode of *Nat Geo WILD*. For most people, their hierarchical status does not materially impact their chances of surviving the night to see a subsequent sunrise. And for leaders in the pursuit of Uninvolved Optimization, it is, in fact, the *opposite* of established norms in the animal kingdom and ancient societies that ensures the endurance of the enterprise. In effect, we must repeatedly choose to *share* the resources and responsibilities to best achieve security and a confirmed future.

At the same time, not everything has changed with the impressive progression of humanity. The commonality between modern-day Teams seeking unity and long-ago ancestors (who truly did rely on their survival instincts) is now found at the intersection of a healthy acceptance of unremitting work and a finely tuned awareness of present conditions. More specifically, the most successful workplace teams have no tolerance for complacency, and they comfortably demonstrate there is no off-season. The best leaders are only rarely (if ever) hoisting a champagne-sprayed trophy high in the air with the assurance tomorrow ushers forth an extended period free from the progressive demands of increasingly positive outcomes. Instead, the meaningful work is ongoing. It is never-ending. It is, as leadership and management expert Simon Sinek calls it, an "infinite game."[3]

More surprising than the unrelenting demands on new leaders and early-stage entrepreneurs is the inherent vulnerability of any achieved unity. Unfortunately, this cohesive condition can, indeed, be all too fleeting. Even with historically successful Teams, its fragility is an omnipresent threat.

But knowing from exactly where the opposition to our unity imperative will originate—and how it may advance—gives us a fighting chance to fend off the uncaring assault on what is suitably sacred to a high-performance team pursuing its potential. To be sure, we must continually battle these four distasteful foes as they are existential threats to organizational unity.

A Purpose-Driven Delta

We seek purpose in our work. Most fortunately, it is proven to be attainable—and it is inspiring when we notice those who have found it! But at the risk of sounding contrary to popular commentary on the promises of teamwork, you do *not* need a full alignment of *individual* purpose from each participant for collective or long-standing success as an organization. The risk, instead, is greatest when leaders do not know the specific purpose someone attaches to his work and brings into the workplace. The hazard becomes even greater when a leader assumes that each contributor shares a similar purpose to her own or will be moved to meaningful action for the same reasons as those that spur others on the Team.

Please allow me to illustrate further. In a recent hotel stay that was spectacular in every conceivable way, I spent time on my final day on the property asking a variety of employees about the purpose they attached to their respective roles. I did not share with them that I perceived the last few days to be flawless in an environment I customarily find to be unmemorable or worse. The answers were seemingly honest and predictably varied:

- The front-desk associate was employed on a part-time basis while she completed her studies at a nearby university. She has a scholarship for much of the academic overhead—but that award does not pay for her apartment or any non-tuition expenses. This job pays her very well to meet those obligations—and gives her a solid vantage point for one of her admitted pastimes: people-watching.

- The housekeeper quickly quoted her motivating verse from the scriptures. To do so, she politely referred me to Colossians 3:23. Although there are various translations, the New Living Translation version suggests, "Work willingly at whatever you do, as though you were working for the Lord rather than for people."

- The restaurant manager had been a longtime fan of this hospitality brand while a patron in other markets. When this position was vacant and referred to her by a colleague, she was immediately interested. She is now most inspired by the opportunity to oversee an operation that must perform alongside (and in alignment with) non-food departments in the overall enterprise. She wants to "always be learning"—and from the peculiarities of late-night room service to the particulars of banquet services, this role is feeding her appetite for ongoing education.

- Weirdly enough, the valet attendant originally took the position when he did not have a car of his own—and the hotel was an easily obtainable location for public transit. Now he has come to love the friendliness of the guests and his coworkers—and wants to remain in a position to both afford his new car payment and be in an environment where "most everyone is in a good mood."

It would be hard to oppose any of the stated motivations for the individual contributions each employee I interviewed makes. Yet in many organizations, the lack of interest in gaining a more personalized sense of purpose among staff results in erroneous assumptions and wrongful expectations. Supervisors, senior managers, department chiefs, and company owners too often conclude from their own stories that everyone is inspired to earn a promotion, get a raise or beat the quarterly forecast. When these results do not reliably occur, any claimed unity proves to be shallow or is quickly siphoned from the organizational atmosphere.

It is crucial to ensure that you know the underlying purpose of work for each person directly entrusted to you. This is an easily achievable task via warmly engaged consultations. Best of all, these conversations are the greatest means for avoiding the dangers associated with "a difference between two things" (as *delta* is defined by Oxford Languages[4]). Gaining clarity in any individual's personal purpose should help shape how we evaluate their suitability for a specific role. This insight crowds out the space otherwise available for a "Purpose-Driven Delta." Additionally, when we elect to proceed or continue with someone in a role, this knowledge of purpose further provides a custom framework for us to effectively communicate instructions and expectations. Most valuable, this knowledge establishes an authentic connection that is perceivably sincere and strategically effective in its deployment.

Ultimately, for leaders who present a service proposition through others, there are only two options available for mutual and material success in your ability to build and maintain unity across your Team.

1. Logically and legitimately conclude that the specific purpose of each individual *can*, indeed, operate in concert with the

expectations of their role and the objectives, priorities, and mission of the organization.

2. Logically and legitimately conclude that the specific purpose of each individual *cannot* operate in concert with the expectations of their role and the objectives, priorities, and mission of the organization.

When the latter of these options is realized, light might be immediately shed on previously overlooked or ongoing concerns. Confirmed wedges rooted in disparate purposes cannot be left unaddressed between a Team Member and the organization. When such neglect occurs, the delta broadens, and the potential for rising discord only increases. Just as much, the quality of individual contribution likely decreases and myriad consequences disperse into formerly unified places. At the earliest stage, and for the sake of those who are served and who have a stake, the gap must be bridged or annexed. While the stated purpose of any individual will be unique in its own right, it must not collide with the purpose of the organization. When such transpires, changes must be made by the individual and/or the organization to achieve a comfortable coexistence—or the current arrangements must be dutifully dissolved in the rightful name of unity.

Disagreement and Disappointment

Oh, how it is that the two words that comprise this tamable foe hardly suggest a warm and attractive workplace environment! And, for sure, both contribute greatly to the dissatisfaction found in some of our most important occupational efforts.

But take heart! In organizational life, Disagreement and Disappointment are unavoidable—but a negative impact from their combined existence is *entirely avoidable*. Even better, a leader who can master proper introductions of these themes—and manage their frequent presence—will prove a worthy abolitionist of disunity!

The key is to give Disagreement and Disappointment a proper status in the organization. As surprising as it may be, these forces are irrefutably beneficial additions to any organizational ecosystem. In fact, they should be welcome conditions by any member of a high-performance Team.

Here's why: in an organization where there is almost always collaboration, there is seldom consensus.

Let's dissect this usually unacknowledged reality even further . . .

If we are on a Team where ideas are encouraged, opinions are valued, and empowerment is extended in the pursuit of better results and Uninvolved Optimization, the statistical likelihood that each contributor will perpetually complete tasks in an identical fashion to his or her colleagues is 0.00 percent (and that is if we round up to the nearest 0). The same is true relative to any universal agreement on fresh ideas or preferred routines. It is an unrealistic presumption. And we do not need a citation of research to support these claims, as our own experience presents all the data we need. We *regularly* disagree with others, and we likely wrestle with disappointment *all the time*. These are common affairs in any organization where the sum is truly greater than its parts—and where there is a belief that power and progress are found in diverse experience.

As soon as we strive for an environment rife with creativity and widespread contribution, we must also cede that consistent and complete alignment of thought is a mathematical impossibility. This is not just a restatement of Sun Microsystem co-founder Scott McNealy's "disagree and commit" lesson, as popularized by Jeff Bezos.[5] This precedes such solid counsel. As leaders, we must bring Disagreement and Disappointment to the fore as integral companions on the journey to Better or Best Yet. We should be direct and open with our Teammates. Once each Team Member accepts that Disagreement and Disappointment are necessary cultural ingredients, they become effective tools protecting and even *engendering* unity. They are simply the rightful byproducts of consistent collaboration.

And they are always worth it.

As a final note, it should be comforting for leaders to recognize that it will likely *not* be the same Team Members who are perennially disappointed in every decision made or every action taken. And it will likely *not* be the same Team Members who always disagree with you or each other. Instead, you can rest assured that every significant contributor will get more than their fair share of fruitful dissatisfaction . . .

Solved ... But Unresolved

This foe often becomes the devious offspring of the misunderstood pair of Disagreement and Disappointment, especially when a leader is not monitoring those in her care. At its core, Solved But Unresolved is unaddressed disappointment on the Team. It is connected to a historical instance that was seemingly solved—but emerges in the present as not fully resolved. It can prove silently destructive because it is not always overtly attached (or visible at all) to a collective decision, highly observable result or standard operating procedure. It may be the residue from being denied an anticipated promotion or be later found in the percentage points associated with a deserved merit increase. It may surface as a formerly unexpressed sentiment after a dispute among constituents, or it might reveal itself in an ongoing moral divide between personal practices and company policy. It could even be evident in a rift among colleagues that originated way outside our traditional organizational boundaries. It is certainly not unheard of that a lover spurned or a friendship burned becomes prime fodder for our foe to make daring moves of ruination inside our establishment.

Let us consider some examples that may seem all too familiar (even though they are fictitious):

The company memorandum from months ago clearly stated who was elevated to the role of Vice President, Sales & Marketing . . . and who was not.

The investment in a new point-of-sale system has already been made and fully paid—and it's time to get on board.

He already moved his belongings out of their once shared apartment—and there is no going back.

Paternity leave has always been unpaid in this organization and pet insurance has never been subsidized. The benefits package, meanwhile, is not likely to change any time soon.

Applicable examples are exhaustive and exhausting. Without exaggerating, the catalyst for our foe's emergence might literally be anything that has already been determined and decided.

Again, we must remind ourselves that just because an issue is solved (or decided) does *not* mean it is equally resolved. Someone remains peeved about an outcome from the past—and it has now spilled onto the pages of a new chapter. Simply put, healthier organizational behavior has not yet transpired when there is evidence that present-day problems are directly linked to an event in the past. Something must be done. And where the remedy with Disagreement and Disappointment puts some of the responsibility on others to preserve unity, the opposition with this foe needs to be slayed by the leader alone.

This can only be done through direct contact with the source of discontent that has now metastasized into disunity. Yes, the more convenient and comfortable alternative will be to do nothing and to depend on the passage of time to take care of the trauma being inflicted on a formerly unified cadre—but the leader *cannot* pursue this primrose path.

Any unresolved disagreement, disappointment, anger, hurt or frustration that is discovered or even suspected needs to be addressed. And promptly. Not doing so will result in a Team that is, at a minimum, out of alignment. More likely, it will cascade into valuable members questioning or working against a healthy culture. When this happens, Solved But Unresolved gains an ally—or builds an allied coalition—on the inside. It is simply true that any foothold of discontent that remains active holds the likely (however unattractive) prospect for growth. Like a surgeon, the leader must heal, neutralize or remove the infection before it spreads further.

Of course, there are reams of published research on conflict resolution. As conflict is verifiably common in even the most service-centered organizations, it would behoove any leader to absorb and consider as much of it as possible. At the same time, it is important to note that overpowering Solved But Unresolved is not conventional conflict-related combat. After all, we are *not* ironing out a difference of opinion or mediating in the interests of multiple parties. Our specific task is to determine whether someone (or multiple persons) can productively accept the solution that has been elected and the decisions that have already been enacted.

With this in mind, properly categorizing the root cause of our formidable foe can help conjure a remedy. There are three most common reasons I've found unity comes under attack through Solved But Unresolved: internal conflict, unpopular decisions, and poor performance.

Internal Conflict

For inter-personnel hostilities, you must have an undeniably difficult conversation with both (or all) Team Members who are experiencing friction . . . Yes, at the same time. And in the same place, if possible.

From the onset, the intent is purposefully twofold:

- To state and demonstrate the sum is greater than its parts
- To reach consensus that the future of our organization will not be held hostage by any personal history.

Whether the issue is inside or outside the organization, it matters not. For sure, a rift can be explored more deeply when it is a legitimate workplace matter. But even in the most personal of situations among Team Members, the scenario at hand can be referenced in permissible terms to ensure the objectives and progress of the larger Team and the organizational Mission are not compromised. Those involved must understand there are consequences when it is—and no one is exempt from holding this standard. Despite their previous encounter with Disagreement and Disappointment, they must also acknowledge that the organization's compass still points forward.

Unpopular Decisions

When there is obvious—or even sensed—resistance to a decision made by the leader that is affecting Team connectivity and morale, the befitting forces of Trust and Transparency should be immediately called upon to restore unity and return the focus to the work that lies ahead.

Of course, to capably summon these assets, leaders will need to have made previous deposits of those same characteristics into the emotional and intellectual accounts of their followers. If this has not yet transpired, the following suggestion has no merit. There is preceding work that needs to be done.

But when a leader has already successfully banked these prepayments, the direction for our next few steps remains superbly clear: straight ahead. After all, the historical evidence of Trust and Transparency credibly frames even unloved pronouncements. Even better in these uncomfortable situations, it rightly shifts attention to a leader's responsibility and authority to make unpopular choices for the longer term and greater good of the organization. Such a hard-earned and necessary platform supports both requests for support and calls to action. And it often sounds like this: "I know many of you are opposed to my recent decision. I hear and feel your unease. I am grateful for it. And to some extent, I share it. You know it is rare when I invoke my role to reinforce my responsibilities. But I'm doing it here. I need and I expect your support with this."

In these instances, the past may be summoned and the future may be referenced—but it is the clarity of expectation and an expression of appreciation for the current effort that carry the moment. I have found this is equally true whether an individual matter or a company-wide consideration.

And for those who cannot honor such explicitness for support, a divergent path for them is also becoming clear . . .

Poor Performance

In high-performing organizations, direct and detailed feedback is the strategic bridge between expectations and results. Leaders should be able to travel unhindered back and forth across this most valuable of organizational viaducts with ever-increasing comfort. Moreover, teams, departments, and individuals should be accustomed to this movement and anticipate it accordingly.

Feedback is given. Feedback is received. Feedback is suggested. Feedback is sought.

Even so, there will always be unease if performance is lacking and when standards are compromised. The same is true if results are unconvincing or unclear. To no surprise, this impacts the sense and presence of unity. Fortunately, there are two enduring elements of dialogue that greatly assist with giving proper feedback and may become a leader's trusted allies. They work to focus the discussion and install boundaries as to where such discussions— sometimes difficult discussions, to be sure—can go. In turn, they defeat ambiguity and they cultivate consensus. They are:

1. Rhetorical questions
2. Audible responses

The following conversations are hypotheticals. Even so, they may directly reflect those necessary in your organization. Please take particular notice of referenced norms and established protocols.

Example 1

LEADER: Landon, I want to be sure you were properly acquainted with the KPI we established for the growth of our YouTube channel. There were two elements. Can you recall them?

LANDON: Yes, we were going to double the number of videos in our library and increase our subscribers to seven hundred and fifty.

LEADER: That is correct. How are we doing on these targets?

Example 2

LEADER: Brooke, these imperatives were most recently emphasized during your initial training session as a new district manager. So without wanting this to sound like a pop quiz, can you tell me each of our Core Values that come to mind?

BROOKE: Sure. The themes are Respect Others, Share Resources, and Serve Always.

LEADER: Great. Well done. And now with that institutional knowledge as a foundation, can you help me understand the continued absence of weekly schedules for your kitchen managers and line cooks on our scheduling app?

Example 3

LEADER: Carissa, I understand you've been with us for less than three months. As such, it is possible we've not yet stressed the importance of our Satisfaction Guarantee enough. Do you have a general understanding of what this guarantee says to our patrons?

CARISSA: Not really. Not yet, anyway.

LEADER: Fair enough. In essence, we will *always* provide a refund or exchange for anyone who is disappointed in the performance of their purchase. With this in mind, how do you think your recent response to a longtime customer that there was "not anything you could do" because the purchase had "been made over thirty days ago" went over with her?

These examples are not sophisticated. And whether as a consumer, Team Member or leader, they are easily relatable. But most importantly, they reflect the practice of a leader who is committed to correcting inaccurate behavior, ineffective action or incomplete results. Applying rhetorical questions and encouraging audible responses make for an objective exchange that can be easily documented for an employee file and doubles as an open runway for effectively specific feedback.

Tolerated Treason

Some words just sound particularly menacing when used outside of their traditional context. Take the word "sin," for example. This word is likely laced throughout sermons, homilies, and faith teachings each week in places where people gather to reflect upon certain spiritual beliefs. And though "sin" is unlikely to be celebrated in these settings, it is also doubtful its use in churches, synagogues, mosques, and other houses of worship will be surprising or cause listeners to conclude a message went too far. However, the use of this same word in workplace, academic or public spaces is almost nonexistent. For a term that finds rightful synonyms in "crime," "error," "mistake," and "misdoing," why is it that such a concise and widely embraced word like "sin" is so conspicuously absent from these other environments?

I've found in my own (admittedly limited) research that it is because the word itself invokes a sense of seriousness *and* judgment that puts an unexpecting audience on uneasy alert . . .

The same phenomenon appears to be true with the word "treason." If this term is not used in a historical or espionage-related context, it seemingly comes off as even more grievous and punishing than its companions "disloyalty" and "deception."

But as we begin to unpack the characteristics of this far too familiar foe of unity, we are going to call it what it is. And it is, indeed, treason. It is an ugly act of betrayal.

To be sure, it is also incumbent upon us to be damning and judgmental when it shows up at our doorstep. Leaders with mission work that matters must simply exile it from the organization.

To do so, we must first understand what it looks like and how it appears in an organization or on our Team. And just like with nations where such an offense is, perhaps, punishable by death, stamping out treason begins with consistent public proclamations. These communications remind us of the organizational essence that is the reason for our very existence.

From there, our unity-motivated nonnegotiables must become impenetrable.

A House Divided . . .

To show the dangers associated with organizational treason, let's use an example that has an almost universal application. IHG Hotels & Resorts is a conglomerate of more than six thousand lodging locations, across nineteen brands, with both corporately owned and franchised operations. The stakeholders are many, including guests, employees, shareholders, franchisees, suppliers, and business partners. Their stated organizational purpose is to provide "True Hospitality for Good." Cover-page commentary on their Social Justice & Diversity webpage includes the evergreen adage that "actions will have a more lasting effect than our words." One of three core actions to which the company has devoted itself is to "Advocate." This includes a pledge to "support important causes in the fight for equality and implement policies within our company to support these principles." Even more specifically, a commitment connected to this initiative includes an internal mandate to "require [a] diverse candidate shortlist and interview panel processes."[6]

Per IHG's annual report, we are now cresting four-plus years since this editorial was created and circulated.[7] As such, IHG senior management must now be very mindful of—and on the lookout for—instances where this statement of intent may not be actualized. Whether it is regarding an open position for the head of housekeeping at a franchised location in Des Moines or the decision-making process for determining the landscaping maintenance firm for the resort in Dubai, any person of authority who does not subscribe to the clear directive of IHG's core actions is, you guessed it, treasonous. After all, to show indifference to IHG's action plan is not just to ignore a publicly stated policy but to boldly and blatantly undermine a tenet essential to the spirit of the IHG constitution. To be sure, I am *not* suggesting any such antipathy or obstruction currently exists within IHG—I would not know. Nor is it our collective concern, as we each have our own organizations to which to attend.

To put it concisely, if we make it a statement of fact, that is how we must act.

As Abraham Lincoln more aptly stated, "A house divided against itself cannot stand."

In other words, where there are strong and stated convictions, there can be neither resistance from, nor a recess for, our ordained promise keepers—our Team Members. These are the persons who serve as an example for our new arrivals and our welcomed outsiders. These are the ambassadors who exhibit the character of our brand and the sincerity of our promises. These are the influencers who have prime-time status with those we serve and those who we hope will join us. The condition of unity is in our hands—and theirs.

As leaders, we can accept an imperfect decision following a complex consideration. When a desired result comes up short, we can still respect the concerted effort that preceded it. And we can even celebrate mistakes made in the pursuit of a better product. But we can never compromise on our principles. And we certainly cannot allow the comfort of the moment to shadow the importance of the future. We cannot afford even a slight chisel in our reputational bedrock. Even when we are already overwhelmed and understaffed, we must never accept even the smallest degree of treason, for it will pierce and drain the organizational lifeblood that flows through our mission, our core values, and our behavioral standards.

And with that, we have exposed the four fiercest foes of unity. For sure, unified organizations must also be fortified organizations. Even with their cover blown, our foes will be forever intent on scaling the walls of our fortress to ransack what we suggest is sacred. They will always have a Trojan horse at our gate, loaded with temptation and unwise compromise, as we facilitate strategic growth and administer resource allocation. They will not relent. They will not rest.

And neither must we.

It's the Mortar:
Involved Maximization Imperatives for Chapter 2

1. Reread—and, if possible, commit to memory (your own modified version is fine!)—the definitions of both Uninvolved Optimization and Involved Maximization which precede chapter 2.

2. Find no less than one person inside or outside your organization with whom to share these definitions *and* your intention to be increasingly mindful and proactive about UO and IM. These people should have a reliable ability and level of comfort to provide sufficient accountability to you.

3. Schedule a meeting in a location chosen exclusively as an optimal venue for maximizing productivity. Be honest. Do not let convenience or other typical considerations creep into the selection. For bonus points, scan your schedule to determine where you will be stationed for your various conference calls and videoconferences this month. Are these locations *really* optimized for these activities?

4. Take ten minutes to consider if/where unity in your areas of responsibility is currently lacking or potentially jeopardized. Carefully determine which foe is responsible for the absence and/or is threatening your confidence. Then . . . make notes and take action!

CHAPTER 3

Stuck in the Middle with Me

Humility, Aside ... Everything Really Does Depend on the Leader

My primary retail business was born in the immediate aftermath of September 11, 2001. Like most who are old enough to remember this miserable day, I can still vividly recall my whereabouts and responses to the ongoing rollout of information and necessary adjustments . . . I will forever be fueled by this tragedy, as it was the catalyst for my journey to the service industry. It was my calling to enroll in the daily service of others.

The following are a couple of brief excerpts from a blog I published after this business had reached its five-year mark. In combination, they reflect why I was where I was—and why I went where I went. Most importantly, they helped me prepare an early premise for why it is, indeed, the mortar (and not the bricks).

Excerpt 1

It is my opinion that every American of voting age can recall intimately personal details from September 11, 2001. For my generation, this is our Pearl Harbor. We can remember exactly where we were, as well as some of the disbelief, sadness and shock that went rattling through our mind and body when we saw images from, heard about, or even eye-witnessed this formerly inconceivable attack and ghastly tragedy.

For me, I was in a bright, smallish conference room in Tampa, Florida, at a Coca-Cola Bottling Company facility. After the first plane hit, we briefly paused to hear the report of a seemingly unique aviation accident. We had no sense of the events to come—and we plowed on with launch plans for a new beverage nearing its introduction date.

When the second plane found its target, it was without delay that we were interrupted by the news. The meeting was immediately suspended—and the formerly unfathomable played out for us on a television mounted in the corner of the lobby.

Excerpt 2

Initially, it was nothing more than the volume of noise coming from the exhaust pipes on the speeding Harley–Davidson just north of Ocala that stirred me from my robotic state. This renewed consciousness presented me the opportunity to observe him from my rearview mirror to my front windshield, as he overtook me. The American flag, secured happenstance to the double-bucket backrest, was twice the size of the transport. The speed of the motorcycle obligated the flag to shutter fiercely in the air. I depressed the accelerator hard to maintain my view of—and my fraternal contact with—the rider.

With the eventual realization I had my borrowed sedan at an uncommon speed for its traditional use, I eased the pace. I soon lost both sight and sound of the motorcyclist. As he sped away, tears began pouring down my face. I punched the triangular symbol identifying the hazard lights and pulled over to the shoulder. Through watery, blurry eyes, I stared blankly at the now empty and sun-splashed roadway . . .

It was clear much was going to change in the world I knew. And I knew I needed a change, too.

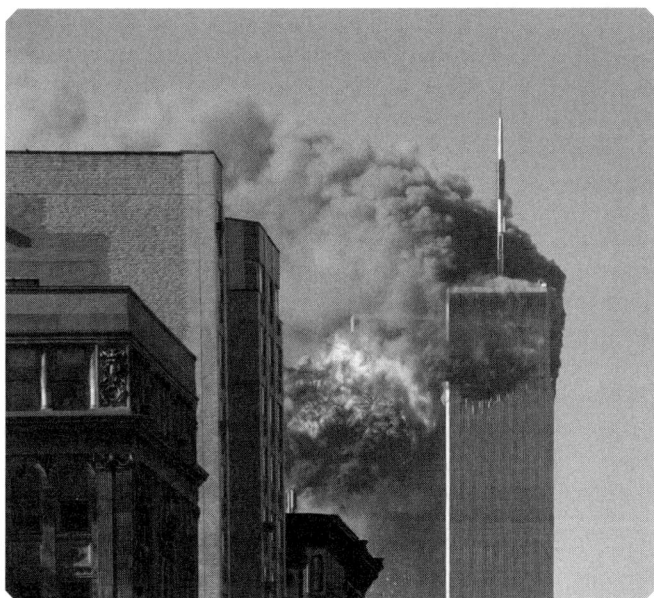

The Twin Towers exploding after being struck by two planes, September 11, 2001.
Reprinted with permission by Flickr user TheMachineStops (Robert J. Fisch).

From Pain Comes Purpose— and from Nothing Comes Something

What followed my interstate tears in a commandeered rental car on September 11 was a state of restless sleep in my own home . . . In heavy darkness the following morning, the opening editorial session for a business plan commenced. My whispered declarations from the day prior inspired a Mission Statement almost immediately.

I had benefited physically, intellectually, recreationally, and socially from committed involvement in an active lifestyle. I had completed one-hundred-plus marathons and ultramarathons, won races at every distance from five kilometers to fifty miles, participated in some of the world's most prestigious endurance events, and had a publishing deal for a book to reinforce my authority as a resource for local runners (*Atlanta Running Guide*, Peachtree Publishers, 2003). My fitness routine had nearly become my singular purpose.

But now, seated in silence at my kitchen table, the deafening echoes of the day prior beckoned me to a future where my competitive spirit was no longer solely purposed for my own benefit.

I had little doubt—and there was ample published research to confirm—that many people for many reasons would benefit from being more fitness-minded. I reasoned (and still assert) that better relationships, communities, classrooms, organizations, leaders, and families emerge when a disciplined, meaningful, and enjoyable approach to health and wellness is embraced. As James Clear, author of *Atomic Habits*, has suggested in his weekly newsletter, "If you can only pick one habit to build, exercise might be the one. Everything is downstream from how your body is functioning."[1]

Still, neither my history of hard workouts—nor my recently composed Mission Statement (*To grow, support and enhance an active lifestyle in and around Atlanta*)—offered me any natural advantage in a retail environment or service-based endeavor. With only brief stints as an uninspired server and bartender, my customer service experience was marginal. As a retailer, it was altogether absent. An honorable mission guided by the painful motivation of the 9/11 terrorist attacks was a fine place to begin—but I was certain there would need to be a far better foundation from which to build to *really* get started.

PASTE: Personal Core Values That Keep It All Together

Mission Statements. Core Values. Promises, purposes, and plans. Each concept deserves its time in the spotlight. And when drawn together, they comprise concentric circles overlapping both personal growth and organizational life.

I'm an admitted fanboy of all of it.

I'm the author and overseer of a Personal Mission Statement, multiple Organizational Mission statements, a Guest Promise, and a line-up of Core Values that directly link to my businesses, my family, and other prioritized elements in my life. Each year, I also spend numerous days evaluating organizational performance connected to Key Priority Indicators and assessing the progress made with quarterly and annual plans. These various considerations act as waypoints and watchtowers from where I may take helpful vantage. And in the pages ahead I will continue to share and celebrate their importance and influence, as they are simply integral to the pursuit of Uninvolved Optimization. They are, in fact, also near-daily accomplices to Involved Maximization.

But when I retreat to the earliest days of my entrepreneurial story, I will admit that none of these concepts and practices contributed to any initial progress. They did not matter. They didn't even exist.

How could they?

After all, these often popular and recommended declarations must come from somewhere. Like it or not, when we intend to make something from nothing, the only place to start is with ourselves. Personal commitment must precede confident pronouncements. You are the commanding agent of change. You are the origin story. In these instances, it does unquestionably begin with you.

Perfectly enough, this sometimes difficult acknowledgment links back to our prologue, where you may recall the definition for our utmost ingredient: "Mortar is a workable paste . . ." And, man, what a paste I found it can be! This forthcoming PASTE was my starting point—and acronymically speaking, it remains the most reliable substance in any endeavor I pursue. I believe this is the mortar that matters most for leaders with a mission to move ahead. And for aspiring leaders in our industry, experience tells me this is also the PASTE on which service-minded possibilities are predicated. Like its clay-composed counterpart found in impressive construction projects everywhere, it enables so many interesting possibilities . . . and never ceases in its effort to hold everything together.

P: POWERFUL PERSONAL PRODUCTIVITY

Leaders are not necessarily the smartest person, most talented resource, or biggest personality in the room, on the team or with the organization. But—they do *not* get outworked by anyone else. Not for long, anyway. And since everyone gets the same amount of time each day, productivity becomes the metric that becomes the best predictor of results. The most productive leaders get the best results. Equally important in an age of abundant distractions only an arm's length away, those who are most productive are also those who are the most discerning and intentional with every moment of their day.

A: ACCOUNTABILITY

When leading projects and people, the quantity of timelines, deadlines, appointments, commitments, and expectations is undeniably substantial. The ability to succeed in finite time with almost countless tasks is fully dependent upon an equal ability to prioritize and organize accordingly. Without a doubt, personal *and* organizational credibility is always on the line. And as a result, we must take specific action, honor our commitments, and make stuff happen. For our sake and the sake of others, we do not *just* manage. We claim ownership! We own our time. We own the duties ahead. We own the results from the past. They are ours. And if they are incomplete or substandard, they are *all* ours.

Accountability begins with holding ourselves accountable. It matures from holding ourselves accountable to holding others accountable. Anything less than complete ownership of each element we've commissioned threatens the confidence we want (and need) others to have in us *and* those who surround us. For good reason, no one confidently follows a leader who cannot be held accountable to herself. The rhythm of leadership suggests we grow increasingly comfortable with our vulnerabilities. And before we know any outcomes, we would be wise to embrace humility. Nonetheless, in a never-ending battle with uncertainty, we must be a leader who quietly tells ourselves—and truly believes—"This is on me."

S: SERVICE-CENTEREDNESS

Contrary to conventional thinking, a leader works for more people inside and outside the organization than anyone else on the Team. Reporting structures and org charts, be damned! The most successful leaders and entrepreneurs in the service industry know full well that they do *not* actually work for themselves. Instead, they selflessly avail themselves in work that is to the benefit of others. And critically, they are mindful of the ever-gazing eyes of others, knowing their every action will be a cue to the Team. A leader's duty, after all, is to initiate and sustain an unfailingly exemplary level of service to all constituents.

T: TRANSPARENCY

The development of productive and ever-improving systems requires a Team focused and interested most in the effort at hand. Leaders must not leave those contributing to such important work to wonder (or worse, worry) about other organizational factors or personal considerations that are unproductive and distracting. Unending transparency ensures everyone is confident to do their best work by being provided the most accurate and necessary information available. Even better, transparency creates a culture where asking questions and expecting straight answers is validated and encouraged. To be clear, there is nothing about the organization or the objectives that should be kept from those most closely aligned with the work being performed and the results being pursued.

I will introduce an enlightening case study from my retail space of Sporting Goods that unequivocally depicts how this leadership principle is expertly employed. For those who resist such uninhibited transparency, this example will likely do nothing to allay concerns that an approach with this characteristic out front can be paralyzingly hard. Even so, I believe the most proven leaders instinctively know there is no law in leadership that prohibits what is personally burdensome from being an effective ally to what is organizationally best . . .

REI: Presenting a Clear Picture

"When we've had to make difficult decisions like these in the past, you've shared clear feedback asking for more transparency and time to understand what's happening—and why."

This is verbatim commentary from Eric Artz, CEO of REI Co-op in 2024, in a company memorandum.[2] It came to employees less than six months after the organization let almost three hundred in-store associates go . . . and it was in advance of cutting three-hundred-plus more staff members in distribution centers and at headquarters. Artz went on to say, "I am sharing these details with you this morning so that you have a clear picture of what will happen today and in the days to come. Decisions like these—with real impacts to people's lives and livelihoods—are the most difficult that I must make as your CEO."[3]

An article in *Sporting Goods Business* went on to detail that the changes in headcount were driven by financial necessity and were done through a strategic approach that evaluated team structures against business needs.[4] I estimate it was a critical and overdue exercise to eliminate redundant and increasingly irrelevant roles. On paper, every leader knows this to be sensible and necessary decision-making . . . In practice, we also know this to be a difficult situation traditionally done in extreme secrecy until the blade falls.

Most interesting to me, the report by *Sporting Goods Business* on this objective reality at REI included an impressionistic analysis. And while uncommonly threading both approaches, it provided the recipe for transparency to be repeatedly successful in our own application. More specifically, the article's headline was that REI "Forecasts Revenue Decline for 2024" and quoted extensively from the CEO's letter—yet it also subjectively offered, "The letter appeared to be genuine, empathetic and clear."[5]

Exactly.

E: ENTHUSIASM

Success is not likely to be achieved without struggle; undesirable and highly intimidating challenges simply come with any worthwhile endeavor. In addition, industry veterans know that service to others is not a craft where you can acquiesce to those who dampen a Team's energy. As such, maintaining genuine enthusiasm for what you are pursuing is mandatory to endure the leadership rollercoaster. Your enthusiasm naturally draws others to you and to the project at hand—and when this happens, it enables opportunities to specify your Mission, provide direction, and effectively communicate with those who will jointly determine the success of your ambitions.

For sure, each of the PASTE attributes is a conscious choice made frequently. There are no hacks or shortcuts to trim the distance to these conditions or that allow us to let up on the required discipline to maintain them. It is a daily grind with no shortage of possible shortfalls. Fortunately for those who execute this regimen with persistence, there is a useful and suitable reward. To be specific, it is when this PASTE hardens that we can build with conviction!

Let's get to work! And let's start with that to which we can attach all that follows . . .

A Day Earlier and a Decade Later: The Importance of Organizational Core Values

Composing and communicating Core Values is BIG work that must withstand a heavy load. Like New Year's resolutions, countless organizations have scripted such for favorable change only to fatigue or falter before realizing the desired results. Equally unfortunate, there are millionfold examples where the exercise to introduce Core Values was completed—but important decisions were soon made without any reference to the posted values themselves, leading to avoidable mistakes. It is wasteful to spend time penning organizational values that become nothing more than baseless filler for unadorned walls in a commercial space. If Core Values are only rarely consulted, you are better off without them.

When utilized cogently and consistently, however, bold and unequivocal statements cast a clear vision and establish a deep sense of purpose. More tangibly, they set a true direction on the road to Uninvolved Optimization. In fact, to steward well-founded and effectively implemented Core Values is to expertly engage in metaphorical mapmaking. A master cartographer, you will be!

But we cannot rush it. Steadfast disciplines do not materialize or come to have meaning in mere moments or even months. Organizations that have not yet scribed Core Values—or do not currently ascribe to them—should be careful not to trade a powerful and eventually established principle for a quicker completion or swifter adoption of less significant possibilities. From their seeding to their gradual impact, Core Values make a singular promise: the work they demand will be arduous but rewarding.

For my primary business, I made two unrushed—but time-bound—declarations near the outset:

1. If my business was to prove an exception to the statistic reported by the U.S. Bureau of Labor that nearly 50 percent of new enterprises suspend or cease operations before the five-year mark, I would have our most popular company trademark tattooed on my body in a conspicuous location.[6]

2. If we achieved the disturbingly rare distinction of serving others and having a profitable business after a full decade, I would author Core Values and instill them deeply into our organization.

For the pledge that came first, I had two staunch exemptions from the body ink. Specifically, if I were entangled with—or climbing out of—either bankruptcy or divorce court at the time of the sixty-month milestone, the tattoo gun would remain unfilled. To me, organizational survival with that type of personal sacrifice or collateral damage did not suggest such an overt commemoration. And like is often the case with uneasy entrepreneurial humor, the commentary I still share when asked about the now somewhat faded tattoo is tinged with the truth that "I only narrowly avoided both . . ."

For my organizational Core Values, there were a few central beliefs that would buttress the ten-year gestation period:

1. As decidedly undisguised declarations of who we are *and* what we strongly believe, these statements would have a rightful impact on our reputation with both internal and external constituents.

2. It will always be that those who are affected by our Core Values will be in various stages of their own journey with our organization. The requirement to be both timely and timeless is essential and unceasing.

3. The critical, unending task of effectively articulating Core Values is made easier when the pronouncements themselves both remind us of our past successes and ensure us of their unquestionable value for the future.

To be sure, one-hundred-plus months may be an overly long observation period—*but* a confidence-securing display of consistency must precede statements made under the brightest of lights. In fact, the grand unveiling of Core Values for any organization should be a billing with both a "warm-up act" and a "headliner." The former should be represented as "historically confirmed capabilities," while the latter as "proven characteristics that are as important as ever." They forever tour together to underpin ironclad commitments.

I have found it is equally wise to exercise restraint against any temptation to erect organizational Core Values that are founded on given authority before earned credibility. It is undeniable that this hard-earned asset takes time to develop—but you must be certain such exists. The truth is that even the most polished roster of organizational Core Values will not germinate in an organization where the credibility of the leaders is not fertile enough to nourish them. Authority alone does not optimize the soil or ripen the harvest. Said differently, mix your PASTE first.

Lastly, for those who already have powerful Core Values proudly posted and reliably performed, there is a common oversight that can be quickly addressed: in too many instances, desired results are achieved, and progress is made—but the leader makes no official or meaningful effort to vocally associate the accomplishments with the values that have helped manifest them. Whether you are an entrepreneur in an organization of one—or a Team Member in a department of too many—YOU get to choose whether YOU make it standard practice to refer regularly to the values penned and the Mission stated. YOU decide whether it sounds trite, trivial, or cheesy to connect a difficult decision or recent success to declarations some may have forgotten (or never knew existed!). YOU have the choice to take an unpopular stand, with purposefully shared principles as your steadfast escort. Accomplishments and key moments are *always* prime opportunities to bolster tradition and celebrate central beliefs.

Again, it all starts with YOU.

And I'm so glad it does!

It's the Mortar:
Involved Maximization Imperatives for Chapter 3

To help illustrate this chapter's Imperatives, I'm going to share the Core Values from one of my primary businesses. For the two-part assignment that follows, there is no need for me to provide a deep context regarding the business itself. Suffice it to say, it is a retail operation that leads with customer service and recognizes its dependence on those within the organization for its acumen in this respect. These two assignments precede a final recommendation to begin crafting, revising, or validating your own organization's Core Values.

Part I

Here are your specific tasks as you consider the values outlined below:

1. With each of these four values, make notes first on how *you* feel your organization or Team would represent them. In other words, if you had to adopt them as your own, where would delight be found or doom creep in? It is okay to overthink it. In fact, it is important to cite the excitement and inspiration, as well as the disappointment and frustration—not to mention any other feelings—that may result from comparing your organization to another. The forthcoming statements that poke you most viscerally are tickling your nerves for *good reason*. As pastor and author Andy Stanley says, you should "pay attention to that tension" when making those big, important decisions.[7] With this context, if there is a statement you like and has potential application to your enterprise—but seems like a stretch for your current Team to embrace—you must note and address it during this exercise.

2. With your senses now awakened, consider the hallmarks of your organization or Team on your best days and through your most sensational seasons. Please continue to be generous with your notes.

3. With equal clear-sightedness, please consider the most prevalent characteristics of your organization when uncertainty (or worse) seemed to lurk around every corner, and difficult decisions filled every cranny of your operation. Try not to recoil from these unsatisfying memories, as these notes, too, are important.

Your output from this exercise should be unbridled and unfiltered. There is no remembered detail or personal observation about these potentially commonplace occurrences that is too small. With your recollection of both the good times and the lamentable moments, we are seeking the principles that anchored your actions and showed resilience against the strong winds. We are also documenting attractive behaviors that likely have not yet projected an aura of reliability with your Team. Altogether, you may find yourself reflecting on a memorable action taken by a single Team Member . . . or a regrettable decision that was approved by the board of directors. It matters not. At the bottom of your sheet, tablet or document, record these moments that had an impact on you, to whatever length is necessary.

Part II

The next part of the assignment will be to travel throughout your organization—and into your various agendas—to evaluate which of the *favorable* estimations from your list are currently present and properly revered. As you encounter evidence of any obvious esteem for a prospective Core Value, add commentary to your notes. Your notations can be protectively objective or boldly subjective—but do be specific. Be very, very specific. These captured instances will become markers of validation when the time comes to illustrate your proposed Core Values to others. Like much of modern history, stories of significance were deliberately recorded to preserve their lessons, not to mention corroborate that they actually happened. Day by day and week by week, these observations will test your theories as to what can be held sacred. As decisions and investments are made—and as actions are taken and priorities are established—noticeable themes will emerge.

Pay close attention, too, to anything that opposes your emerging principles. Your Core Values cannot hope to survive when there is no instinctive, immediate repudiation of behavior that is adversarial to your prospects. If a Core Value is breathed into existence—only to be suffocated by a parasitic custom that is contrary to its very nature—what will follow will be a humiliating, damaging, and disappointing death, indeed! It is better to quietly discontinue consideration of a prospective Core Value now than to have to publicly defend one that gets put on trial later for negligence or overstatement. In an organization's relationship with its Core Values, opposites do not attract. More pointedly, antithetical behavior cannot be justified.

Here we go! Again, please take careful heed of the thoughts that cross your mind as you read the Core Values that follow.

Our Best Business Asset Is Our Team

We develop talent from within the organization so a healthy information exchange is always available, productivity is always visible, and Leadership Team positions can almost always be filled from the current roster. Everyone begins as a Guest Advocate (read: Customer Service Manager or Sales Associate) and no one retires from this position.

Make It Better

We desire a culture that demands and expects continuous improvement. We will build our business fully dependent on each Team Member's respective and recurring personal commitment to such. And while we recognize the tension that always accompanies the innovation and constant change required to make things better, we also vow to embrace and conquer it!

Always Choose Service Excellence

We cherish the numerous roles our Guests ask us to play for them, fully recognizing that friendliness and genuine interest in their pursuits will always be the underpinning of any relative success we achieve. We focus firstly on our Guests; all else follows.

We Take Fun . . . Seriously

We demonstrate how fully capable we are of growing our business, pursuing our passion, and increasing our potential, all while maximizing the amount of fun we have *and* that we bring to others.

After you've completed both parts of this Imperatives assignment, you are ready to compose, reconsider or reintroduce Core Values for your organization or Team. You are ready to transform your notes and notions into words that convey the bedrock of your department or organization. It is my preference for the leader to first do the initial composition on her own. As the initial draft is ready, a few valued Team Members should be brought along to strength-test the arguments and assist with their clarity. The statements should be concise, while the descriptors should be specific. Yes, phraseology counts. Each of your terms will likely be nuanced—but they must still come together to make a definitive statement. As progress is made, it is wise to enlist the input of others who write well and whom you would trust to script the leanings of you and your ad hoc steering committee. Of course, preferred AI resources should be employed as dutiful assistants for editing and clarity.

Above all, on the journey toward publishing or re-presenting your values, consider how the statements will be used. Here are some of the likely applications:

- They will be or become reference points when you interview prospective hires to determine if a proper fit exists.
- They will represent the ongoing expectations of recent additions to your Team and long-standing contributors alike.
- They will serve as a valuable context for both difficult discussions and difficult decisions.
- They will present reasons to celebrate everything from successful seasons to the specific action of a single colleague.

In the end, if you are like many leaders who do not yet have Core Values planned or fully penned, you will likely wish you had started sooner. But, alas, no more! Yesterday is gone. The time necessary to arrive at this state of readiness was well spent. Now you can make a powerful vow to begin, resume or revisit what is core to your organizational raison d'être and joie de vivre. Start immediately—but do *not* rush it. Make your observations. Take your notes. Share your findings. Discuss your impressions. Do the work. Get it done.

The benefits await.

CHAPTER 4:

Experience Matters

Overused and Under-Understood

The word "Experience" has been laced into the retail and restaurant industries as a specialized term for more than three decades. It easily preceded the rise of mass merchandisers, curbside pick-up, the advent of e-commerce, and the rightfully reported fickleness of shoppers and diners. From my days at The Coca-Cola Company, I still remember the word being used regularly in discussions about the "action alley" at Walmart—and how to "plus-up" a towering twelve-pack display of soft drinks the week of the Super Bowl, priced at two for five dollars.

Yes, Walmart. And soft drinks (at those prices!).

And with all due respect to Sam Walton—perhaps the most successful retail entrepreneur of all time—it is my confident estimation those canvassing an aisle in one of his stores right now are hardly basking in the warmth of a glowing experience . . . Not by the standards most of us would assign, anyway.

But let's not get ahead of ourselves. After all, what *are* those standards we would assign?

Perfectly enough, that question may identify why this incredibly overused word—*experience*—is so darned under-understood. I've asked everyone from CEOs of Fortune 100 companies to small- and medium-sized business owners to savvy consumers for their definition of this word. And even with the latitude of consideration each deserves, the length of pause before any personal definition is shared with me is likely greater than would precede the same individual's carefree use of the word in public . . .

And my educated guess is this: you, too, have used this word somewhat recently, perhaps regularly—perhaps even emphatically—without giving forethought to any universal meaning it may hold.

Fess up.

It's true, isn't it?

Yeah, me, as well. For a long time.

So what are we to do?

First, let me submit a definition on which all can agree. And I freely admit that the origin of this forthcoming definition is a bit questionable: the worldwide web. Despite volumes of a contrary opinion, I know not everything found on "www." is true. ☺

But I have used this definition in front of tens of thousands of retail industry leaders and alongside consumers on many days . . . and I've yet to encounter opposition as to its validity. To be sure, I've gained an over-whelming consensus of its appropriateness. Here it is:

Experience (ik-speer-ee *uh*ns) *n.*: the totality of the cognitions given by perception; all that is perceived, understood and remembered.

Despite my affinity for this definition, let's take a second to express some collective gratitude for the semicolon . . . But the "totality of the cognitions"?

What the heck does that mean?!

And "given by perception"?

Say what?

Exactly.

But we'll come back to that leadoff terminology. Let's move past that mumbo jumbo for now—and check out what's on the other side of that heroic semicolon. With relatively basic comprehension of the English language, we more easily recognize the elements highlighted in the back half of this definition. Perception. Understanding. Memory . . . We can tangibly grasp how those capacities contribute to our inherent ability to describe an "experience" to someone. And they certainly give foundation for how we internalize one. Most pertinently, this definition demonstrates why we can absorb experiences differently than the person next to us—or even as the same person the next time we are in an identical or similar domain.

Brilliant. "All that is perceived, understood and remembered." We now have our working definition of "Experience." And we can begin being mindful of such as we take inventory of our respective business *and* our own consumerism. All that is perceived. And understood. And remembered.

Perfect.

Shall we move on?

Sorry. No. Not yet . . . Not so fast.

First, we need to acknowledge something we knew before we settle on this definition. Even though we previously used expressions containing this word without really knowing exactly how we were defining it, we still knew (and always will know) this: experiences can be good—or they can be bad. Favorable, or unfavorable . . . After all, if our own very human existence relies on perception, comprehension, and memory to define an experience, we instinctively know it's not all utopian.

Plenty of experiences suck. Like a vacation with no special memories. Or a fine bottle of wine with no meaningful conversation . . . Or all the many other various "experiences" we understandably prefer not to recall.

And as obvious as it may be that the work we conceive, anticipate or do is all intended to deliver a "great" experience, it does *not* make it less true that our intended audience might still have an entirely opposite experiential outcome. It is indeed verifiable that there is an enormous spectrum as to how others rate the quality of any given experience. Without debating the fringes, let's just say the realm of possibility for (almost all?) experiences is largely in between "perfect" and "unacceptable."

And yet, this is *good* news for you and me!

You see, for all of us, as both consumers and Captains of Destiny, I have found that a careful grasp of this reality only further qualifies our senses;

it puts us in an advantaged position to consider the complete landscape of where "Experience" resides in our consciousness *and* in our operation. Said differently, this heightened awareness of those wide-ranging possibilities associated with "Experience" becomes a unique strength—even a super-power—that can profoundly impact every part of our business. This is where the "bricks" and "mortar" of our bricks-and-mortar operation come together. Our "Experience" is, ultimately, where that which is visible in our enterprise meets the hard work that is often unseen. Readers and friends, we have no other choice . . . We are—or must become—bona fide experts on "all that is perceived, understood, and remembered!"

The Most Important Word of ALL

"Is that all?"

I'm glad you asked. And your word choice is perfect.

Because before we go any further, there is another part of this definition of "Experience" we must tend to, grab ahold of, and become genuinely comfortable with.

It's the "All." And it is, frankly, the most important part of the definition. As in "*All* that is perceived, understood, and remembered."

Perfectly—and not so coincidentally—this is also where simplicity in the leading statement for our definition can be found. After all, "All" is the far more concise way of alluding to the "totality of the cognitions"—right there, waiting on the launch pad for those easily digestible concepts like perception and cognition and memory. Just maybe we did not need that semicolon to save us . . .

But let's check ourselves. Because here is the way this concept is usually received when I include this content in my keynote work.

ME: "All right, *all* that is perceived, understood, and remembered . . . How much?"

AUDIENCE: "All."

ME: "Yep. All. Got it?"

AUDIENCE: "Yes. But . . . really? All?"

ME: "Indeed. All. All means all."

AUDIENCE: "Well, that sounds impossible. How about 'most'? Like 92 percent or 99.5 percent."

ME: "Sorry, y'all. It's 'All.' Like 100 percent. You know . . . all."

AUDIENCE: "So, nothing else really needs to be said?"

ME: "That is correct. In other words, 'That's ALL, folks.'"

Environment & Interaction: Together. Forever.

Before I explain how to orchestrate an operation ruthlessly and unapologetically committed to making the notion of "Experience" an asset, let me assure you a sense of foreboding is normal. After all, domesticating "Experience" in your organization will require a lot of work. And embracing the "All" of it will be never-ending. It will not be easy . . . and it may not ever get any easier.

But it will be worth it. And it is manageable.

More notably, when I eventually came to fully understand the entire post-semicolon definition of "Experience," including the "All" contained therein, I also realized there are but two elements to which all aspects of a "retail experience" connect:

1. Environment
2. Interaction

Let those terms soak into your consciousness. If possible, bathe yourself in the images that come quickly to mind . . .

Now, let's consider a few retail-experience-related items together:

The timeliness and pleasantness associated with an in-store or on-phone greeting?

That's Interaction.

The cleanliness of a restroom or the brightness of lighting in a fitting room?

Environment.

The expectations for all Team Members when presenting the check to a table of diners and/or the conclusion of any sale or consultation?

Interaction.

The volume or genre of music being played from speakers overhead in a hotel lobby or the content of conversation overheard from the associates?

Environment.

Now, think about it yourself . . . Let your mind wander. Consider where you are right now. Recall where you were yesterday. Retrieve a special memory from your past. Everything you can conceive fits nicely into one of these two buckets. In fact, the real challenge (after you give up the game of trying to think of something that does *not* fit into one of these classifications) may be determining placement for recalled experiences you rightly believe could be dumped into either—or both.

Next (and even better!), take a field trip. Or go out for a coffee, or attend a game, or run an errand to (finally!) retrieve that item you need to finish that long-procrastinated project. And while you are completing this assignment, be incredibly mindful of your task. Submerge yourself in every detail that will soon surround you. Make sure each of your senses is vigilantly focused! Consider carefully and *really* listen to every word that is spoken. Be observant of each gesture and take note of every visible interface, whether directly involving you or not.

Environment and Interaction. Environment and Interaction. Environment and Interaction.

For leaders, this exercise is not to be conducted as an informative, one-time, presence-of-mind experiment. It needs to be a way of life. You should shift from the standard habit of having to consciously turn on or turn up such awareness to only occasionally giving yourself permission to turn it off or turn it down . . .

Environment and Interaction.

You now see how "All" is, indeed, *a lot*. Moreover, there is the complicated reality that not everyone's "Experience" is the same. Every person does *not* perceive, understand or remember every *thing* the same way. When I hear the music, it's too soft—but a great selection. But when you hear it, it's way too loud and an awful choice. When I ask for insight to where the hummus is located, I appreciate the personal escort to aisle seven. But when you inquire the whereabouts of the guacamole, it's an unwanted intrusion to have a stranger alongside you on the trip to the produce section while you finish the call with your pet sitter . . . We will surely get to how to best manage these discrepancies and be bold and confident in the choices we make pertaining to "Experience." But for now, let's simply acknowledge it is (deep sigh) substantial, ongoing, and complex work.

Experience by Committee: A Group Project Committed to Genuine Progress

Bishop Desmond Tutu was right about a lot of things. But the widely attributed adage that is especially applicable to the potentially overwhelming efforts with "Experience" is a sage parallel for the (even if unlikely) consumption of the planet's heaviest land animal: "There is only one way to eat an elephant: one bite at a time."

And that's the way it is with assessing and continuously improving the "Experience" in our organizations. Whether you are a food truck operator with only a couple dozen square feet under your temporary control or the vice president of stadium operations for a National Football League team that permanently occupies a dozen city blocks, it is a massive task that can only be done successfully when it is sensibly cleaved into reasonable portions.

So that this massive responsibility is more easily consumed in my organizations, I have parsed the critical elements of Environment and Interaction into two "Excellence in Experience" subcommittees. More descriptively, a specific task force is assigned to any conceivable element associated with "the Environment we provide for our Guests." We simultaneously install colleagues who are focused exclusively on all that is connected to "the Interaction we have with our Guests." Along with on-site biannual "tours" of each business unit, these subcommittees are responsible for documenting each item they've come to believe could be enhanced and advanced. The documentation is not immediately concerned with feasibility, cost or complexity. After all, the initial part of this exercise is only to capture each instance where these three to five subcommittee individuals believe improvement can be demonstrated.

This oversight produces a task list that is consistently updated and eventually transitioned to the appropriate leadership personnel for consideration and action. There are simple fixes that can be done within hours or days of the submission, while other items must be more thoughtfully scheduled or budgeted. Items not given immediate attention are placed into an "Experience Holding Pen" for future consideration. The "detainees" of this exercise are documented *and* addressed during the next round of annual or strategic-planning exercises. For the sake of the experience we provide for others, final decisions and future allocations on the committees' findings can then be made, as appropriate and actionable.

Most gratifyingly, the practices of the Excellence in Experience committees produce the following organizational benefits (alongside the experiential improvements themselves):

- The cumulatively healthy list of suggested enhancements and modifications to various procedures and in-venue considerations becomes a list of reminders *and* a roster of accomplishments for the committee and the organization to evaluate and celebrate.

- The documented items that have remained unchanged for twelve or more months have been confirmed—even if unstated—by leadership as unimportant *relative to other elements and priorities*. No mystery remains as to whether near- to midterm change is likely in these areas. An expedient review of these long-neglected tasks demonstrates that only philosophical or personnel changes can likely elevate their standing.

My final tip for this recommendation is a word of caution: it is easy to hear this suggestion and immediately qualify or disqualify various members of your current team for either or both subcommittees. But I urge you to not be so hasty!

And here's why: just as our requirement as leaders is to engage all our senses and to be a relentless observer of all that transpires around us, we must also ask the same of our Teammates. *All* our teammates . . . For sure, this will be an easier assignment for some than others. At the same time, exposure to these concepts and their accompanying exercises will be beneficial to anyone involved. Meanwhile, this exercise is only maximized when we have committee members who are selected without bias and are legitimately diverse. In fact, it is through this very commitment that we can be assured the output is intelligently reflective of *all* the persons whom we intend to better serve and delight!

The Experience Committee should likewise be formed and organized to receive and rotate team members regularly. My experience suggests a two-year term, with no more than half of the subcommittee members rolling off the committee each year. This length of service ensures the proper balance of veteran participation for the sake of intent and procedure, while also making important room for a fresh perspective and an unvarnished lens for viewing both the (supposedly) bright and (potentially) dark spaces in the existing experience. It also acknowledges the likelihood of turnover and transition.

Above all, leaders pursuing Uninvolved Optimization—and thus committed to the demands of Involved Maximization—must display their dedication to this initiative. Whether loyal customers or casual observers, everyone already knows the importance an organization places on customer experience starts at the top. And notably, when ownership or appropriate senior leadership is enthusiastically engaged and visibly appreciative of the Experience Committee, the harvest from this initiative is accelerated. Best of all, taking this lead helps to uphold the standards of customer Interaction without the need for the leader to facilitate each Interaction on her own behalf! The personal time savings here, compared to other ways a leader could spearhead quality assurance, is significant. The acquired insight also goes beyond traditional evaluation. Through the subcommittees assigned to Interaction and Environment, leaders are given a window into both the current caliber of the offered experience and the impressions of key Team

Members. The leader who champions "all that is perceived, understood, and remembered" has visibly picked up her trowel to expertly layer a rich mortar of keen awareness with the nearby pile of bricks to build the stable walls of a remarkable retail experience.

An Ode to the "Experience Economy"

My office at The Coca-Cola Company was on the twelfth floor, with eastern-facing windows overlooking the Atlanta skyline. The sill underneath this vantage point in each office on these middle floors was a popular location for employees to place awards, distinctions, photographs, and memorabilia that deserved attention. Not only was the surface sturdy and ample, but the contents thereon could be easily observed by the frequent hallway traffic when the door was ajar. For my colleagues, it was primarily commemorative eight-ounce glass bottles of Coca-Cola Classic, stuffed polar bears, and trinkets from an extensive company-licensed merchandise collection.

For me, the ledge instead became a shelf for an impressive display of books.

It was a facade.

I knew the specific titles could not be seen from the hallway—but the mere presence of a robust, private library would *surely* give the appearance to passersby that a studious and driven worker occupied this space. More so, I imagined my curated collection worked to dispel any narrative that national class ultramarathoners do not also make significant occupational contributions. The books were an organized army, subtly strategic in their effort to push back on occasional comments I heard from unconvinced coworkers made in the spirit of "Does anyone who runs eighty-plus miles every week really have any remaining mental energy or time to do real work?!"

To be sure, I had read a few paragraphs in some of the books on the windowsill . . . but most were without a page ever turned. The tomes languished like trophies in their high school hallway case, hidden behind the expansive city view that was just beyond it. My regular glances toward the window perpetually failed to go beyond a cursory scan of the words and phrases on the vertical seams.

Except once. And only once.

It was the font that first caught my attention. More specifically, there was a print/cursive combination that seemingly danced off the spine. *The Experience Economy*, it read . . . I instantly remembered its origin, as a friend had given it to me when I started realizing my dream of opening "a running store." Now, as I surveyed the collection from behind my desk, all the other titles seemed to fade away . . . I swiveled in the direction of my glance, rose from my chair, and approached the sill inquisitively—but cautiously. My unhurried pace to the window represented my doubt: "Could there be something here worth more than its contrived visibility?"

Surely it is unlikely that any single book can act as an exact how-to manual for your service intentions or aspirations; nonetheless, absorbing content that provides nourishment for any embryonic notion is crucial. As American architect Daniel Burnham has famously been attributed as saying, "Make big plans; aim high in hope and work, remembering that a noble, logical diagram once recorded will never die, but long after we are gone will be a living thing, asserting itself with ever growing insistency."[2]

Thus was the impact of B. Joseph Pine II and James H. Gilmore's *The Experience Economy* for me with my first business. There were two themes from this manuscript that had a powerful impact on me in my inaugural entrepreneurial endeavor. Even today, they continue to guide certain decisions and practices relating to the retail experiences my Team and I offer. Let's address each.

1. In the first edition, "Experiences" were placed at the apex of the Value Proposition spectrum. This placement was notably above more widely understood marketplace drivers, including commodities, goods, and services. As a predictable example, a coffee bean is a Commodity, while a can of Maxwell House is a Good and a cup of java served with an Egg McMuffin is a Service. On the other hand, the book's example of a trip to Starbucks—or that espresso from your favorite locally roasted, locally brewed purveyor, served in a fancy mug, with latte art featuring an Olympic wreath encircling the top of your drink—is an Experience. The authors empirically contend it would be only those who successfully craft an Experience

that could have a real influence on their margin and anticipate future success. More descriptively, Pine and Gilmore wrote it as follows: "[Companies] that thrive will do so because they treat their economic offering as a rich experience—and not a glorified good or celebrated service—and will stage it in a way that engages the individual and leaves behind a memory."[3]

2. Every place of business (and elsewhere) is a stage on which a performance is being given. We are all performers—even when we think no one is watching. As a result, we must consider our service and occupational actions as artistry on display, caring for and being mindful of each little detail. Even if it is not viewed as "theatrical" per se, our organization very much crafts a performance in all that we do. The authors continue to help us see that our marketplace offering very much includes staging, a script, actors, and a plot.[4] And no matter our profession or product, we aspire to bring the audience to their feet in applause, wanting more—and wanting to see and share the experience again and again and again.

At the risk of a spoiler, I will also mention my key takeaway from the second edition of *The Experience Economy*, published more than twelve years after the copy that produced the content referenced above (and that I still repeatedly devour). In this later release, there is a twist: those of us whose organizations have benefited from the creation of experiences are put on notice—for our authors crown a new champion of the economic spectrum. To be specific, economically advanced societies have now entered the *Transformation* economy. And there is no turning back! It is decidedly incumbent upon leaders to recognize something that *only* creates a special memory is no longer enough. We must rather participate with those we serve in a true—and total—transformation.

Wow. Let that sink in. (To learn more about *The Experience Economy* and related work, be sure to visit www.StrategicHorizons.com.)

Go. Get. It.

My previous skepticism regarding the value of a personal library is now long gone. To me, we constantly need information and inspiration to discover new possibilities for our service-first endeavors.

Fortunately, helpful resources now materialize with barely a few taps on the keyboard. We can read the suggestions immediately, have the proven plans delivered tomorrow, and automate the insight to arrive in the manner and rhythm we desire. No longer does the distance that separates us from our peers—or the death of the greats who preceded us in our pursuits—prevent us from tethering onto what others are doing or how it was done!

It's that easy. And it's that hard . . . because each of us must still go get it. Leaders have immediate access to more information than collectively exists in the best university libraries. Whether we engage this bounty circumspectly—as I did the books beneath the windows in my office—or whether we do so with zeal, we advantage ourselves greatly when we make regular use of the vast access we have at our fingertips. Even when our network is unimpressive and our experience is limited, there is no unmovable barrier to continuous improvement. Order the book. Read the blog post. Download the document. Claim the insight contained therein for yourself—and put it to good use.

It's the Mortar:
Involved Maximization Imperatives for Chapter 4

For leaders in the service industry who are serious about achieving Uninvolved Optimization, there is only one proudly predictable Involved Maximization Imperative that comes with this chapter—and it is one of the most important and nonnegotiable imperatives you will find in this book: the formation of an Experience Committee.

When an experience consistently depends on delivery from—or the involvement of—the leader, organizational growth is capped. No matter the efficiency or proficiency achieved, even the most inspired artist will reach her own capacity. We must instead equip and enthuse others to perform the service we have perfected ourselves—and to which we've staked our personal and professional reputation. The Experience Committee is a means to this end. Its material existence, coupled with diligent execution, effectively disseminates the messages meant to convey what matters most. Beyond the resulting productivity, the committee also makes it both fun and fashionable to "sweat the small stuff" while striving toward your utmost service proposition.

These are the ordered steps to appoint and anoint your committee:

1. Whether with your Team, your department, or your company, gather to discuss the provided definition of "Experience." Allow each person to comment on the definition and provide the opportunity to share a personal experience and what they perceived, understood or remembered about it. It matters not whether the experience recalled is favorable. The aim is to highlight the importance and inherent existence of "experiential awareness." As the stories are told, these will be tailor-made moments to encourage colleagues to level-up their senses! Most importantly, be on the lookout for Teammates who are particularly enlivened by this exercise or who seem to be noticeably engrossed in the details they recall or hear from others. Along with a request for volunteers, you are fairly—however surreptitiously—determining who should participate on the inaugural Committee.

2. Use some of the content from the shared memories to consider with your Team the gigantic implications of the word *All* in the definition of Experience. Reassure the Team that any sense of overwhelm or lack of certainty as to where to begin is natural and welcome.

3. Present the two concepts associated with the Everything of Experience in the context of our relationship with Guests, Customers, and Clients: the Environment We Provide, and the Interaction We Have. As a basic understanding about Environment and Interaction develops, prompt a discussion about tactical approaches to cultivating positive, memorable experiences within your respective department or enterprise. Let Team Members create helpful categories in which to organize their approaches.

4. Conclude this exercise by indicating there will be two subcommittees for the soon-to-be-formed Experience Committee. To no one's

surprise (and to everyone's delight!), there will be a subcommittee for both Interaction and Environment. Ask for volunteers. Close the meeting and discussion with a timebound indication of when the inaugural committee members and assignments will be announced.

From here, leaders will have decisions to make for the placement of individuals on the Experience Committee and the Excellence in Experience subcommittees. Do not overthink it. Just get started. You can ensure a continuously improving experience in your operation by simply keeping the concepts of Environment and Interaction top of mind! And if you hold consistent meetings with your committee members, while ensuring there is always a genuine interest in their reporting and scripting of action steps, the compounding of worthwhile benefits will commence. Most importantly, the groundwork you've laid—and the commitment you've shown—with the Experience Committee will make clear your path of travel from Involved Maximization to Uninvolved Optimization!

CHAPTER 5:

Empower the Tower!

Why Building "Broadcast Towers" Is as BIG as Ever

The Tokyo Skytree, Japan. Reprinted with permission by Flickr user Jun Seita.

This is an unaltered image of the Tokyo Skytree. The snapshot is stunning by any standard, as it depicts the world's tallest broadcasting mechanism.

But what does this unrivaled behemoth of broadcasting bandwidth have to do with us? (You and me, that is.)

I am glad you asked. And here is the thing: it is just a visual. Another analogy, really. Whether you have seen the Tokyo Skytree before—and regardless of whether you were aware of its "World's Tallest" distinction—something like it has been erected on the property of your business. It is right outside the front door! The deposits you and your Team have collected by successfully serving others paid for its installation.

To be precise, such impressive communications potential has been historically labeled as "word-of-mouth advertising." And though such sky-high imagery would be an outlandish backdrop in U.S. History books, the metaphor could carry the same context in the period preceding the Revolutionary War. After all, merchants trading for a fur pelt on the banks of the St. Lawrence Seaway were just as greatly dependent upon the vocal accounts of others as we are now. Maybe even more so! After all, the choices with whom to do business in that era were truly life-and-death matters. There was a thin line between credibility and survival.

More recently, we've used terms and tactics like social media, influencer marketing, review sites, group chats, and virtual communities for this same purpose. The ability for any individual to share his or her thoughts on any interaction anywhere has never been easier! Even the newest customer-facing enterprises can expect commentary from patrons to pop up quickly and with ease across the internet.

But because of the current accessibility and ubiquitousness of these online outlets of commentary, retailers, restaurants, and other service providers are now resignedly accepting the role of the fluttering flag—instead of that of the prevailing winds—with personal comments published about their enterprise. Like with a prized painting hanging in a familiar hallway, we barely slow anymore to observe the masterpiece! Even with a long-standing and proven history in the world of commerce, favorable commentary is mostly deemed a passive asset (that is, one not requiring active management) and often relegated solely to viral visibility. In essence, we grow comfortable in the shadows of our own Tokyo Skytree, while only rarely affixing our gaze upward to grasp its actual power and potential . . .

More curiously, we allocate time for meetings to, again, hear the pledges of supposedly better SEO (search engine optimization). We purchase questionably compiled lists of total strangers so we can add them to our content-marketing distribution. We budget for paid social media as an accepted cover charge. We complete tutorials on geofencing, algorithm enhancement, internet advertising, CRM (customer relationship management) software usage, and other relevant promotional resources to improve our connection with prospective customers and provide them information more effectively . . .

To be sure, these tactics are deservedly popular. Without question, they can be worthwhile and productive. I am confident that some of them have earned their place in your marketing mix.

But there is also a renewed sense of urgency among many leaders today to discover and harness that "best advertising" resource. To them, this opportunity feels more authentic than some other currently popular options. Throughout history, it has always been reassuring to know the people we serve today will capably carry our reputation tomorrow.

Fortunately for organizations delivering remarkable experiences, the beneficiaries of our efforts have communications capabilities that rival those of entire municipalities only a decade ago. Their ability to swiftly and broadly convey perceptions and memories in real time and with hyper-specificity to an engaged audience about our brand and enterprise is undeniable.

Valued Customers *and* Invaluable Communications

As you may have noticed from previous pages, in my primary retail business we refer to those we serve as our "Guests" . . . Yes, this term is synonymous with customers, patrons, and clients in other organizations. In a general sense, we could split hairs and further refer to these persons as shoppers, passengers, diners or members. But high above these preferred terms and their nuances, there is another term that uses the Tokyo Skytree to connect them all together with metaphorical prowess.

Our valued Guests are not merely a conglomeration of individual consumers—they are our Broadcast Tower. This moniker applies to all who are served by our business or have an encounter with our brand. It reflects each constituent's almost effortless ability—even inherent nature—to communicate their experience with us to others.

Fortunately, with the delivery of a consistent and remarkable experience, the Broadcast Tower concept builds momentum easily. It is, in fact, before a word is said or any action is taken that we can commit today's task to deliver service that builds a wonderfully favorable collection of Broadcast Towers. We even have the power to continually reinforce our Broadcast Tower metaphor. Whether citing service-forward observations from the day prior in a Team huddle or while celebrating a positive testimonial from social media before a board meeting, reminders that every interaction is the intentional construction of a Broadcast Tower should be pervasive. After all, the messaging radiating from these towers speaks to the heart of our business, our organization, our Mission, and our possibilities.

Ready! Or Not?

To determine if you're ready to boost your message across all available airwaves, please recall an interaction with a *recent* customer, client or guest, whether from a casual observation or firsthand involvement.

All set?

For sure, these two freshly conjured images—the Tokyo Skytree and your recollected portrait of a memorable engagement with a recent constituent—are, in essence, the same. And to ensure they are connected, we must ask ourselves the following question with sincere honesty.

Here it is: Are you certain you would celebrate and embrace the messaging that the "Broadcast Tower" from your memory would likely compose?

Now, bring to mind a few more interactions, with the same intent. At some point, be sure one or two interactions you evaluate are *not* ones in which you directly participated in the service delivered, as finding confidence in others is crucial in the pursuit of Uninvolved Optimization. Then, as a fitting conclusion to this exercise, imagine a detailed recap of the recalled experiences as a text message sent by the customers—our Broadcast Towers—to their family members. And in a moment of complete candor, permit yourself to voyeuristically read this fictional correspondence . . .

As a gut check, do you delight in what you're likely seeing in this exchange among loved ones?

For those who are courageously truthful and would admit nervousness around any public or shared review of the recollected experiences, I respectfully—but heartily—recommend you review the concepts of "Environment and Interaction" and the assignment of developing Core Values before further considering our customer base as a key marketing element. Our mighty Broadcast Towers have no inherent bias for favorable discourse. We already know bad experiences transmit on the airwaves just as fluidly as good experiences do. Radio silence exists no more for any retailer or service performer! This is why you must first do the heavy lifting that comes with the formation and continuous progress of your Experience Committee. So if necessary, temporarily retreat back to those pages. Reread those words. Create your action plan. Make candid assessments and commit admirably to putting first things first!

If you are currently among those who have survived and addressed the otherwise inconvenient truths about customer experience in service environments, know that there are now tactics reserved for businesses where "talk value" is real value. After all, your service proposition has attained a hard-earned, noteworthy status: It is robust. It is reliable. It is remarkable. And it is worth sharing across all available platforms. Here you have a unique opportunity to engage in the prestigious work of enacting what I call the "The Rightful Rhyme."

Simply put, it's time to "Empower the Tower!" Because like with all good broadcasting instruments, we should not just build them tall... we should also power them up.

Ultimately, this rallying cry initiates an amplification of the voices of our satisfied patrons—our Broadcast Towers!—who have enthusiastically joined us on our summit to the peak. Plainly speaking, there is is no worthwhile humility found in being shy about the spectacular service you deliver (and, perhaps, guarantee) . . . It is *not* an act of sensible modesty to keep rightful praise to yourself. In fact, it is potentially selfish to bury a headline full of hope when you have a product that will make the lives of other people better. It is repeatedly reported that over 90 percent of consumers make purchasing decisions that are influenced by recommendations and online reviews.[1] As an initiative, Empower the Tower proclaims that it is time to *maximize* the chatter! After all, when a beautiful service proposition is paired with a powerful broadcasting source, the opportunity to bring similar satisfaction to even more deserving members of the community is mightily boosted.

Below you will find some of the most effective pathways (out of otherwise numerous possibilities) toward a more sizable and effective platform from which to broadcast a redeeming message about the services you provide. While some options may apply most effectively to specific situations, you will find each provides a no-cost-to-low-cost opportunity that is perpetually fueled by your level of service. They work both externally to drive more traffic to your enterprise *and* internally to generate more momentum for your Mission.

Here are some first steps to make the most of your Broadcast Towers:

- Ensure the placement of permanent or scrolling testimonials in a prominent location on the homepage of your website.
- Institute social media features with an "Ambassador" of the day/week/month, featuring a recent customer and including details of the experience and the transformative outcome.
- Utilize POS-enabled software—or a personal note with a link—that sends a message of gratitude, as well as a brief survey, to anyone who has made a recent visit (purchase).
- Use the results from a recently conducted Customer Satisfaction survey on your website, in your company meetings, and with your advertising.
- Display a reminder at checkout about the preferred online review site for the establishment and a humble request to consider leaving an honest review (do *not* limit responses by qualifying, "If you were pleased").
- Create an invitation for patrons to send a note, recording or video message that can promptly be shared with the leadership and the rest of the organization at an upcoming activity (perhaps an Experience Committee meeting!). Every customer should at a minimum have easy access to an e-mail address of someone in the organization who is connected to the experience and who has an appropriate level of authority and a responsibility to respond. Although response times are predictably more measured when addressing concerns, a prompt reply when receiving or noticing a favorable review only deepens the connection between patron and provider!

As you consider these suggestions, you will undoubtedly have more ideas as to how to utilize your fans in a manner that makes their "word of mouth" ever the mightier. Jot them down, and don't hesitate to try them out. Again, featuring the work you've already done—*and* the favorable impact you've already had—in your communications is both smart *and* generous. No matter what you sell or offer, others want to experience the same joy as those already celebrating their satisfaction with your services!*

The Cycle of Satisfaction

Below you'll find another visual I use to complement conversations about the Tokyo Skytree and the unbeatable power of our Guests proudly serving as Broadcast Towers for our endeavors. It reflects the chronology that precedes our opportunity to Empower the Tower, illustrating how we regenerate the satisfaction patrons derive from our services in a cycle that continuously unites the Sales Associates with the Marketing Department (even if they're the same people!) . . .

The Cycle of Satisfaction

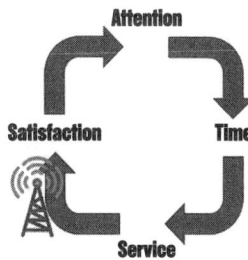

The Cycle of Satisfaction shows us four ordered and recurring elements for service-minded enterprises to put their good reputation to work for an

---

* Please keep in mind you cannot use testimonials without permission or without an effort to protect someone's identity. It is always recommended to ask a customer for permission when they indicate or express gratification. Most people are genuinely enthused to represent your service-rich enterprise because of how you so favorably impacted them. Again, most people do not wish to keep good news to themselves! Conversely, if you do not have expressed permission, abridging names as "Mike C." or "Mike from Atlanta" is acceptable.

even more favorable future. Please note where in the sequence the broadcast tower is located. That placement is not a happenstance.

Here's how it works:

We objectively understand the attention of others is the fundamental basis of any existing or anticipated success achieved in the service industry. If you get no one's attention, there is no success. It is that simple. And the more attention your enterprise gets, the better your prospects for increased success. Attention must be a strategic pursuit.

The importance of attention is not so much because of what it is . . . but, instead, because of where it *leads*. "The notice taken of someone or something" (as "Attention" is defined by Oxford Languages) is the prized precursor to obtaining "the golden opportunity": someone's *time*. We know this to be true from our own experience. Whether labeled a diversion (social media scrolling), obligation (parent-teacher meeting), special occasion (date night with spouse) or priority (core strength workout), something has first drawn our attention to such activities before we committed our precious time to them . . .

For retailers and other consumer-facing industries, the successful acquisition of someone's time crescendos in the opportunity to improve, weaken or destroy the relationship!

Many marketing-focused theses rightly suggest that time is the bridge that connects attention to money. I teach the analogy of ATM to my retail industry colleagues. The automatic teller machine—or "ATM," as it has been dubbed for decades—is that ever-convenient pipeline to our accounts that are eligible for withdrawal through the reserves available from previous deposits. Similarly for those of us with something to sell, we only realize deposits when we garner the A̲ttention of someone in a way that presents us with an allocation of their T̲ime that eventually results in a sale to acquire their M̲oney. In linear fashion, it is an A-T-M effort. Attention snares time . . . and time controls the outflow of money.

In financial terms, attention is the underpinning of all spending. We must secure and purpose the attention of others accordingly.

So, yes, attention leads to time that leads to money—but whether money is obtained or not, the Cycle of Satisfaction should *not* be disrupted. As you can see from the graphic, money is not part of the rotation. This is lucky for us!

The omission of money from the Cycle of Satisfaction saves us from a hard stop in the cycle itself due to that which may be outside of our control. Said differently, there will be occasions when we successfully capture our prospective patrons' attention—and we rightfully honor their precious time—but no sale transpires. If this were not true, retailer conversion rates* would always be 100 percent. And they are not. Therefore, we must remove "money" from the Cycle of Satisfaction. After all, the immediate acquisition of revenue is *not* the primary objective in the work of turning previous shopper visits into a valuable marketing asset. The objective is to build a Broadcast Tower that we empower to provide us additional opportunities to perform the same valuable service to others—which leads us to the keystone concept in our Cycle of Satisfaction.

In our unending effort to build Broadcast Towers for our enterprise, we must not construe satisfaction with the product or service sold to be the same as satisfaction with the service received. You see, our emphatic friendliness when someone leaves an item on the counter in a last-minute decision to forego the purchase or our visible empathy when someone concludes *not* to drive that car off the lot has the same intrinsic ability to be as impactful as handing someone a receipt or shaking hands to signify a consummated arrangement. Fittingly, it is *service* that last precedes the construction of a Broadcast Tower—it is also the electric current that juices it up! As the cycle reflects, it is neither the effort to gain someone's attention, nor the time necessary from someone to make a sale, that anchors this modernized word-of-mouth advertising—it is not even the sale itself. As has always been the case with this type of marketing effort, our tower is completed in the homestretch that connects the delivery of service to an end state of satisfaction.

If you find this difficult to grasp, consider these real-world examples that are *without* a sale to cite:

- We recommend a real estate agent to a friend in a city where we looked at houses—but, ultimately, elected not to take the promotion that required a relocation.

---

* A retail conversion rate is calculated by dividing the number of sales transactions by the total number of visitors. This figure is then multiplied by 100 to get the conversion rate as a percentage.

- We send contact information to our future daughter-in-law for the helpful florist who could not accommodate our last-minute Valentine's Day delivery.
- We tell everyone in our workplace about the friendly and knowledgeable sales associate at the bedding store who made you a new authority on mattresses, even though you must wait a few more paydays before you can purchase a new one for yourself . . .

When we focus on the service offered as the means to the satisfaction—and not the sale or the resulting revenue—we increase the number of opportunities to build Broadcast Towers. Just like the wide receiver who desires the single-season record for touchdown catches, the odds for success rise when the number of balls thrown in our direction increases. For customers in a full-service environment, the service received—not the sale completed—produces the satisfaction that compels them to speak favorably on our behalf. By comparison, these satisfied shoppers will throw more balls in our direction—that is, return visits and confident referrals! Our conversion rate with customers will occasionally get bruised—but the satisfaction rate *never* should. Most importantly, the more Broadcast Towers we can confidently empower, the higher the likelihood we set seasonal records of our own!

Returns, Refunds, and Exchanges

As an instructor, I am admittedly pleased with audiences that embrace my content suggesting Broadcast Towers make no distinction between a successful sale and a fully satisfying interaction. Low-price and closeout retailers notwithstanding, I have found the adoption of this mindset to be relatively quick and mostly complete . . .

However, I am regularly faced with others' concern relating to one all too common scenario where there should be no distinction between sales and satisfaction: refunds, returns, and exchanges.

Ugggh. And before I make the case to allow the Cycle of Satisfaction to be the prevailing premise for your policies in these areas, I will fully admit that the devoted retailer in me does not like these interactions any more than you do. Occupational hazard. Unavoidable reality. Cover charge. No matter how I term them, I, too, wish such episodes did not exist.

But they do. And they likely always will. In 2023 the National Retail Federation indicated these incidents were at an all-time high. For brick-and-mortar operations, the sum of returns was 10.02 percent of sales, while online retailers had a whopping 17.6 percent of all sales returned.[2]

We can understand returns simply as the diminishing certainty any patron feels regarding their purchase. This alteration of confidence can be tracked to myriad causes, including the cognitive dissonance experienced when product performance differs from expectation to a disapproving spouse when hearing the cost. No matter the reason, the new request or expectation is for us to complete a return, issue a refund or facilitate an exchange—and it's an irritation and an expense for us.

Nonetheless, please receive this: the dissolution of a sale does not need to be the dissolution of satisfaction. As we learned, customer satisfaction in a full-service environment is not about the sale, anyway. Returns and refunds, even though entirely unwanted and a confirmed expense, should be viewed as another opportunity to influence the messaging from our Broadcast Towers. Unless we're certain we do not wish to do business with this entity again—*and* we genuinely do *not* care about the messaging this tower will broadcast—the Cycle of Satisfaction should persist. And for the best results in these undesirable occasions, we service providers must continually prioritize our devotion to the inherent heeding found in "all that is perceived, understood, and remembered."

For additional context, my retail businesses have a "100% Satisfaction Guarantee." This means someone can return a purchase at any time for any reason. In addition to the signal it sends to the purchaser whose certainty in the purchase has changed, it creates a uniformity of Uninvolved Optimization across my locations and various enterprises. Any subjectivity with a policy that has parameters for when a refund can be given is eliminated! I've heard the naysayers of this approach ad nauseum on the likelihood of fraud and being "taken advantage of." And I will not refute that such has transpired on limited occasions. However, in three-plus decades of retail across multiple channels, a profound realization regarding returns still stands: most shoppers dislike making returns almost as much as retailers dislike taking them. Discontented shoppers are consistently thankful for the permission when they need it, but very few people want to involve themselves a second time in something they initially estimated would be a single interaction. In addition, the discomfort that research suggests consumers feel about (especially brick-and-mortar) returns helps naturally tamp down higher return percentages.[3]

To best demonstrate how satisfaction can soar even when a sale goes south, testimonials from my business within a year of the publish date of this book include the following:

"If you're in the market for running shoes, I highly recommend this place! They have incredible customer service. I bought a pair of shoes here and when they turned out not to be the best option for me, the team worked with me to arrange a return and find a better fit. Great experience!"

—Ashley G.

"Very easy process and GREAT customer service. I ordered the wrong size and was able to return those and received a new pair all in less than a week from the original order."

—Solomon T.

"I returned a pair of shoes I had for six months that were peeling on the inside of my right foot. The store took the shoes back (no problem!) and ordered another pair of the same shoes. I received the new pair within one week. I am completely satisfied with the service and my purchase—and I will tell others about my fantastic experience!"

—Fergie C.

I could add many others. This approach works! I firmly believe service providers with onerous, subjective or complex return policies must take a closer look—and a longer view. Yes, it needs to be tracked, monitored, and properly budgeted. And with shipping costs, online retailers will need to offset the likely higher net margin loss elsewhere. But the investment made in a frictionless and easily executable return policy is an investment in the construction of your Broadcast Towers and the Cycle of Satisfaction.

As a final word on this topic, it is important to recognize that having a consistent return policy is not the same as "Always Doing Business with Everyone." Whether we're willing to admit it or not, having to happily take a return sometimes begins with foolishly making a sale . . . Said differently, most POS systems can easily identify shoppers who are serial returners or exchangers. Although it is rare, we reserve the right to occasionally suggest—despite our best efforts and genuine desire—that our records indicate we are not seemingly able to find a solution or an appropriate product for someone. After all, a product that is never sold by us is not nearly as eligible for return to us . . .

It's the Mortar:
Involved Maximization Imperatives for Chapter 5

1. Complete an audit of reviews and testimonials about your business or Team. This may include everything from Yelp and Google reviews to Glassdoor and TripAdvisor. While the highs and lows of praise and criticism need to be properly managed, achieve a productive comfort with the validity behind most of the commentary. This type of assessment should, ultimately, be assigned to a senior employee to complete no less than two times per year.

2. Teach and discuss the "Broadcast Tower" concept with your Team. Use some of the most specific Guest, client, or customer reviews discovered in the recommended assessment above to demonstrate the power of these communications. Just as importantly, connect the highlighted comments to the definition of "experience" (and all that is "perceived, understood, and remembered").

3. If most of the recent commentary found through the assessment is favorable, prepare to utilize such positive reinforcement in a growth-minded manner (see step 4 below). If, instead, the assessment has revealed an inconsistency or liability in your service or product that detours too many constituents on their journey to Satisfaction, this must be addressed promptly. The assessment should serve as a baseline so that

a similar exercise can be completed in the future *after* addressing where the "mortar is not bonding with the bricks." Even though all comments found in the reviews are subjective, comparing the volume *and* theme of testimonials over similar periods will produce objective data.

4. If the assessment suggests the delivery of a consistently satisfying experience, it is time to "Empower the Tower." With your Leadership Team or key advisor(s), select two tactics from the menu provided in this chapter or devise a few alternative methods for utilizing these positive appraisals of your business. For maximum results, put the high praise to use both externally *and* internally.

5. Return to the Cycle of Satisfaction. In a brief recess from Service, sincerely consider how you are currently acquiring the Attention of others. Empirically speaking, what is working to fulfill this most basic requirement for survival and growth? And what is not? Especially consider what role the experiences of others are currently playing in the quest to acquire increasing amounts of attention.

6. Meet with others who impact and influence your policies around refunds, exchanges, and overall customer satisfaction and discuss if each of these respective policies is simple enough in design and effectively practiced across the board. If there is a way to further quantify the conditions of your current policies (number of returns or exchanges, percent of sales returned, etc.) and/or determine the costs associated with a more liberal approach, inject such into the conversation. Tilt the policy more (if not entirely) in the direction of those you serve. For the sake of clarity with each policy, and doubly to ensure that the road to Uninvolved Optimization continues to be laid, ensure ease and consistency with the details and execution. Make the necessary changes and make plans to evaluate the results in six to twelve months with the same costs and objective criteria incorporated above.

CHAPTER 6:

There Is Nothing Special about Being Exceptional

We Must Make It Cultural

Remarkable service in any environment can be easily placed into two simple classifications: Exceptional and Cultural.

When it is the former, there is no guarantee it will occur again. In fact, in most instances, it won't. As the root word suggests, it was the rare exception to the otherwise common norm. It was, simply, someone having a good day. Or the fortuitous luck of the draw by you as a patron with the server or sales associate who had your cards. Heck, it is for good reason we rightfully suggest the toughest customer to satisfy is the person who had an awesome experience the *last* time he or she visited . . .

For just a few seconds, consider this hypothetical: the impression made on someone who had a wonderful engagement with your enterprise only to have it bested in an even more recent interaction.

Wow. Amazing, eh? How powerful is that notion?! Even just the thought of a repeated occurrence that is fantastic—and getting better each time—moves us.

Now let's return to the more likely reality. As we do so, make an important mental note *not* to confuse the term "exceptional" with "impressive." To make this clear, please consider this potentially uncomfortable (but true) statement: in many organizations, impressive moments are an exception. The same is true when you substitute "impressive" for "outstanding." Or "transformational." Or any other synonym we desire to repeatedly hear in regard to our service proposition.

We'll remember that when someone has an awesome experience—even just once—he or she can serve as an effective Broadcast Tower for your operation or ambitions. He or she may very well tell friends, neighbors, coworkers, and family members about what transpired. While basking in the immediate afterglow, it is almost certain a recent patron will sing the rightful praises of their time with you! And in the coming weeks and months, if something reminds them of their experience, they will pipe up and regale an audience with a memory that serves your enterprise well . . .

So, yes, this Exceptional experience is valuable. Very much so.

At the same time, please understand this distinction: retelling a positive episode from your life is *not* the same as presenting your hard-earned, battle-tested credibility to someone with whom you have influence. It is not the same as honoring your relationship with someone you care about with a bona fide recommendation.

Think of it this way: remarkable service that is Exceptional will result in the retelling of a positive and productive story about your enterprise when it is relevant and recollected.

But remarkable service that is Cultural? That will result in proactive, implicit referrals of your business that arrive with regularity. Even better, this type of referral evidences the extreme confidence necessary when someone puts their reputation on the line. Even though *your* service proposition and performance are outside of *their* realm of control, *your* consistency and *their* satisfaction negate the inherent risk that always accompanies a personal recommendation. Said differently, all they have "perceived, understood and remembered" is too credibly and reliably special to keep to themselves!

In short, it is when your service and the experience you deliver become Cultural that the real magic happens. This is when the pilings go deep—and the sky is barely a limit for the reach of a Broadcast Tower!

Those who feel compelled to pursue both personal *and* organizational potential feel no temptation to settle only for what is deemed "exceptional." Instead, these persons and their organizations embrace soaring expectations for their products and services. They publicly commit to the formidable challenge of sustaining greatness on an uncommonly dependable level. They decisively lean into the norms and traditions associated with an incomparable brand of service excellence. And in myriad ways an undeniable culture shines through both themselves and their organization as they masterfully perform the meaningful work they genuinely feel called to do for others.

Let's Define "Cultural"

For years, it has been increasingly popular to highlight the importance of "culture" in an organization. A cursory query of the word's etymology produces topics ranging from the beneficial bacteria in yogurt (*cultures*) to identifying the relevant dangers and/or merits relating to the root word (*cult*). While this etymological trivia can be interesting and handy, we must not miss the figurative forest for these correlative trees. Formal definitions of the word provide retailers with everything needed to analyze whether a service-first culture has been reliably established. Let's consider two entries for *cultural* from America's leading and largest provider of language information, Merriam-Webster:[1]

- the characteristic features of everyday existence shared by people in a place or time
- the set of shared attitudes, values, goals, and practices that characterizes an institution or organization

Oh, these definitions are so rich! And so clarifying. For those who wonder whether they have enacted a service proposition that makes them eligible for Uninvolved Optimization, the required standards are found in its parameters:

- Is remarkable service a "characteristic feature of everyday existence"?
- Does remarkable service "characterize (your) institution or organization"?

To achieve a long-lasting "Yes" in answer to these essential questions, I recommend a process of implementation and evaluation that is academic in name, yet elementary to administer: the Service Quotient. Playful in its moniker, it remains serious in its intent to ensure that your conscientious customer service is not only pervasive throughout your organization, but indisputably Cultural in its nature.

The Service Quotient focuses on specific characteristics vital for a superior service proposition. An operation that repeatedly demonstrates real aptitude in applying this system of measurement can lay claim to all the benefits available to an authentic culture of astonishing service! On the flip side, when there is not a methodology that is consistently practiced, we instead become unconfidently dependent on only the "exceptional" to sustain and garner more positive attention for our organization.

Introducing the Service Quotient (SQ)

The Service Quotient (SQ) packs all of its meaning into the name itself: it is a way to measure the amount or degree of a well-defined quality or characteristic relating to the service an organization provides. And like the far more widely known Intelligenzquotient, in its original German—what we know as "IQ"—it evaluates a person's ability to master designated capabilities. In essence, our test has swapped the pursuit of determining human intelligence with determining suitability for a service-oriented role.

At its core, I have discovered six traits that must be ever-present for optimal service performance in a retail environment. And, oh, how I wish the initial letter of these attributes could be jumbled or sensibly ordered in a way that produced a pronounceable acronym. Man, I've tried! But ultimately, I was left with a choice: change the components of the Service Quotient to enable a cool acronym or do away with a mnemonic device and further commit to the characteristics that have brought continual success to the organizations with whom I have participated and consulted. I trust you will respect my choice.

Our exploration of each of the Service Quotient's characteristics concludes with a simple-by-design form and grading system. Together both have overarching goals to remind us of our need to leave first base and to help us determine whether such strategic latitude dependably exists. When your organization achieves the desired scores, the service culture is enviably favorable and completely suggestive of a meaningful mortar awaiting more bricks!

Friendliness

It is not happenstance this first SQ characteristic is placed where it is. Friendliness simply sits atop the remaining SQ characteristics. Scramble the others if you wish, but leave Friendliness alone at the peak.

For more than a decade, I've written a personal note to any Team Member who is commendably referenced in a testimonial about our company. This feedback might come from a review site, through our website, or even as a personal e-mail to me or another Leadership Team member. Regardless of the origin, if it mentions someone who represents our brand, I read every word. After all, this is a Broadcast Tower transmitting discourse about the cornerstone element of our business! And in thousands of these affirming endorsements, the most noted favorable trait by our Guests regarding a Team Member is "friendly." It is not even close to what our patrons appreciate most . . . By a landslide, it is friendliness.

As I've realized the magnitude of appreciation for this characteristic in these reviews, I've also become increasingly observant of Friendliness being displayed inside our stores and amongst our Team. I now believe its vital importance in service-based affairs is simply because

1. it makes a good interaction great, and
2. it makes an average (or worse) interaction better.

When our organization shares information to help someone improve their daily routine or better understand possibilities or circumstances, Friendliness only complements this feedback and our desire to enhance a relationship. When an engagement is less spectacular—or even undesirable (think about the considerations we discussed with returns and exchanges in the previous chapter)—Friendliness has the power to bring down walls and lay a shared road for all parties to explore together. . . . And, of course, even in the common occurrence of an inaugural visit to an unfamiliar environment, a friendly welcome puts everyone more at ease!

Finally, the trait of Friendliness must also be prominently on the radar when conducting interviews for service-related roles. A business that wishes to emanate sensational Friendliness must present job offers only to those who are unmistakably friendly people!

Patience

Let's get this out of the way: not wanting to acknowledge that some situations and some people can be difficult does not make it any less true each will eventually present themselves. Even you and I experience moments of uncertainty, confusion, and discontent. With this understanding, we know our organization is only fully dressed for service when clothed in the increasingly elusive characteristic of Patience. And as with all SQ characteristics, this is not an optional skill for those who have targets associated with revenue growth and customer satisfaction survey results. But unlike the other qualities found on our SQ, Patience more often reveals itself as a reactive response than a proactive gesture. Like the hockey goalie who does not flinch or blink when the puck heads toward the target at ninety miles per hour, we must similarly condition ourselves when a burdensome customer or a grueling instance comes our way.

Because, boy, oh, boy, they will . . .

All the time.

And when we pre-decide that Patience will be our unblinking reaction, our service is moved into an advantaged position to stand up as a standout.

Empathy

It is unlikely there is an SQ trait that requires more research—or demands more of a service professional—than does Empathy. When surveying the Wikipedia page for this term, we find the following:

> **Empathy** is generally described as the ability to take on another's perspective, to understand, feel, and possibly share and respond to their experience. [It can be] broken down into more specific

concepts and types that include cognitive empathy, emotional (or affective) empathy, somatic empathy, and spiritual empathy.[2]

In industries and instances in which service is part of any formula for success, an emphasis is properly placed on the ability to "share and respond" to another person's experience. Putting ourselves in the shoes of others from the clues we have sought—and the fair conclusions we have drawn directly from them—is both demanding and rewarding work! It requires immense intentionality, astuteness, and dexterity. Most of the qualities in our SQ are demonstrated similarly, if not identically, across persons and situations. For Empathy, however, our efforts will be as unique as the people and circumstances we encounter. Empathy must be customized. Made-to-order. Build-to-suit. The caliber of our Empathy will be dependent upon the thoughtfulness of our questions and our commitment to diligent listening. For a usefully basic example, let's look at a business-relevant context for someone selling shoes. An empathetic response to a person who needs to eliminate foot soreness to teach mathematics to middle school children every day will look and sound markedly different than it would for an anxious Guest who has registered for her first half marathon.

In our commitment to remarkable service, the vastness of circumstances should not dishearten us. Instead, it should only remind us that each unique encounter presents us the opportunity to do the absolute best we can to genuinely learn about the person in our midst. As we combine this noble effort with our service intentions, we cannot help but adjust our perspective to better understand those we desire to assist.

As a final note on Empathy, please keep in mind that expressing open excitement for someone else is as connective as being sympathetic toward him or her. If there is a mistake I witness too often, it is made by the attentive listener who is verifiably good at feeling the pain or burdens of others. Yet, when good news is shared with them by a patron, friend or teammate, their reaction is unspectacular and unintentionally suggests they are not impressed or do not care. Let us not forget that being visibly moved by the triumph of another can be the sweetest empathy of all. So, sing that birthday tune to a stranger with glee—and raise your hands high in the victory celebration for a colleague!

Willingness

It is a misperception that someone working in a service role has a natural willingness to help others. Let us not pretend! It is like assuming all physicians and nurses are healthy. We know better. We have had our own experiences inside service establishments that refute this assumption. Sad, meet True.

To state it plainly, a legitimate demonstration of Willingness goes noticeably *and* enjoyably beyond what is expected. To *really* assist someone with an undertaking, we cannot be defined by service basics or confined by the premise of a job description. We openly welcome situations and requests that require discomfort and sacrifice. We have a penchant for both anticipating needs and delivering pleasant surprises. And we get involved with tasks and circumstances beyond the norm and the generally expected to manifest how comprehensive a service role can be.

When evaluating the characteristic of Willingness, do not get juked by solitary—or even spectacular—gestures of kindness. Willingness is not simply an act or an action that is taken for the sake of sport or story. Instead, it is a state of mind. Of perpetual existence. I have been asked the question, "When am I most likely to see this trait exhibited by our best Team Members?" More so than any of the other traits associated with our SQ, the answer is easy: All. The. Time.

With customers. With teammates. With others. With everyone.

Enthusiasm

So here it is. The term you may have hoped you would not see on this list. It is the quality you already know you cannot fake—and, perhaps, cannot afford. It is tough to quantify, harder to evaluate, and darned near impossible to build effectively into a training plan. But as Ralph Waldo Emerson so accurately penned in his essay "Circles," wherein he argues that everything in the universe is connected and constantly in movement, "Nothing great was ever achieved without enthusiasm."

Like it or not, "eager enjoyment" should be a cover charge for entrance into your organization. It should be expected of any visible member of the organization. And it should go beyond an excited appreciation for the products served and showcased. In essence, there needs to be a palpable Enthusiasm for service itself! For example, any sporting goods retailer can likely find a tennis enthusiast to oversee the Racquet Sports department. However, the supervisor who staffs this portion of the business with individuals who—even more so than a stated love for the sport—have a visible enthusiasm for helping others get better and enjoy the game more is what will propel this department to its potential. It is no different for the Business Development Manager with innovative software to sell. If Enthusiasm is exclusive to the features of the product, it severely limits the reach of our excitement for the resulting benefits to the purchaser! Always be on patrol for where Enthusiasm is lacking.

To emphasize the importance of this SQ characteristic from another angle, I have a couple of quick—but potentially uncomfortable—questions related to *your own* previous experience within a job, role or responsibility for which you had very little enthusiasm:

How was your attitude?

How was your performance?

Honesty, please.

I may not know you. But I know you. On a good day in this sad season, the best answer possible was "passable." Most days, it was worse.

When we present our customers to those on our Team who lack Enthusiasm, we take significant risks. During staffing shortages or exceptional circumstances, an absence of this trait may be briefly unavoidable (even if only barely digestible)—but if SQ evaluations regularly present a dearth of Enthusiasm, it is downright dangerous. A regular lack of enthusiasm gnaws at the core—the purpose—of an organization. Like a termite infestation, structural damage will eventually appear, with a costly result of needing to rebuild from the ground up. And finally, because this characteristic is so tough to train, make no mistake: any supervisor with an absence of this quality is more likely the enemy than an ally.

Gratitude

There is wonderfully no shortage of compelling commentary these days on the benefits of grateful living. It is, simply, a ground truth. In her writings about happiness and work, *Forbes* Senior Contributor Tracy Brower concludes through her research that "Gratitude is a powerful positive force. Far from a fluffy or frivolous concept, it has real impact on physical health, emotional wellbeing, motivation, engagement and belonging." She goes on to say, "Gratitude is also a 'gateway emotion' of sorts. Philosophers over the years have suggested it's the greatest virtue because it leads to so many others. For example, appreciation of someone can grow into love, gratitude for what you have can lead to greater satisfaction and loving your work can lead to improved performance."[3]

Oh, the mellifluous sounds of Dr. Brower's wisdom!

But also a cautionary consideration regarding such inspiring insight: the increased societal awareness of the benefits of Gratitude can cause us to erroneously conclude it is a preexisting condition in a service-based entity. Unfortunately, it is not. Yes, thanking someone as they exit the building with a purchase—or ensuring that "Thank You for Your Business" is stated at the bottom of an invoice—are common and recommended practices. Even better, these gestures, alongside so many others, can be centralized, corporatized, and systematized. But for our establishments to truly thrive, we must go above and beyond with additional gestures of gratitude that become an extraordinary fixture in our service proposition. Here are just a few I've seen in recent travels that have made an impression:

- A handwritten thank-you note from the sales associate on the "Come Back Soon" postcard dropped in my bag of purchases
- A scribbled note of appreciation from my server on the Styrofoam cup given to me with my to-go order
- A personal e-mail from the owner of a company from whom I purchased lawn care equipment the previous week
- A jovial and affirming escort to the front door with the store manager of a popular Mediterranean market after purchasing ingredients for a new recipe I wished to try

As leaders, it is our role to foster an atmosphere replete with visible thankfulness! As with each element in our SQ, it starts with YOU. Make no mistake, a leader's outright gratitude is a powerful energy source—and it transfers well. In addition, a workplace environment infused with considerable gratitude is the sign of an organization with admirable levels of occupational satisfaction. When we have Team members whose gratitude for the work they perform increases by the day, we have people who are becoming more engaged with our Mission and our potential. Best of all, Team Members who are genuinely grateful for their work (and wages!) emit corresponding thankfulness to those in their care.

A Form for Service Function— and Your Permission Slip to Leave First Base!

As previously suggested, FPEWEG is not much of an acronym for the ingredients in our Service Quotient . . . But rest assured, commitment and near-perfect consistency with these characteristics provide a path to service success. I have seen this desired result in retail sectors of every kind.

Of course, the subsequent requirement for the adoption of FPEWEG is the implementation of a Service Quotient Evaluation for the service providers on your Team. In the end, it is consistent oversight of the SQ that makes unbeatable service a Cultural norm in your enterprise. Furthermore, continually emphasizing and administering the SQ not only shines the navigational beams on the unceasing importance of meaningful engagement with your patrons but obligates us to pair the SQ traits with the required competencies in every service role in your organization. As influential management consultant Peter Drucker would agree, "What gets measured is what gets improved." Best of all, favorable SQ Evaluation Forms double as permission slips for leaders and entrepreneurs to leave first base and move toward new areas of opportunity.

As no surprise, the SQ's evaluative process makes another strong case for Uninvolved Optimization. In fact, the intentional empowerment of others to steward this process helps initiate and validate the effort. Even better, veterans of this process will bring an appealing sense of organizational tradition that cannot be discounted! The level of confidence you place in others to assist with the evaluations will be commensurate with the level of capability they exhibit in the SQ themselves.

By design, the SQ Evaluation Form, as well as the rating and scoring systems, are simple. The process uses existing customer interactions to make it unintimidating and straightforward. To be specific, the observer is simply going to watch and note how ingrained the SQ characteristics are in front-line sales associates. If this exercise can only be done with the customer's awareness, do not hide the fact that the presence of multiple associates is because of ongoing training. Patrons are always further assured when they witness the importance of customer service in an organization.

In the end, this is an evaluation completed through observation—with timely feedback and instruction. In essence, it is coaching. And for those who are less inclined to relate to our baseball/softball-inspired "leave first base" metaphorical mantra, feel free to find acceptable substitutes. No matter the vernacular, every at-bat with a customer is a "time such as this" moment to hit a game-winning grand slam and build a Broadcast tower of immense size!

Service Quotient Evaluation Form

Friendliness

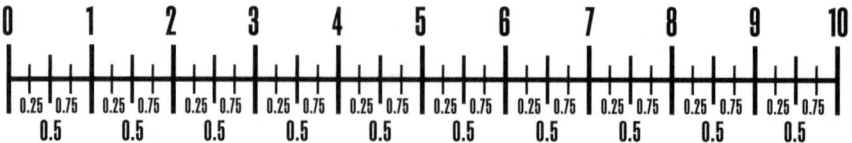

Patience

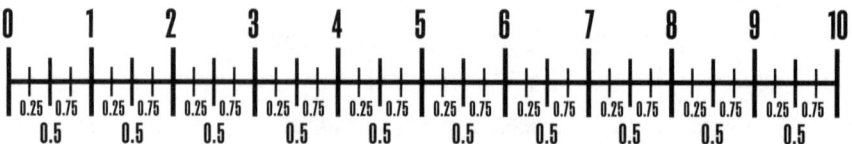

Empathy

Willingness

Enthusiasm

Gratitude

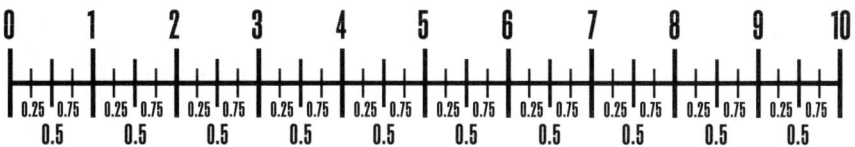

Service Quotient Evaluation Form Scoring Guide

Ace   (Total Score: 60–59)

These persons on your Team get it. All of it. They understand the business *and* exemplify the SQ. All the time. In addition to creating opportunities for them to engage more customers, clients, guests, visitors, and patrons, we are wise to suggest to others in our organization that they, too, observe the behaviors of the Aces on our staff. From the front line to the Leadership Team, we can all learn from them. Especially when there is a Team of Aces

facilitating interactions with those who provide revenue, leaders and entrepreneurs have an awesome opportunity—if not an obligation—to leave first
base and make plays elsewhere on the field.

Starting Pitcher (Total Score: 58–55)

These Team Members are likely key holders to any real estate you operate
and any aspirations you possess. Along with the Aces, they are who you
bring to the reception hosted by a new or valued client. You habitually count
on these individuals for good reason. And as they are continually able to
include a lofty SQ score on their résumé, you will—and *should*—feel ever
more confident in giving these men and women the ball and sending them
to the mound. Even better, when you make a play a few dozen feet from first
base, you will be able to rest assured that they'll be standing on the base in
your absence—smiling back at you, ready to receive the ball.

Trusted Reliever (Total Score: 54–52)

This person in your line-up is satisfactory. When sickness, vacation schedules, and staffing shortages arise, we are thankful for these Team Members.
To be sure, they are not an Ace or a Starting Pitcher. However, they can be
largely trusted with any pipeline you are trenching toward organizational
prowess and profitability with customers and clients. Of course, our Trusted
Relievers should be perpetually motivated to achieve higher scores, especially
if merit or compensation increases are mutually desired and anticipated.

Bullpen Performer (Total Score: 51–48)

For those who know baseball or softball, they know the "bullpen" is located
away from the dugout, where the rest of the Team spends its time (when not
on the field). In these sports, the separation of the bullpen from the nucleus
of the Team serves both strategic and tactical purposes. Such is *not* the
case with the SQ. Anyone with Bullpen scores is essentially separated from
others in our organization for additive training and coaching. Yes, they are
acceptable in a pinch. But if we have a host of Bullpen Performers making
most of the pitches for us, we are surrendering to a degree of mediocrity
their respective scores guarantee. In the context of Bullpen Performers, our

ability to leave first base also becomes significantly constrained, as electing to do so would assuredly put our organization at risk.

Minor Leaguer (Total Score: 47–44)

There are only two assignments for any Team Member who achieves the score of Minor Leaguer: Rookie or Rehabilitation. For what it is worth, the same is largely true in professional baseball. If you have someone who is new (a rookie) to your organization—naturally requiring development to reach their utmost potential—this status may be rightfully assigned. For our Minor Leaguers who are rookies, we should simply undertake a continued effort to ensure an adequate understanding of expectations and procedures. At the same time, the conspicuous Cultural norms and routines of others on the Team will be at work positively influencing these newest teammates. When propelled by these two forces, there is every reason to believe performance and scores will improve!

Conversely, a more tenured Team Member who achieves the scores of a Minor Leaguer is likely "injured" . . . or worse. Depending on their past performance, the decision will be whether to rehabilitate them—or cut them from the roster. The status of Minor Leaguer is normally a relatively brief stint: improvement or recovery either happens or it doesn't. There is no former star on your Team—or the Toledo Mud Hens (a minor league ball club affiliated with the Detroit Tigers), for that matter—who will accept a less prestigious status for too long. If progress is not made expediently, this person will stop coming to the stadium on their own . . . or you will have to ask them to clean out their locker.

Losing Pitcher (Total Score: =/< 43)

All organizations make mistakes. The history of professional sports is overcrowded with bad draft picks and unrealized potential. Properly termed, these are sunk costs to an establishment that are playing out in front of us in realtime—and throwing more good money and otherwise productive resources after a "losing" cause is fruitless. More frankly, it is stupid. For good reason, it is no secret that the best coaches must cut the worst players from the Team.

As we conclude our celebration of the Service Quotient, allow me to address the potential discomfort that travels with any announcement to your Team that the SQ's characteristics will be monitored, evaluated, and scored. In their own way, leaders must establish the Service Quotient as the critical mortar supporting a significant investment in organizational bricks. Whether done through simulation, shadowing or any other means of respectful administration, every constituent should be motivated to embrace the chosen tactic to ensure your service foundation. Where there is truly a service *culture*, there is only a desire to encourage and deepen the sentiments contained therein. These skills may be basic—but they are not common. And it is only when SQ scores are both impressive *and* recently achieved that certainty exists that the SQ characteristics are firmly embedded into individual and organizational behavior.

It's the Mortar:
Involved Maximization Imperatives for Chapter 6

1. Introduce the Service Quotient to your Team, department or organization, including an overview of each element. Although the SQ has the most obvious application to the front-of-house and customer-facing roles, it is recommended all Team Members be made aware of the components and their respective focus. If remarkable service is to be cultural, these characteristics should be prominent in all areas of the workplace and in every interaction with constituents. Do not preach that which will not be practiced.

2. Bring each element of the SQ alive through discussion and shared examples where the traits have had an impact previously (personally and professionally). If there is strong evidence of another service-related characteristic that has consistently produced desirable results in your organization, add it! Ultimately, this is *your* Service Quotient.

3. Travel to the front lines of your operation—that is, where service is being performed. At the onset, make sure Team Members are aware your presence (and that of others participating in the evaluation) is connected to the Service Quotient. Whether perceived initially as a

tactical installment or a strategic initiative, advanced notice will help communicate the intent and reinforce the specific components. Be sure to share SQ scores promptly with Team Members and comfortably discuss where enhancements to referenced behavior can be incorporated. With the exception of those who were likely bad hires, the inaugural assessments are not occasions to express concerns associated with organizational fit or longevity. Keep the dialogue focused on the characteristics of the SQ. Like all employee-related feedback, ensure a date is included and put the documentation in the appropriate file.

4. After the initial round of assessments, convene with Team Members who made the observations and reported the scores. Accurately determining the value of the SQ and its degree of penetration throughout your organization will be dependent on the quality of the oversight! Make notes and suggestions as to how the process can be improved. Determine the frequency with which such evaluations should be administered. The size and complexity of your organization or department will rightly impact the necessary cadence. From daily to biannually, the answer is yours to determine—keeping in mind that less than once every six months is just too infrequent for impact.

5. Collect, capture, and document your new trove of qualitative data! As you input and analyze the details, look for themes. Are there organizational strengths or advantages that emerge? How about areas of liability or weakness? As the leader, it is your responsibility to report back with the current findings. The size and composition of your operation will help determine the audience. A "State of Service Address" or report can be generated from this exercise alone. Such a summation should be done regularly and completed alongside the findings of the continuously captured details.

6. Commit to the process long-term. Although advanced notice for the assessments becomes unnecessary once the practice has been firmly seeded in your enterprise, regular references to the exercise and recent findings are strongly recommended.

Section I Summation

Section I received the subtitle "What Feels Good Is Really Hard" because of a stark paradox that exists within its content. We instinctively sense—both intellectually *and* emotionally—that continuous improvement in serving others is a worthy, honorable pursuit. It is also easy to comprehend how training and, ultimately, trusting others on our Team proves productive—and gratifying. And we do not need industry-leading consultants to present new research any of us can already do ourselves.

Yes, the allure of Uninvolved Optimization is understandable.

Even so, gaining the necessary confidence to leave first base does not come easy. The efforts necessary to form Experience Committees, build Broadcast Towers, ensure organizational longevity, create an irresistible service culture, and institute the Service Quotient are now known. There may be no complex arithmetic or sophisticated scientific formula for success associated with these concepts—but the recommendations take consistent diligence, constant awareness, and intentional, thoughtful oversight. At times, they also require an almost intimidating amount of time to generate tangible momentum.

But do not be deterred!

Even though these processes may be daunting, we know the results are worthwhile and *truly feel good* when achieved. In our own journey—or through our observations of those we admire—we already have sufficient evidence of how effectively this "mortar" bonds people to our plans and potential. Meanwhile, the Involved Maximization Imperatives provide a proven path forward. But more importantly, it should now be apparent as to the best way to actuate the processes of Section I: Just. Get. Started.

SECTION II

Hard Skills
What Feels Hard Is Really Good . . .

The most successful retailers acknowledge the critical importance of soft skills—the people skills and emotional intelligence at work within their operation. But they also know the advantages stemming from such practices are not enough on their own to achieve an organization's full potential. For maximal prosperity, the qualitative inputs of soft skills must be paired with processes markedly more objective and quantitative in nature.

Welcome to Section II!

For this material, I have culled specific hard skills that are commonly missed, or otherwise misinterpreted or misapplied, by retail organizations—always to the detriment of their potential. Service-centered businesses must obsessively pair their remarkable service proposition with a great aptitude for resource acquisition, allocation, and management. This, too, is necessary mortar to keep our bricks firmly in place!

Let the debate rage on behind us as to whether hard skills are easier to master than soft skills. No matter the outcome, we know hard skills can be especially hard to achieve. As a fair warning, the forthcoming lessons and recommended practices may resist your advances. For those who are naturally oriented toward service, an equal bent toward mathematical formulas and other task-oriented arithmetic is atypical. For some readers, these elements will require a disciplined and steady grind. For others, the lessons will be downright demanding of their full attention and repeated consideration. But for all who aspire to Uninvolved Optimization, skillful oversight of key performance metrics matters greatly. Here we'll explore proven prescriptions for this industry of which we must be keenly aware and sufficiently versed. In this section, we will qualify and quantify direct marketing, business development, procurement, sales management, and strategic planning for retail operations. The resulting combinations of skills will enable you to interact with the marketplace in a deservedly more confident and definitively more measurable manner.

As a final and expected reminder in the wise pursuit of Uninvolved Optimization, leaders must also ensure the content in Section II runs deep within the organization. I should have made this commitment in my own establishments much sooner. It was at a glacial pace I came to understand the only role I play more valuable than practitioner with these quantifiable elements is that of the tutor. As an entrepreneur *and* as a parent, the self-manufactured encumbrances I foolishly installed around these raw retail realities still bother me. They likely always will.

"I love when people who have been through hell walk out of the flames carrying buckets of water for those still consumed by the fire." Oft attributed to fellow enterpriser Stephanie Sparkles (Bliss Cakes founder), this quote encourages all of us who have learned valuable lessons "the hard way." Truth be told, this book is a personal attempt to manifest such a mindset . . .

A Gleeful Arrival Gone Awry

Nine months after opening the doors to my first retail business, our daughter, Monica, was born. Out of a gleeful arrival too quickly emerged obvious signs to the birthing team of respiratory distress. An eventual diagnosis of surfactant dysfunction proved to be a significant challenge that initially saw no signs of improvement. It then transitioned to an extended stay in the neonatal intensive care unit, with my daughter and her physicians fighting for her life.

As if it were yesterday, I still remember peering through the same glass that braced me from collapsing from sadness and uncertainty. She was encased in a clear box, with only wires and tubes penetrating the enclosure.

And, man, the wires and tubes! There were so many of them!

I knew this discomforting entanglement was doing work that gave us our only hope my own arms would ever wrap her in a similar fashion . . . Still, this wee inaugural environment for my daughter looked blankly uncaring and utterly uncomfortable. In stark and somewhat sinister contrast, the otherwise wonderfully cozy and ceremonial pink-and-light-blue blanket initially prepared by the maternity staff remained perfectly folded and entirely unused. It lay untouched in a nearby location that was almost equally as agonizing for me: my wife's recovery room. Our previous success in an identical environment with our son—and our natural anticipation—had suggested we embrace this setting for celebration and family bonding.

Now, it was anything but that. My wife, Inge, and I were both disconsolate. We were scared and downhearted. And confused. Everything we witnessed was both unexpected and thus unconsidered! And no one with any medical authority had any material answers for us. We were left unattended for hours in her hospital room to exchange estimations on our own.

And none of them were likely accurate or helpful to our state of mind.

Of course, we shared a thankfulness Monica knew not of her own frailty or our unbridled anxiety.

As I still recall this occasion with vividness, I also know there are all too many who can picture this scene in their mind with expert clarity—from just a brief description—because they, too, have been in a similar situation. Without knowing the specific stories, I still pray for those in such a season. Included in these prayers is hope for the presence of mind to properly put first things first—*and* for the existence of advanced preparations made in the absence of any rationale to do so. I know now it is these previous efforts that enable rightful prioritization. And I include this petition because I have been on both sides of the well-founded order in my own efforts. Yes, with my son, I walked away from my business for more than two months to care for him, my family, and his recovery. The trust I confidently placed in our Team—with clear-mindedness per the processes developed, the systems constructed, the culture so intentionally built, and the standards instituted—was the basis for what so importantly ensured my involvement where my involvement mattered most!

But fifteen years earlier, I am still sad and embarrassed to say the same was not the case with my daughter.

With my in-laws in town and willing to assist with our son, I left my wife in our sorrow, prior to her discharge from the maternity ward. And with the only certainty we had with Monica being that she was not leaving the hospital anytime soon, I was pulled headlong into my occupational tasks. Without deeper consideration, this seemed the only acceptable choice in light of my family's needs. No one else was going to do what needed to be done at the store. Or on the spreadsheet. Or with the accounting software. I felt I had but a single choice: to get back to work. After all, we came to the maternity facilities with a clear intent and an obvious objective.

But we came up short.

Stiff-arm the pain. Repress the despair and disappointment.

And get back out there to take charge of those tasks and considerations under the demand of personal control.

So to my store—to my own service business—I went . . .

And I stayed there.

And I stayed.

And stayed. And stayed.

Sure, I made visits to the hospital. In fact, after my wife was cleared, we were allowed a thirty-minute visit to the neonatal intensive care unit each day. We had several options presented to accommodate our schedule . . . and we selected the 9:00 p.m. option each time, as it allowed me to close the store every evening and be away from the business when I believed the least amount of my own contribution was required.

The Bookend

It is often contended that prioritization is best reflected in how moments and monies are spent. For what it's worth, I believe this assertion is true.

Most of the time . . .

This assertion is faulty in scenarios when no other perceived options exist to manage something else that is critically important—even if it is *not* the top priority. When this occurs, discomfort and psychological dissonance despotically escort the situation. While my daughter was in the hospital, those closest to me labeled my time back in the store as an unsurprising coping response to the concerns I had with her health. While this assessment undoubtedly carries truth, I do not deceive myself: Everything from the stability of my nascent business to my fiscal responsibility to cover health insurance premiums and treatment costs was also on the line during her hospitalization.

To this day, I believe the decisions I made while the well-being of my daughter remained uncertain to be acceptable. I hold no reservations as to how our beautiful baby girl was ushered into this world. Yes, her present-day health, her incredible accomplishments as a teenager and young woman, and her successful management of lingering neurological complications over the years greatly impact my viewpoint. My family would even go so far as to say our experience during the first few weeks following our daughter's birth ultimately had a positive impact on us and has continued to instruct us throughout our lives.

But . . . I do have regrets. Even more so, I'm reminded of the Brené Brown quote shared earlier that Regret is a "fair but tough teacher." I have come to understand and accept that the passion for my work—and the even loftier purpose for me with parenting—is a blended and full-circle experience. And for me, my daughter's poor health at the onset of her life will now forever serve as a sort of bookend.

Not a book, mind, you. A bookend. An unsparingly honest assessment of my absence from my family during my daughter's health challenge is that I presented myself with no latitude or opportunity to choose better. With every decision I made before her birth—and every action I did not take—I painted myself into a claustrophobic corner I could not feasibly flee.

The instance with my son's accident serves as the backside of this idiosyncratic sibling bookend. As restauranteur Will Guidara learned from his dad (and shares in his book *Unreasonable Hospitality*), "Adversity is a terrible thing to waste." And so it is that I learned much from February 21, 2005, when my daughter was born distressingly unwell, through January 12,

2021, when my son was involved in the deadly traffic accident previously detailed. This education involved a predictable mix of observation, trial and error, unexpected events, and some disciplined study and research. Some of my increases in knowledge were the product of clear intent. Other gains were happenstance, transpiring through processes akin to osmosis or the application of a heat press by simply showing up, being present, and being willing to submit myself to my surroundings and my intuition.

But most importantly was the realization that the ideas, tactics, processes, and standards shared on these pages needed to exist elsewhere in my organization. It was not through individually applying my skillset in my business that helped me transform my response to the separate incidents of trauma with my children. It was, instead, the achievement and application of these skills by those with whom I found a dependable reliance. There were exactly 5,542 days that separated my daughter's dangerous birth from when I was given my son's prognosis as unlikely to survive. And as much as I sincerely hope the bookends of personal growth and organizational development for you are not easily interchangeable with my story, I do wish for you to achieve a leeway of choice regarding your future actions and decisions because of the intentionality you put forth *right now* in your own areas of influence and responsibility. You see, training a Team Member, clarifying an expectation, building a remarkable service culture, fine-tuning a process or implementing a system—among so many other kindred considerations—does not happen without forethought, commitment, focus, and execution. Especially knowing how much you cannot control, do everything you can *today* to avoid a painful choice that someday pits where you critically matter against your most critical matters. This is where the intent of Involved Maximization first meets the objective of Uninvolved Optimization. Grab hold! Do not wait. Plan *now* so that you are prepared later to always make decisions with the utmost discretion. Put your personal and organizational potential into motion. And build from there. The time is now. The world wants more of you. It deserves your best . . .

Friends, we're not done yet. A deliberate transfer of proficiency to your Team for the skills that follow is more bonded mortar for your organization so that it may confidently continue to build.

Let's carry on!

CHAPTER 7:

Take It from the Top—After All, It Always Starts with Topline Revenue

The Three (and Only Three) Ways to Grow Revenue

If only as a primer, let us consider a fundamental principle of sales growth that some know, and others quickly comprehend: There are only three pathways to increase revenue in your business. That's it. If incremental topline growth is the target, it's just that simple. There are only three pathways.

As you read the overview of each, feel free to challenge this definitive statement. And, of course, if you come up with something novel suggesting I've omitted other possibilities, please do drop me a note! Also, while considering each description, play no early favorites. Each growth pathway has a potentially different level of importance depending on the industry it calls home. From a strategic standpoint, each possibility likely enjoys different seasons of contribution in a growth-minded organization, depending on current trends, resources, and, most importantly, priorities.

Meanwhile, it is appropriate to acknowledge it is infrequent that total revenue—or even revenue growth—is the *most* important financial consideration for an enterprise. For good reason, it is *profitability* that remains the paramount pursuit. We will cover this topic in greater detail in a forthcoming chapter.

But here's what we already know: most of us cannot save our way to prosperity. We are wise to first enroll ourselves in the duty of generating and growing income.

Let us now explore the three ironclad pathways for revenue gains.

Pathway to Revenue 1: Conversion
Get More Purchasers to Visit the Enterprise

This is the hard truth: increasing the number of visitors to a domain (on-site or online) is meaningless to revenue totals unless there is a tangible transition of that visitor from "Browser" to "Buyer." This required changeover connects to the term we defined in chapter 5: *conversion rate*. In the end, we must be sure there is an adequate—if not ample—number of Purchasers (buyers) amidst all the otherwise appealing characteristics associated with leads, prospects, impressions, followers, fans, clicks, views, and downloads. No matter the marketing hype, nothing beats a Purchaser! To demonstrate conversion—and to distinguish a "target audience" from a "paying customer"—let's use an example. If Restaurant A has 150 persons darken the doorway to review the "$14.99 Lunch Menu" above the counter but only has a third of them elect to place an order (50 patrons and a conversion rate of 0.3333), the number of actual purchases are less than they are at Restaurant B, which may only have 75 total visitors, but 70 of them submitting an order.

Of course, the conversion rate is significantly higher, too, for Restaurant B (with a rate of 0.9333). If we further assume Restaurant B has a similar lunchtime offer with items priced at $14.99, we can also determine the revenue difference. Even though Restaurant A had twice as many visitors, Restaurant B had $299.80 (20 × $14.99) more in income.

The arithmetic for these conversion rates is simple, while the impact that improved conversion rates can have on your business is significant. For the absolute best results, we have a dual responsibility. We must attract more visitors *and* affect more Purchasers. In retail terms, it is a mandate to "increase traffic *and* improve conversion."

Pathway to Revenue 2: Frequency
Get Semi-Frequent or Infrequent Purchasers to Visit More Often—and Make Purchases Every Time

Remember this: It is not frequency of visit, but frequency of *purchase* that really matters. The difference is often imperceptible to the casual observer . . . Fortunately, there are tools and tallies to capture critical data and demonstrate the difference. Frequency is our means for when the same person or entity makes multiple (or many!) purchases at different times.

As an example of this principle, our Team hosts free "Social Runs" in my Run/Walk-focused sporting goods stores. These weekly occasions are expressly created to be enjoyable and promote collective accountability for fitness routines and step-count totals. But make no mistake: someone who comes every Tuesday night to participate in the free Social Run—but never buys anything—is not a frequent *customer*. He or she is a frequent *visitor*. Yes, he or she may be an awesome ambassador for our brand. And, for sure, these organized gatherings are evidence of the goodness of our Mission "to grow, support, and enhance an active lifestyle." But when evaluating the extent to which income has increased through frequency, there is only quantifiable value in Purchasers who come back (again and again and again) *and* verifiably make additional purchases each time.

The most arguably popular tactic serving this concept is to implement loyalty programs. Whether a grocery store, a favorite coffee shop or through a hotel operator, promoted rewards are dependent upon devotion despite the alternatives. The benefits are not originally offered in the pursuit of more Purchasers; they are primarily available for the sake of incenting more purchases from the same Purchaser. And when implemented successfully, this programming has a material impact on revenue totals. To better quantify the potential impact of frequency, let's pretend we know someone likely to order an Americano in an establishment two hundred fifty times in a year (I'm not sure who this could be . . .). At an average cost of $4.50, here's the difference in total revenue depending on whether 10 percent or 50 percent of these purchases are made in the same place. Again, keep in mind that these revenue totals are without adding even one more unique visitor or customer.

25 × $4.50 = $112.50
125 × $4.50 = $562.50

As you consider our first tandem of means to grow revenue (conversion and frequency), keep in mind that every time there is an increase in visits, visitors or return visits, there are additional opportunities to acquire an actual purchase. Said differently, we have more chances to improve our conversion and/or frequency. Do not begrudge those who visit often but only purchase rarely. If we cannot solve how to get someone to make a purchase more than 5 percent of the time they visit, we can work to increase the number of visits they make. After all, even if someone only makes a purchase 5 percent of the time, they will make twice as many purchases in forty visits than they do in twenty visits. Moreover, the same "group runner" who participates regularly in the activity I referenced above is more likely than a first-time visitor to take notice of new arrivals or any merchandise now on markdown. The same is true with website patrons. A website that draws substantial traffic for shopper research will yield tangible commercial benefits when new services or products are announced as "Now Available" on a homepage. The same value is found in a weekly blog that repeatedly brings readers to the same digital destination with products or services simultaneously for sale. There is no doubt "content marketing" has a direct connection to revenue when it increases online visits and influences purchase frequency.

It also sets us up perfectly for our third and final means to increase revenue . . .

Pathway to Revenue 3: Transaction Size
Get Purchasers to Purchase More Than Planned While Inside the Enterprise

Did this third means of revenue growth make you think, "Would you like fries with that?" Or, "Do you want to purchase trip insurance before checking out?" If so, you get it. This is an unmistakable attempt to elevate sales totals. And it is visibly connected to our final device: *transaction size*. In slow traffic seasons, it matters greatly; in the busiest of times, this consideration becomes a powerful pairing with traffic increases to truly maximize revenue to the fullest!

Consistent with *conversion* and *frequency*, let's bring in some mathematics for clarification. Doing so will highlight why sales training programs emphasize this theme so consistently in the curriculum. There are thousands of possibilities to set the stage. As I recently returned from the dentist's office, I'll recount—and quantify—my experience.

My visit was a standard cleaning and inspection. This is not covered by my insurance program, so I'm out of pocket $139.00 for the services included. I make this visit twice per year, with an annual forecast of $300.00 on my home budget spreadsheet . . . While at the dentist, however, a service not included in the cleaning was suggested: a teeth-whitening session (maybe I should rethink all those Americanos . . .). The cost quoted was $80.00. To have this added to my biannual routine, my receipt total would have increased 57.5 percent per visit and added $160.00 to the annual income for my dental clinic. As is easily evident, upselling and adding services can make a meaningful difference to sales totals. Wonderfully enough, such growth possibilities with transaction size exist without needing to generate more traffic or incent additional visits by the same patron. In the moment, it is the only means to higher sales. When done properly, it can also intensify and amplify customer appreciation for our salesmanship. My friend, Dan Mann, author of *ORBiT* and *Leading Change*, often tells the story of his first mountain bike purchase. Stranded six miles from his car, he endured a long hike cursing the salesperson who did not upsell him a flat-repair kit and a spare tube.[*]

Transaction size is also inextricably connected to price adjustments. Inflation is the obvious macroeconomic condition connected to

---

[*] To be clear, highlighting this available methodology to grow revenue is not an endorsement for offering or selling something not genuinely beneficial to the customer. Absolutely not! Instead, when associated techniques are performed properly, this is, simply, presenting additional possibilities or features to Purchasers in a meaningful way that suggests their life would be demonstrably better with this additional or more expensive prospect.

purchasing—or spending—more than planned or desired. But whether proactive or reactive, an increase or decrease in the price of products materially impacts revenue. If someone purchased four hundred gallons of fuel from somewhere for $2.79 per gallon last year but pays $3.14 per gallon this year for the same volume in the same place, the incremental revenue for the reseller is $140.00. Of course, this is *not* to suggest a profit increase in the same amount. It is only when all acquisition and operating costs for the fuel reseller are the same, less or at a lesser rate of increase that gross or net profit begins to increase.

To be sure, every price increase comes with an inherent risk. Whether a strategic plan or a simple decision to pass costs along, Purchasers may decide to seek an alternative, do with less or altogether do without if or when they realize a higher price. And, similar to poor service and product dissatisfaction, price increases often produce a newfound willingness in customers to try a different product or to shop elsewhere for the same product. If price increases are the chosen tactic to achieve a higher average transaction size, keep in mind it offers no guarantee the number of total units sold will remain the same. To demonstrate the risk, let's go back to the gasoline price increase examined above. Let's imagine that a Purchaser decides to resist the increase by taking public transportation for some occasions, thereby reducing her fuel consumption by 25 percent. As a result, the purchase of three hundred gallons (instead of four hundred) at the higher price (of $3.14) reduces the annual income to the seller by $174.00.

A. 400 gallons × $2.79/gallon = $1,116
B. 300 gallons × $3.14/gallon = $942

In this example, the average transaction size is higher—but the number of transactions is fewer. More notably from the arithmetic, we can determine that our Purchaser must buy no less than 356 gallons annually at the higher price to match or exceed last year's spending total. When we forecast revenue, we must always assess the possible risks and rewards of the ever-present option to raise prices.

Prioritization Precedes Plans

Comprehension of where revenue expansion originates is not enough on its own to initiate or expect sales increases. Yes, growth is grounded in these three pathways to revenue—but the power source driving increased sales is only activated when we are fully mindful of some other underlying factors.

For a moment, let's pretend we are partners with a gourmet popcorn and specialty candy purveyor. Much of our business is done online and fulfilled through efficient shipping procedures that send our products to all fifty U.S. states and Canada.

However, as e-commerce sales have plateaued, we begin to seek growth from our lone brick-and-mortar location. If we can facilitate the desired revenue increase, a rollout of additional stores is likely.

In the Land of Make Believe, we will call our shop Sweet & Salty's Flavor Factory.

A new residential development nearby presents a fresh setting for our aspirations of growth. As with all opportunities, we need to prioritize the circumstance accordingly. With commendable conversion rates (everything smells so good!), we are understandably tempted to pursue a recently discovered "Welcome to the Neighborhood" mailer. The proposal for participation in the mailer itself was thoughtfully created to assure our decision-making awareness of a clear target market. And as the spokesperson for the program indicated from his own research, the premise seems to follow in the footsteps of every online and in-store marketing investment we've ever commissioned. The visibility of our recent campaigns seems to infer that Sweet & Salty's strategy for sales growth is primarily about finding New Purchasers.

Without question, a direct-mail campaign follows suit. And the pitch is straightforward and compelling! It is almost without forethought we set aside $2,000 toward the proposed effort to introduce us to the new arrivals in the nearby neighborhood.

Shall we sign the agreement and write the check?

No. Not yet. We are not finished . . . Today is different. This time let's draw the possibilities out further. Now that we know more, we have more to consider.

To get started, let's be mindful of the other prospective growth contributors. These are the ones that have seemingly been historically abandoned by Sweet & Salty's: Frequency and Transaction Size.

A financial commitment to the mailer likely stamps out a separate strategy aimed at increasing visits by previous shoppers who only make one to two purchases per year. For $2,000, we could give away a lot of our signature caramel popcorn to those who do return! In addition, we already possess these patrons' email addresses for the purpose of providing receipts or shipping confirmations. For those who have not "opted out" of communication from us, correspondence about an offer to "Get a Free 4 oz. Bag of Caramel Popcorn with any purchase of $15.00 or more!" could easily find its way into their email inboxes for *free*.

Are we even mildly enticed to deviate from our conventional marketing? We may not yet fully recognize this as a "frequency play"—but it feels different . . . And with a zero cost for the email addresses and a total production cost of barely $1.50 for a bag of caramel popcorn, it sounds like it might be less expensive.

What to do?!

As with most decisions, it is time and/or money that mandate we choose at all. There is always a finite number of plans we can make and priorities we can firmly establish. As such, we must be deliberate in our priorities.

To make this recurrent—but difficult—choice of where to best allocate resources, we must be doubly objective. Said differently, we need to be keenly aware of the three pathways to revenue. We should also remain unapologetically unbiased about whether our growth tactics target New Purchasers, increased frequency or a higher transaction size. As we said at the onset of this chapter, each possibility is likely to have its own time in the spotlight for organizations where growth is perennially critical.

To conclude our example with Sweet & Salty's, please consider the following hypothetical to help make the final decision*:

---

* Please note this is an example (not a recommendation); for comparison's sake, the options are underlined.

Average transaction size at Sweet & Salty's for the last twelve months: $17.80

Average number of visits per customer for the last twelve months: 3.25

New Purchases by Prospects in New Neighborhood

Estimated number of adult occupants in new neighborhood: 700

Typical 1-year conversion rate for new neighborhood mailer: 12.5%

Recommended formula: 700 × 0.125 × $17.80 × 3.25 = $5,061.88

Increased Frequency by Infrequent Purchasers

# of Past Purchasers who only purchased once or twice in the last twelve months: 3,230

# of Past Purchasers with whom we can connect via e-mail: 2,841

Average transaction size of these Infrequent Purchasers: $20.21

Comparative conversion rate for typical email campaign: 12.5 percent

Recommended formula: 2,841 × 0.125 × $20.21 = $7,177.08

In this example, both the total number of persons who are Infrequent Purchasers and the average transaction size for this person are higher than the related numbers for our New Purchases prospects. Again, this is fictitious for the sake of displaying a formulaic approach—but it reminds us that the bigger opportunity may not lie where initially assumed. Some assumptions are also made to enable the calculations (like using the previous average transaction amount to represent the future average transaction amount). But assumptions are never escapable when making forecasts! And to properly steward our resources—and empower others to do the same—we must habitually perform exercises to determine which means of increasing revenue are likely to be the most productive. In this example, if we could only choose one initiative—or only had $2,000 to spend—we may very well determine we should finally send that note to our Infrequent Purchasers.

Prioritization Guides Plans

After a thorough examination of various growth opportunities, single or multiple sales growth priorities can be appropriately declared, stated with clarity, and reinforced through repetition. Balance sheet improvement through sales growth will almost always help align an organization more than cost-cutting measures.

But stay alert! This is where common—but avoidable—mistakes are made. More specifically, this is where gaps between the stated growth priorities (i.e., improved conversion or frequency or increased transaction size) and the distribution of resources can develop.

Let's consider some real-world examples where I've witnessed misalignment.

Example 1

We'll first consider the case when we had a talented general manager in a relatively new business unit in our retail operation. He introduced his annual business plan for his newest store by stating, "As everyone here knows, this location is less than two years old. As such, we are going to continue with—even amplify—our focus on driving more awareness of our presence in this market, while maintaining the high levels of conversion we've already established in a brief period. The plan I will outline today is going to indicate how we intend to drive more customers through our doors."

This is a solid beginning, as it clearly indicates that increasing store traffic and sustaining attractive conversion rates are going to carry the plan. For new and established businesses alike, this consideration is often the first *and* best way to ensure a continued existence. Get more Purchasers to visit the enterprise! We were on track. We eagerly waited to hear about strategies and metrics with which to evaluate the soon-to-be shared recommendations. And if the suggestions came alongside an attractive volume projection and a reasonable budget request, it was going to be a grand slam!

But the presentation soon fell apart, with the plan's first tactic centering on our Apparel category. This may sound acceptable until you know this part of our business is only a single-digit percentage of total sales.

Moreover, its counterpart, our Footwear business, constituted over 70 percent of recent revenue. The plan and budget request went on to assert a need to transition from plastic-molded to premium wooden hangers to better showcase our featured clothing collections.

And suffice it to say, the funding needed for a storewide transition was not insignificant . . .

Please give some thought to where errors and inconsistencies in the planning occurred here. We will soon come back to this scenario, with indications that highlight a specific mistake made by retailers all too frequently.

But first, let's consider another example.

Example 2

While consulting with a restaurant owner who was often at full capacity at dinner—but desperately wanted additional revenue growth to compensate his kitchen staff more generously—I explained the three pathways to revenue. In response, he confidently (and perhaps correctly) stated that an increase in average ticket size was the most attractive and immediate path to achieving his financial desires for his business. He soon went through options to achieve his objective. His ideas included price increases on his most popular items, increased emphasis by servers on the à la carte salads, and a tableside presentation of tantalizing desserts. I was thrilled with the way he grasped which of the three revenue growth pathways should be his focus. I was also impressed with the eventual on-site implementation. These tactics connected seamlessly with the higher receipt totals his satisfied diners would gladly pay after uttering the most famous of all food service phrases: "Check, please."

But then . . . Ugggh! My favorable impressions faded when I visited his website. The imagery and messages were outdated and disconnected.

As part of this exercise, please take a moment to think about how digital resources could support a restaurant's efforts toward revenue growth while on the pathway to increased transaction size. We will come back to this example in just a few paragraphs.

Some Who Wander Are, Indeed, Lost

For now, let's return to our general manager with the strong opening for his Annual Plan—and the befuddling budget request that came with it. To be clear, his initial strategy was decidedly suggestive that more traffic was what was most needed for prospective sales growth. Yet even with the aid of bright lights and big windows, even the closest passersby would not likely notice the new hangers. Moreover, this tactic simply provides no discernible basis for a footwear retailer to capture the attention of prospective visitors. Imagine the ridiculousness of an accompanying advertising campaign with the message, "Now Proudly Featuring Wooden Hangers!"

Of course, if the strategic focus were, instead, increasing transaction size by getting customers to purchase more while inside this store, the tactic of converting the admittedly cheap-looking plastic hangers to those with an attractive walnut finish might make sense. After all, this tactic would potentially draw more attention to each apparel collection and may even give the merchandise in a lower-volume category a more premium appearance. In essence, the 70 percent of visitors who make a footwear purchase might begin buying apparel more frequently. If this occurred, it would certainly increase the average transaction size.

But that was not the stated intent. Fortunately, the disconnect between declared priorities and requested resources was discovered before any expenditures of either time or money were committed. Simply put, our general manager strayed from his stated priority. I refer to this mistake as as "tactical wandering." Had we not course-corrected to the strategically decided destination, those resources would have been lost. Forever. From another angle, those resources would have been misspent—and they could never be reclaimed or redirected toward programming that accurately reflected the stated intent to improve the total number of transactions.

Since none of us has the resources to pursue every growth possibility, we must ensure a clear alignment of our intentions with our ideas and investments.

As we conclude this chapter, let's return to the efforts of the restaurant whose online presence was less than savory. You may have already devised some smart online tactics to support the strategic effort to increase the size of each ticket. Your ideas may include mouth-watering pictures of the new desserts on social media, or an "Eat Your Salad First" enticement on the takeout app or website landing page, or a mention of all the fresh ingredients found in the recipe for last month's most popular menu item through a weekly blog or a monthly newsletter. And, of course, all these ideas (and likely many others) nicely complement the stated plan and solidly fit the objective.

Unfortunately, strategic alignment was *not* what I found. As I canvassed the digital media being employed, all of the assets were dedicated to a "Join Us for Lunch" campaign.

Bah!

Again, it is not that an effort to expand the lunchtime business is altogether inappropriate. It is just not consistent with the agreed-upon priority. It is not congruent with where the owner made the biggest investments for sales growth. If the strategic focus had been instead on *frequency*, I would have felt no such disappointment. If the proprietor believed the most viable route to higher wages was through revenue increases from those who already visited for dinner— but now could (and would) do the same at a time of day with plenty of seating capacity—we were potentially on to something clever . . .

The business's lack of alignment is clear when comparing the practices inside the restaurant with the primary messaging outside of it. Our assessment illuminates inconsistency between the leader's vocalized objective for the eatery and the execution of specific tactics through key resources. We must avoid such a scattershot approach to growth—or as Jim Collins and Morton T. Hansen convey in their ageless literary work *Great by Choice*, "uncalibrated cannonballs flying all over the place."[1] Our responsibility is to bring order to our resources and constantly steer our strategic assets in the same direction as our stated priorities. Drumbeat discussion on the three pathways to revenue and growth—and carefully aligned intentions—keep us on track to reach our potential. Our direction is clear. Forward, we go! Equally important, an organizational familiarity with this approach confirms a commitment to Uninvolved Optimization, freeing the leader from having to constantly determine if growth priorities and available resources are situated properly.

It's the Mortar:
Involved Maximization Imperatives for Chapter 7

1. Select a current revenue growth plan or tactic for your business or department. Determine its proper classification as a conversion, frequency or transaction size initiative.

2. If you're in an organization or on a Team where revenue increases are not specifically connected to the three pathways to revenue, offer or make plans to teach an overview of each. Use recent efforts as examples to help determine where you are seemingly declaring your growth priorities.

3. To ensure a full understanding of conversion, frequency, and transaction size, develop a prospective growth plan attached to each. It does not matter if it is probable or even realistic. The intent of this exercise is comprehension.

4. As comprehension is achieved, consider where financial and personnel resources are currently deployed in the name of growth. Are they logically aligned with the growth priorities identified in your examples from Imperative 2?

5. We are in Section II now. We can no longer avoid the necessity of computations! As such, select a growth target. It can be specified in either a gross revenue increase or a percentage gain. Either way, show off the arithmetic that validates the merit of this pursuit. For bonus points, determine how to get to the same increase through a different means of growth.

CHAPTER 8

Strategic Multiplicity

Doing Various Things at the Same Time ...
So You Can Always Do What Matters Most

Even if only out of long-standing habit, many retail industry leaders believe doing many things at the same time—*and* concurrently working across multiple ways to grow sales—is achievable. Even necessary—if not expected.

It is my conclusion these leaders are correct. This can be our modus operandi.

Even better, we—as inspired Masters of Making Things Better—can accomplish multiple high-stakes initiatives simultaneously!

But it also remains true that notable combinations of physical or mental activity cannot be done in the same instant . . . Most of us cannot even apply a modest focus to two elementary tasks in unison. In the same time frame, maybe. But not synchronically.

So, what gives? Can we move more than one rocket ship onto the launch pad or not?

The ability to leave first base is the bridge that spans the chasm separating those with momentum on multiple fronts from those relegated to a singular pursuit. As a reminder, the definitions and examples for the various types of revenue growth found in chapter 7 were *not* about which option is most popular or superior. Each is valuable in its own way. And each is qualified to be a top priority, whether by itself or beside another means of growth . . .

A Method for Multiplicity

Parallel efforts to improve conversion, frequency and/or transaction size should be embraced. Again, several pursuits of growth *can* be undertaken at the same time. It is my finding that retailers achieving sustained growth make it a common practice to (at least) *consider* growth across all three of the available pathways. This does not mean each of these is always of equal priority—or that each prospect for revenue growth should be perennially pursued. Instead, as the seemingly best opportunities are illuminated, growth priorities are established.

Of course, seasoned service providers already know there are no reliable shortcuts for revenue growth. Empirical success through each or any means of growth requires strategic planning, hyper-crisp execution, and clear-eyed attention toward an objective. And for maximal results, a proven methodology for taking on multiple pursuits must be instilled. Said differently, we must ensure a method for our multiplicity!

I have discovered two inherent obligations to do this effectively. In both, devotion to specificity is required, as it sets the direction and determines the course. To be specific with the required specificity ☺, it is the What and Who associated with our pursuits that must be declared and documented. The obligations are as follows:

1. We must specify with tremendous clarity the growth pathway and the strategic plans associated with any forecasted sales increase.
2. We must assign Team Members (including yourself, if appropriate) to specific tasks in the pursuit of such revenue growth.

Introducing the OST Framework

If only to state the obvious regarding our three pathways to revenue growth, we cannot pursue improvement in any of these areas if we do not know our *current* performance in these same areas. Before we dive into the recommendation that follows, here are the metrics for which you must have valid data to perform this exercise:

- Total number of visitors (or prospects or leads)
- Total number of transactions (or receipts or sales tickets)
- Total sales volume
- Total number of purchasers contributing to total sales volume

Do not let the term "Total" mislead you. If the increases sought are departmental or categorical, the information acquired should be a departmental or categorical total (instead of a "grand" total). You must also use the same time frame for each metric to ensure "apples to apples." In the end, revenue growth is the manifestation of a higher number of sales tickets of the same average and/or a larger average total on every sales ticket. Nothing more.

And certainly nothing less.

Given the required data, it is likely no surprise my recommended approach is grounded in traditional goal-setting terms. It flourishes when the pathways for growth and the desired outcomes are clear and measurable. To ensure their presence, we thread <u>O</u>bjectives, <u>S</u>trategies, and <u>T</u>actics together in a pyramidal fashion.

It is the OST Framework.

As an initial example of this model, we will use a single-store retailer of casual footwear with multiple and coexistent growth initiatives. This blueprint is equally advantageous for other service businesses, nonprofits, restaurants, and online sellers. You will quickly observe how each Strategic Focus in this example is aligned with one of the three pathways to revenue growth. While each Strategic Focus contributes independently to an overall growth Objective, the growth Objective is, of course, pursued collectively and collaboratively.

For each strategy, there is also a Strategy Lead who reports results and provides proper accountability for all Team Members implementing the supporting Tactics. Meanwhile, Strategic Themes concisely provide an overview of intent and serve as a tactical umbrella for the specific actions planned. I will comment more on this element following the example.

Most notably, the OST Framework provides clear evidence that we are strategically pursuing our Objective through simultaneous growth on multiple fronts.

Objective

Achieve gross COMP sales growth of no less than +5.5%, while maintaining a gross margin of >/= 45.0 by December 31.

Strategy #1	Strategy #2	Strategy #3
Strategy Lead: **Mike**	Strategy Lead: **Tricia**	Strategy Lead: **Shanta**
Strategic FOCUS: **Conversion**	Strategic FOCUS: **Transaction Size**	Strategic FOCUS: **Frequency**
Strategic Theme(s)	Strategic Theme(s)	Strategic Theme(s)
• Community outreach	• Premium products • Bundled offers	• Digital Marketing

Tactics

Connect with 10 new high schools to develop relationship with athletic department and/or specific teams. (Mike)	Ensure no less than 1 premium-priced model is provided to Guests in first round of choices during full-service fitting. (Greg)	Utilize POS-based CRM system to send email notifications about the arrival of model updates to previous purchasers. (Shanta)
Connect with 3 local hospitals to determine if fittings can be done onsite for nursing staff and rehabilitation personnel. (Heather)	Create specific "combo offer" for those who would consider purchase of both an athletic shoe and hiking boot. (Greg)	Utilize free software to create monthly newsletter for existing database, focusing on new releases and special events. (Shanta)
Connect with each co-tenant in shopping center to discuss prospects of cross-promotion. (Mike)	Implement monthly sales incentive for Team Members who sell no less than 20 pairs of Tier One–priced shoes. (Tricia)	Ensure efforts to begin capturing valid email addresses for no less than 75% of purchases. (Mike)

The power of a Strategic Theme is its connectivity up and down the plan. To better illustrate, please find the reference to "Community Outreach" in Strategy #1. In it, we see a Strategic Theme both inseparable from the overall Objective *and* directly connected to very specific Tactics designed to increase in-store traffic. A well-crafted Strategic Theme does more than represent a Strategic Focus. It proudly serves the Objective and supervises the related Tactics.

As mentioned earlier, each strategy also has a designated leader. Each Tactic is employed by a Team Member (see the assigned names in the example). Yes, the same Team Member can lead multiple strategies or Tactics. He or she may also enlist others inside or outside the organization. This transparency goes beyond knowing "who is doing what" by ingraining an essential unity within the effort. Like with team sports, our OST Framework is a playbook that makes it clear everyone has a role to play in the pursuit of victory. For the lead-up strategy discussions, input from the Team is encouraged. As the OST Framework is prepared, however, it is crucial that comprehension of the strategies and a firm commitment to the Tactics are confirmed by all involved. Accountability is a must. Anything less keeps the first baseman tethered to the base.

Grounded in Growth—Or Destined to the Opposite

To present a contrasting case study where alternative pathways for revenue were not properly considered, I will reference a former footwear retailer where I live. I reside in a lively tourist town in the Blue Ridge Mountains, with an abundance of summer visitors from Atlanta and the state of Florida. They arrive to enjoy outdoor activities and the cooler temperatures at our higher elevation. When I dare go downtown during this peak season, the sidewalks are packed, as pedestrians spill into the roadways, canvassing the food, beverage, and shopping options. For anyone who gives such a passing thought, it appears each merchant is easily surpassing any reasonably established sales target for the month or season.

As a local, I simply applaud the orchestration of politeness demonstrated by those entering specific locations at the same time others are exiting. It is a beautiful collision of congestion and kindness.

But alas, consider my use of the keyword *former* in regard to the referenced footwear retailer. It was *not* a lack of visitors inside this store that, ultimately, spelled D-O-O-M for the now-defunct operation. Instead, it was a bona fide conversion failure, as too many people who vocalized, "Excuse me," while leaving the premises did so without carrying even a single bag or box out the door.

Finding Legacy in a Guest Services Graveyard

There is simply no way to bring that footwear retailer back from the Guest Services Graveyard. As happens thousands of times every year, we are left only with a retail cadaver—and the somewhat cruel opportunity to conduct an autopsy on its demise. In this instance, we can easily identify the fatal wounds from a lack of conversion: lots of visitors, too few receipts.

If the postmortem could breathe life back into the enterprise, we would suggest an OST Framework different than our previous example. Not enough traffic is trouble—but so is plenty of traffic without sufficient transactions.

In any OST tribute exercise for this former merchant, the Strategic Theme would likely focus on getting tourists to start spending while inside the premises. To put it plainly, this retailer needed to close more leads, not increase the number of visitors. And it matters not whether our operation is healthy or has flatlined. Once we sense the means most ripe for growth, we can more easily generate ideas to get us going.

With proper homage to hindsight, here are a few off-the-cuff tactics for the dearly deceased. They aim toward sales growth through improved conversion while *not* emphasizing any need to stuff more people inside the store itself:

- Installing a pleasant store greeter who communicates, "Welcome! Our newest arrivals can be found over there!"
- Prominently featuring in-store signage indicating, "Each Purchase of $150.00 or More Receives a Meal Voucher" at a popular downtown dining destination
- Accommodating visitors with self-service options to comfortably try on shoes and minimize the need for a sales associate to navigate the crowd just to acquire a specific size from the stockroom

The Pursuit of Growth Is Infinite—Our Resources are Not

As a final example, let us consider a hypothetical involving a boot-strapped bakery in the recently restored city center that sees almost nine of every ten visitors make a purchase. In this statistic alone the tenant gets deserved props for its remarkable conversion rate and clearly positive in-store experience. Nonetheless, bank statements depict some very real concerns as to whether cash flow will support operating expenses after a "reduced rent period" expires in ninety days.

It's time again to put our OST Framework to the test!

Our business's conversion rate of nearly 90 percent is a valuable clue for how we might initiate our efforts. With such apparent customer satisfaction, it may be wise to do any or all of the following:

- Find ways to attract more visitors (conversion)
- Attempt to get those already making purchases to spend more during their visits (transaction size)
- Incent those who made a purchase today to return sooner and more often (frequency)

As we see with this example, programming options exist with each strategy. However, commissioning a plan aligned with every means is not always advised or even possible. As we wade through the various options, we must also consider our resources. Only after considering growth options *and* the available or attainable resources can we build the best and most specific OST Framework.

Let's consider a framework, keeping in mind the all too familiar realities of limited resources and seemingly too little time to increase sales:

Objective	
Achieve gross sales growth over the next 3 months that eclipses any prior 3-month sales period by no less than 30 percent.	

Strategy #1	Strategy #2
Strategy Lead: **Fernando** Strategic FOCUS: **Transaction Size** Strategic Theme(s) • **Bundled offers** • **Relevant pairings**	Strategy Lead: **Fernando** Strategic FOCUS: **Frequency** Strategic Theme(s) • **Loyalty programming** • **Digital marketing**

Tactics	
Offer coffee for $1.00 for anyone who purchases a muffin, scone or breakfast cookie before 10 a.m. (Fernando) Create a 12-pack program, where any purchase of a 12-pack of cookies, muffins, specialty doughnuts or bagels can get a second 12-pack for 50% off. (Jason) Remember to ask each patron whether they would like a specialty butter, cream cheese, or bruschetta with their bulk purchases. (Fernando)	Utilize POS-based loyalty program to reward customers with a FREE BAKERY ITEM (of their choice) after each threshold of $50.00 is surpassed. (Fernando) Begin earnest capture of email addresses and commit to a weekly newsletter with indications of new items and attractive pictures of freshly baked goods. (Jason) Provide each patron a bounce-back coupon for a free coffee on their next purchase of $5.00 or more before 10 a.m. (Jason)

Other Benefits of an OST Framework: Mitigating Risks and Reducing Anxiety

You likely had other (even better!) ideas than those found in the above OST Framework to generate incremental revenue for our hypothetical bakery. To be sure, sales growth is rarely stymied by a lack of possibilities. It is, in fact, the variety and number of ways to pursue growth that is overwhelming to most operators. With the aid of credible ideas from colleagues alongside a constant stream of inbound information from outside the organization, the three pathways to growth offer almost limitless possibilities. Ultimately, an OST Framework drives us to a conclusion from the plethora of options and prompts a commitment to action.

In any growth pursuit, overlapping efforts are also a legitimate, long-standing concern. As such, leaders practicing Involved Maximization must regularly confirm proper coverage for their stated priorities—and promptly remove any discovered duplication. A well-constructed OST Framework ensures that roles and assignments are crystal clear, without wasteful replication.

Lastly, an effective OST Framework mitigates risk through its built-in boundaries. As mentioned, a Strategic Theme supervises the Tactics we endorse by ensuring they remain focused on the most relevant and productive opportunities. In the same way it would be imprudent to implement a Frequent Diner program in a restaurant that caters to tourists—and still ends each day with too few tickets—tactical possibilities are naturally refined when filtered through a Strategic Theme and directly connected to a well-considered Strategic Focus.

A Measurable Objective Grounded in Measurable Growth

Though not necessary in every instance, incorporating measurable Strategies and Tactics into the OST Framework brings cohesion to the entire effort. For example, a business's Tactic of handing out five hundred "1-Day Sale" flyers could assist their strategy to grow average weekday receipt quantities by no less than thirty per day, as they both remain subservient to the business's Objective to increase Q3 sales by no less than 3.25 percent. In essence, pursuing the Objective is grounded in achieving the Tactics.

As we compose an increasing number of OST Frameworks, a natural byproduct is to begin communicating in specifics. Said differently, "OST multiplicity begets OST specificity!" We transition from shallow commentary such as "I'm forecasting 5 percent growth in our business" to deeper, more focused clarifications, such as "We intend to grow the business 5 percent primarily through a notable increase in transactions and a slightly higher transaction size. Here is where we're starting." Regardless of an organization's specific goal, the powerful specificity enabled by well-engineered OST Frameworks will be impossible to miss.

Here are some other ways I've heard growth targets introduced in organizations that utilize the OST Framework. The powerful specificity engineered by this approach is impossible to miss:

"For this nonprofit to maximize its potential impact this year, we must grow income no less than $100,000 from donations by those who have contributed only once in the last thirty-six months. This is how I propose we do it."

"I am trying to grow our total sales 25 percent this weekend by doubling the number of diners who add a premium side item to their order. Here's where I need your help."

"For us to add those two positions we discussed at the last quarterly meeting, we need to generate almost two hundred thousand dollars in incremental revenue. My plan to get us there includes increasing the monthly subscription rate by four percent for all users and working with key accounts to double our business in the Hospitality channel by the end of the year. And as I know you'll ask, I do not believe the price increase will result in subscriber attrition of more than five percent . . . Are you ready to hear more?"

We now see how growth Tactics are to be born from a specific Strategic Theme in any OST Framework. In turn, Strategic Themes exist to serve the specific Strategic Focus with which they are aligned. And the Strategic Focus itself, we should remember, is dutifully connected to one of the three pathways to revenue growth. Most importantly, all strategic and tactical elements are subordinate to a measurable Objective that represents the intended growth and the strategic multiplicity promoted and enabled by the framework itself.

It's the Mortar:
Involved Maximization Imperatives for Chapter 8

1. Build an OST Framework for your organization. Be very specific in your Objective. For the Strategic Themes and Tactics, put down both

current initiatives *and* new ideas. Cite the means of designated revenue growth (conversion, frequency and/or transaction size) and determine whether the pursuit is sensibly linear.

2. The inaugural draft can be done by yourself or with companions. As a proper basis, begin by acquiring the information needed to establish current performance with conversion, frequency, and transaction size.

3. Share the OST with a constituent who was *not* involved in its creation. Most importantly, ask him or her to evaluate its clarity and feasibility.

4. After incorporating any useful feedback from step 3, present the OST to your Team, department or organization. Make final changes based on the relevance and quality of this feedback. Ensure an understanding by all involved Team Members that this will be a regularly cited document when assessing performance and progress. In addition, begin to consider and discuss assignments and oversight for each Strategy and Tactic.

5. Make the final assignments and begin the work associated with the Tactics. As Tactics are initiated and completed, take the time with your Team to evaluate the results and progress toward the Objective.

CHAPTER 9

The Creation Story

In the Beginning of Every Relationship . . .

In a book such as this, commentary on emphasizing the importance of "building relationships" is only to be expected. To be sure, relationships in a service-based entity matter greatly. It is mortar! In fact, I agree with Brad Sugars, chairman and founder of the business-coaching firm ActionCOACH, when he specifies, "Business is all about relationships . . . how well you build them determines how well they build your business."[1] And famed film producer and talent manager Jerry Weintraub complements this commentary with an even more direct assertion: "Relationships are the only thing that matter in business and in life."[2]

At the same time, so much good content on developing and nurturing relationships is already available. Go find it. If you are not sure where to begin, I would recommend anything written by author John Maxwell on this topic. It is also my belief *How To Win Friends And Influence People* by Dale Carnegie, originally published in 1936, remains timeless. Meanwhile, Nicolaj Siggelkow and Christian Terwiesch's *Connected Strategy* is a master class on how globally known and iconic brands have used the power of relationships to build impactful and profitable publicly traded enterprises. More recently, Mo

Bunnell unpacks the "Four Gifts"—strategies to build and sustain healthy professional relationships—in his book *Give to Grow*. With a focus on ways to ensure "everyone wins," his expertise on the delicate matters associated with the "Exchange" (as referenced in the pages ahead) is invaluable.

For now, however—and to connect directly with the three pathways to increase revenue—we are going jump the line to focus specifically on external business relationships as real conduits to tangible and recurring income. More so than Guest Services, this content will connect to the theme of Business Development. For many service businesses, a great retail experience not only builds many favorable Broadcast Towers but is also paired with various marketing activities that help to ensure a steady stream of visitors. This is both a fair—and fairly successful—way to build sales volume, presuming both the experience and the marketing efforts are solid.

But we should not stop there.

When we achieve the ability to leave first base, we can go beyond traditional marketing to the general marketplace. We do not need to rely exclusively on digital and social media tools to connect with a predetermined population. This hard-earned latitude allows us to identify and engage with specific entities—persons or other organizations—that can influence the perception and patronage of our business in a meaningful way. My preferred approach will borrow from two terms that are consistently popular in board-rooms and business dialogue. At the same time, my experience suggests too often these words stray from their meaning, get separated from each other or are not aligned with any specific tactical effort. These terms are simply hollowed of their worth when used only in general reference:

Value

Creation

Expressed more perfectly together: Value Creation.

This term expresses itself best in the form of a procedure, not just as an alluring and fanciful, if not often mysterious, point of reference. For me, it is a system oriented toward outcomes and intended for meaningful results. But to fully engage with the forthcoming three-step process of Value

Creation, we must first connect emotionally with each word in this term: Value. Creation. My own definitions do not differ from others published. At the same time, I aim to be concise in order to assist memorization and allow for easy evaluation of whether the concept is actually being considered and administered in the pursuit of growth.

Value: the price relative to quality.

Creation: to design into existence.

Even if elementary, it is crucial to understand that in this definition of "value" there are no inherent connotations to low prices, inexpensive acquisitions or significant discounting. The key is in "relative to quality." I often substitute the word "impact" when "quality" doesn't go far enough—so "relative to impact" can be appropriately applied here as well.

Let's put this important point in context: Whether it is with our money, our precious time or any other thing we trade for something that truly means something to us, the price—the investment—may be enormously high. However, if the quality obtained *in your estimation* justifies the cost, what you have obtained is of *real* value. Yes, the purchase of a Porsche 911 Targa 4S, a matinee performance with your kids when your hourly billable rate is $750 or a stay at Le Sereno Hotel in St. Barthélemy might be deemed expensive, even exorbitant, by others . . .

But it may still hold incredible value to you due to the quality or impact you perceive and experience.

Now, let's move to our definition for "creation." Even while acknowledging various religious teachings, it's still smart to start with the opening of the Old Testament as a relevant use case. Its key takeaway has seemingly been heard by most and memorized by many: "In the beginning, God created the heavens and the earth" (Genesis 1:1, NLT). If we resist the temptation to debate whether the universe exploded into motion, was the origin of an inexplicable gravitational collapse or was constructed supernaturally in a week, this opening biblical statement can be translated as "God designed into existence the heavens and the earth."

And it was good.

As leaders, our goal is to consistently "design into existence" (Creation) something good for others where "price relative to quality/impact" (Value) is acceptable—if not better! I believe the ability to successfully do this is found through the efforts of three critical actions: Investigation, Assessment, and Exchange. Each of these contributes to a repeatable process and actionable plan for legitimate, calculable Value Creation. Additionally, this approach enables and ensures a proper "return" for our efforts in the form of compounding income increases.

Value Creation Creates Revenue Growth through Conversion

Before we fully detail the three critical actions of Value Creation, let's see exactly where Value Creation intersects with our three pathways to revenue growth.

As we discussed, many retail and restaurant endeavors generate traffic (visitors) almost exclusively from walk-ins, word-of-mouth (building Broadcast Towers!), and conventional marketing. For sure, these efforts are productive and likely to forever be an integral part of revenue growth—but our plans for additional increases should not stop there. Proactively maximizing the benefit of our Broadcast Towers and always improving our strategic marketing are fine complements to what is more regularly known in other sectors as "Business Development." As growth-minded retailers, we must abandon the sense that this term is reserved for agencies and enterprises serving others without menu boards or pre-priced products sitting on shelves. And to be clear, this approach is not business-to-business (B2B) *instead* of business-to-consumer (B2C) or direct-to-consumer (D2C). It is directly and comfortably alongside the efforts to serve patrons who are individually visiting your stores, restaurants and websites.

Here are just a few examples:

- Beyond counter signage, restaurants can proactively pursue a profitable catering extension that attentively accommodates lunchtime meetings.
- Beyond an easy-to-navigate Gardening & Lawn Care aisle, a hardware store can proactively seek an equipment contract with the City Parks & Recreation Department.

- Beyond busy weekends, a fashion boutique can contact local employers with a program to offer gift cards as an employee perk or for employee recognition.

The possibilities are truly countless for most enterprises participating in the retail industry. And business development secured through Value Creation is a boon for conversion statistics! We are attracting more visitors who are built-in buyers.

Let's take a closer look.

Transaction Acceleration Programming

In keeping with classic organization-specific vernacular, my businesses have developed the acronym TAP: transaction acceleration programming. To help manage this initiative, store-management personnel set time aside each week to develop a TAP Plan, engage in TAP activities, and invest in TAP possibilities. These conversion-related efforts exist to generate more income from newly created and smartly maintained relationships within a specified "business development zone," otherwise known as a BDZ, which is usually defined by a five-mile radius of anywhere we do business. Although agreed upon terms may include contract pricing, bulk purchases, special discounts or complementary services, the intent is, indeed, profitable revenue. Again, these sales often come from business-to-business relationships (even if nonprofit or governmental), where our products and assets produce a consequential impact for another organization and further our own solid reputation through interaction with those associated with that organization.

The Three Actions for Successful Value Creation

Now, as with the three pathways to revenue, there are equally three reliable, road-tested steps for ensuring we repeatedly engage in successful Value Creation: Investigation, Assessment, and Exchange. Let's explore them each in depth.

Value Creation Step 1: Investigation

Most people can easily recall an instance—or even an intrusion—when we were offered a dramatic promise of help in an initial conversation or uninvited correspondence. It might have been a pledge for more website traffic, happier customers, cheaper shipping options, increased efficiency with payroll processing . . . bigger muscles, a smaller waist, better neighbors, happier kids, less traffic—or all of that and more. And we can admit that when the offer is creative or the database blast lands at just the right time—when we do, indeed, have tangible pain or frustration that could be alleviated by the promised result—we might ask the salesperson a probing question or click the accompanying link to learn more.

But without knowing you, here is what I do know about you: it is rare that you would respond in this way to such offers.

And it is no different for the person on the other side of your advances to initiate, increase or intensify a relationship. The work associated with business and relationship development is *not* merely the accumulation of prospects. And Value Creation has absolutely nothing to do with the number of uninvited calls and messages made and sent.

In most instances, a persistent claim by you to provide a distinct benefit *without* learning more about the actual needs or wants of the prospect is woefully shortsighted. There is credible proof that informs us that customized connections and solutions are best to move people and businesses forward. In fact, it is in this current generation that we have transitioned from the once-groundbreaking B2B selling principles found in the 1985 book *Strategic Selling* (written by business consultants Robert B. Miller and Stephen E. Heiman) to a customer relationship management (CRM) software industry with more than $1B in annual revenues. Business development and relationship building is now big business on its own!

But whether you begin with a decades-old selling plan or an investment in a new cloud-based and AI-driven software, the first step is the same. Effective Value Creation begins with an examination of where and how we can uniquely create value through ourselves or the product(s) with which we are associated. *This* is the Investigation. And yes, to do it properly, we can summon our inner Jessica Fletcher, Veronica Mars, or Sherlock Holmes, as common investigative principles apply in this context in the form of

- research completed with considerable depth,
- discovery of helpful clues not likely residing in plain sight, and
- continual consideration of established facts.

With an Investigation, the foreteller of success in any effort to unlock solutions and reveal new possibilities for an entity you wish to serve is predictable—but it is not easy. The quality of your detective work, in fact, is entirely commensurate with the quality of the questions presented and the research completed. This is as true for a suspect in a scene from a Hollywood crime drama as it is for us when we are having coffee with a prospective client or generating input for an AI language model to automate follow-up with current customers or patrons.

After all, our resources only produce a growth opportunity when they intersect with the confirmed desires of our prospective clients. To regularly arrive at this lucrative destination, we must communicate effectively by making thoughtful queries and listening intently. There is published material in many places—and from many fields of study—to help us improve this skill. Recently, one of my favorite resources comes from Charles Duhigg, whose 2024 book *Supercommunicators: How to Unlock the Secret Language of Connection* explores the importance of "Asking Questions and Noticing Clues." It masterfully underpins any Investigation and reinforces our "curiosity first" approach.

In the pursuit of Value Creation, our Investigation must achieve

- an accurate sense of the required deliverable to be of "value," and
- an appropriate estimation of the impact it needs to have to be considered of "value."

With this end in mind, thoughtful questions must be tailored to ensure success per the definition of "value" (price relative to quality). It matters not whether you've less than five minutes to do this work or are given a half-day to sit with a prospect. Any eventual involvement becomes entirely dependent upon an ability to cogently and convincingly suggest a satisfying return on investment in an area of confirmed importance.

Our investigative work does *not* include pledged efforts, next steps or proposed solutions (hence the use of the phrase "eventual involvement"). In fact, to avoid an overreach in any initial encounter, keep your preconceived notions of how you can help unpacked! Instead, allow your advanced preparations and previous experience to astutely guide your questions. Whether your opportunity is a fully anticipated lengthy conversation or an entirely unexpected brief exchange, the best "Investigators" seek *only* to learn in initial encounters.

Lastly, there is no reason to conceal an intent to use the knowledge gained through your Investigation in your follow-up with your prospect—right down to the very words they used in your initial conversation. Ultimately, this initial effort will only serve to help you develop a compelling plan to create customized value for those who deserve nothing less. It also provides a foundation for the remaining actions in our three-step process.

Value Creation Step 2: Assessment

"Can we *really* create value for this prospect?"

When it comes to Assessment, this is the question to which we must determine the answer.

Our path to enlightenment includes an honest evaluation of three distinct elements related to any potential project:

1. The party for whom you wish to create value (Introduction)
2. The specific needs and desires of this party (Investigation)
3. The resources and capabilities that you and your organization have to create value for the party by reaching their needs or desires (Introspection)

As the terms Introduction, Investigation, and Introspection self-evidently suggest, our Assessment requires both an outward and inward effort. Reconsidering the method of Investigation, we already know that good questions produce truthful answers from those with whom we wish to work. For our Assessment, the honesty, instead, must come from our end. It is only if we are honest in our Assessment that we can produce a fitting answer to the question, "Can we *really* create value for this prospect?"

To demonstrate how this works, I will craft an example featuring a sports franchise. As it will be equally informative for you to put yourself in either the shoes of the Team or the retailer, you can pick your preferred role! This illustration will be sizable enough to be beyond niche—and local enough to be interesting.

To get started, please imagine that your favorite professional sports team would like to acquire a more lucrative partnership in the Automotive category. For the sake of our example, we will also assume the pertinent questions below were asked during the Investigation stage:

- We have read quite a bit online and in the trade journals about the industry and some of your counterparts recently. Still, in your estimation, how has business for you and in this market been for the last 6–24 months?

- In the last few months—or even years—what has been the biggest accomplishment for you and your organization? How about your biggest challenge?

- What does your forecast for performance or growth look like for the next couple of years, or for any period you feel comfortable and somewhat confident sharing?

- What are some considerations that will most likely influence the accuracy of this estimate? Are there any "great unknowns" that could have an impact?

- Of course, we have read and observed much about the culture in your organization. Even so, what do you see and sense is most important for your team/organization to ensure a maximal contribution to the market and business?

Let us pretend we now have the following firsthand knowledge through the answers we obtained from these worthy questions:

- Sell-thru (how much inventory a retailer sells compared to the total inventory they have received) in this market is currently solid across all dealers with truck models—but SUVs are more of a mixed bag and the portfolio of four-door automobiles is soft.

- The top-grossing dealer in the region has had a tough stretch with employee retention in the sales department—and this seems to be impacting focus on programs from the manufacturer, including proper communication and in-house awareness of available rebates, purchasing incentives, and financing options.
- The release of a new fuel-efficient, hybrid SUV model next year is projected to account for no less than 5 percent of all new car sales for the dealers in this market for the twelve months that follow the introduction.
- The phrase "Perform and Play AS A TEAM" is posted in numerous locations of the regional offices. It speaks to a Core Value of the organization—but with only loose parameters from headquarters as to its definition. Even worse, there is no evidence to suggest this rally cry is tangibly meaningful to the local dealerships that showcase and sell this brand.
- The company was previously involved in a sponsorship deal similar in nature to most new offerings brought to them by a sports-related property. It was constructed by and connected to the athletic department of a big-name university not too far from the professional team's metropolitan area. That agreement was not renewed after the initial five-year term, as no one could seemingly cite any benefit to the association.

Every Assessment we do mandates we take the information we obtain and determine if we are genuinely qualified to create any tangible and meaningful value for the prospective partner. We mix the results of our Investigation with candid introspection. In this example—and in our own efforts—we honestly determine whether we have the resources and capabilities to accomplish the outcome expected by the partner. Even if uncomfortable or disappointing, there is always the possibility we are not *really* needed or equipped to assist. In fact, for those who are continuously exploring the fringes of where and how to serve, our Investigation and Assessment will undoubtedly uncover occasions when we are *not* distinctively qualified to create the desired value.

Square peg. Round hole.

Move on.

Fortunately, most Assessments will identify something worthwhile that inspires further pursuit. When this occurs, you will hardly be able to keep the possibilities to yourself! Your enthusiasm for such progress will compel you to share more and, if necessary, sell the likely benefits to your prospective partner even harder

As we return to our example, let's assume the Assessment has deduced that the professional sports team can improve business performance for the automotive brand, as well as its dealers. As such, the initial follow-up from the sponsorship manager at your favorite team could be the following e-mail correspondence to the retailer's regional vice president:

Good afternoon, Taylor!

I quite enjoyed our time together on Monday. THANK YOU for your willingness to share more about yourself and your organization. Not only was it fascinating for me as someone who has a bent toward personal and organizational development, I believe it spawned some legitimate prospects for us to work together. In fact, I now hope you'll allow me to share three thoughts I've had since leaving your office.

For one, the headaches associated with the employee-retention challenges of your top dealer really intrigued me. As the most popular sports team in this market, surely, we can help address that challenge anywhere there are good people—and not an overly bad boss. ☺ We've access to countless parking passes, pregame occasions, club-level seats, concessions vouchers, and the biggest matrix board in the league in our stadium. Let's get these Team Members to the games on a regular basis and give them the VIP treatment they deserve.

Secondly, truth be told, most of the contracts of our bona fide superstars—and even our older veteran players—do not allow us to feature them in team-sponsorship campaigns without an incremental arrangement with the player(s) themselves. However, we have a few younger players and top rookie prospects who do not come with such encumbrances. In fact, they are either required to make a certain number of appearances or they have an agent who is looking for ways to more frequently showcase an "up-and-comer." I could not help but think there may be some solid synergy between these prospects and your new "rookie" hybrid model releasing next summer— let's pair 'em up!

Lastly, based on the elements you could recall from your arrangement with the college I'll leave unnamed, I used my network to determine the likely costs of that deal. For sure, this estimate may be in today's environment, rather than sixty-plus months ago. Even so, I still believe we can construct a partnership that would verifiably engage your dealers, demonstrably showcase the heart of your SUV and four-door portfolio, bring measurable success to the launch of your new hybrid—*and* cost less than two thirds what you paid previously for the former collegiate association.

Could we find time in the next few weeks to brainstorm further? I'm almost certain we can create value for your business and brand in a manner that is customized and complete in meeting some of your biggest objectives for the next couple of years.

Again, many thanks!

—MIKE

In the correspondence above, numerous references are made to the Investigation. Furthermore, specific indications of the desired outcome were derived from the internal Assessment of our capabilities and holdings that could be advantageously utilized. Again, "Value Creation" is entirely based on learning what is important to others and matching it with what is true about us. We want others to benefit from the unique perspectives and qualifications we possess to create obvious and unmatchable value. This is imperative, whether we are serving a meal to a family on the patio of a casual dining restaurant or conversing with the decision maker for a multimillion-dollar contract.

Value Creation Step 3: Exchange

"To love and be loved is to feel the sun from both sides." This quote attributed to American psychiatrist David Viscott reflects what we instinctively know about the best relationships. We have no regrets, doubts or hesitancy about what we put into it—and we are fully satisfied with what it does for us. Even in business, the best relationships are never lopsided or merely transactional.

At the same time, most are conditional.

Our clients and customers are not our kids (despite their occasional tantrums). It is wholly appropriate and always recommended for organizations to firstly service their own best interests. If this does not happen frequently enough, the music stops altogether—and everyone in the room is finished dancing. For sure, delayed gratification may be necessary. And there should be instances where an immediate gain is forsaken for an even grander fortune and future. Such strategic and calculated exceptions may include everything from free samples and introductory rates to "loss leaders" and hassle-free returns. Still, the ultimate and necessary intent remains for us to experience payout from the first position.

In addition, this forthcoming guidance regarding the Value Creation step of Exchange should not be perceived as a slap-in-the-face to "doing well by doing good." I very much suggest making generous donations to every degree possible, and taking care of others, without any expectation of anything in return. For what it is worth, my personal experience also submits that individuals who prove to be total takers on a truly service-minded Team will eventually be organizational outcasts.

But it is not altruism or charity we are recommending in this section. While these actions are profoundly good, they remain unrelated to our aims per Value Creation. After all, for Value Creation to be legitimate and ongoing, it should be understood that conditions must be created so that all parties are satisfied—and remain so. In fact, true partnerships are only realized when there is a recognizable overlap of self-interest by two or more entities.

So, yes, if you get yours, I do eventually need to get mine . . .

For this to occur, however, we need to clearly define what comprises such an achievement for us. And it is here where we find the wheels rattle off the rails too frequently. Many times, they also do so unexpectedly. When this occurs, the surprise is understandable. After all, we learned what we needed to do (Investigation), and we knew exactly what we had to offer for the betterment of others (Assessment).

But in too many instances, we did not fully understand what *we* wanted from this relationship to be satisfied in the Exchange.

Yes, it might just be an "us" issue.

Even so, there are no winners without a strong, shared belief that the partnership is a healthy and mutually beneficial arrangement for all involved. And regardless of the basis for any sloppy or faltering Exchange, shortchanging our own interests spins victimhood in many directions. As with most self-induced wounds, they come to harbor misplaced frustration. This is frustration that often gets directed at others when it should, instead, be an expectation to look more closely at ourselves. It is surely not a selfish endeavor to be ever-diligent in the preemptive work of deeply considering our side of the Value Creation equation. Anything less is unwise. After all, when we are dissatisfied, it is difficult to remain energetic about any agreed-upon arrangement.

We prevent such disappointment by effectively knowing what we really want through the Exchange.

That is: what we really, really, really want.

And when this foundation for truly mutual benefit is built and stable, we will create and exceed the value desired by, or promised to, others.

As we said at the start, Value Creation is *not* a pitch. It's a procedure. Even better now that you have the necessary elements, it's a *plan*. A plan that is specific, orderly, and full of applications that are easy to understand. A plan that can become measurably valuable and never heavily dependent on any single individual. Best of all, it is a plan that always features a process we can faithfully implement and consistently improve.

And it goes something like this:

- We conduct an Investigation of a prospect in the understanding that we are to judge whether measurable possibilities exist to deliver value to current or forthcoming efforts.

- We complete an honest Assessment of our own resources to determine whether there is an arrow—or multiple arrows—in our quiver that enables us to hit the target where the value would be visibly created for the prospect.

- We develop and propose an Exchange with the prospect through the unique resources we possess for something from the prospect that is also unquestionably of value to us.

It's the Mortar:
Involved Maximization Imperatives for Chapter 9

For a retail business primarily reliant on its reputation and marketing plan for growth, it is inarguable that our three-step process for Value Creation is an advantageous playbook. After all, it is always performed alongside a remarkable service proposition and tactical marketing efforts grounded in our three pathways to revenue growth. Especially at the onset, we kid ourselves not—this specific approach toward business development equates to more work.

But man, is it worth it! When Value Creation is done properly, the additional efforts will produce results beyond the existing reputational and promotional yield. Even better, over a longer period these business-development practices become organizational habits while simultaneously producing compounding returns and building many mutually beneficial relationships.

So, where to start?

In our professional lives, "on-the-job training" is a creative phrase for "learning by doing." When done correctly, it also equates to "improving by doing." As you might already suspect is necessary, our Imperatives for this chapter will harness this approach. With Value Creation, there is simply no more effective means! Whether someone is learning a new skill set—or you are wisely pursuing Uninvolved Optimization—these are the ten recommended steps to take and teach:

1. Determine and illustrate a radius from where your business operates to serve as the established BDZ—the business development zone. Depending on your operation, your BDZ may have minimal

or even no geographic boundaries. If you do not already have a preferred software to create a radius for your location, www.Maptive.com/radius-map-tool/ is a solid place to start. Again, for my retail businesses concentrated in urban or suburban areas, we give our BDZ a five-mile radius. In a moderately to heavily populated area, this presents plenty of opportunity to perform community outreach and identify prospective partnerships!

2. Within your BDZ, identify a target you believe would benefit from working with your organization. Whether the products you sell, services you offer, assets you possess, or characteristics you seemingly share, there must be *something* that tangibly connects you to this prospect.

3. Begin the Investigation! From online research and mutual connections in your network, there is much to learn. In addition, there are AI tools that can prepare a worthwhile overview of any prospect for your review and to learn more. In these instances, be sure to validate such information through established sources like company websites and materials published by the prospect (or its representatives). Do not shortcut the preparations of your investigative dossier. It is unlikely that a single tidbit alone can determine whether your initial inclination with this prospect is spot-on or off base.

4. As part of the Investigation, determine a contact strategy. This may be as linear as finding key personnel on the company website or attempting to connect through LinkedIn. It may also be as indirect as asking a shared friend or colleague to make an introduction.

5. As you make your introduction (written or verbal), *concisely* and *specifically* demonstrate two achievements from your Investigation:
   - You've given genuine thought to this connection by completing advanced research.
   - You and/or your organization share something with them, or their organization, that is a worthy consideration.

   NOTE: In your introduction, do *not* offer suggestions or solutions, and (for heaven's sake!) do not use the initial correspondence or conversation to sell your products or services. You are intending to build a relationship. In introductory communication, the objective is to secure a better vantage point from which to continue your Investigation.

6. As you secure an opportunity to learn more and check your research, continue the Investigation through thoughtful questions and truly engaged listening. Regardless of the medium or the audience, the initial session is typically time constrained. As such, clock management suggests a maximal amount of education with only a minimal amount of introduction.

7. From your learnings, complete an Assessment of your own skill sets and your organizational offerings to determine whether there is a meaningful way to create value for this prospect with whom you have completed an Investigation. This is not quick work or light exercise. In addition, you must also determine what you would need to receive in Exchange for the efforts necessary for you to create the intended value.

8. If your Assessment determines a verifiable reason to suggest a collaboration, compose follow-up correspondence grounded deeply in what was learned during the Investigation. Be very specific as you connect what you have learned from your prospect to your known strengths. If you need to establish your capabilities or credibility, use previous work that is relatable and projections that are believable and achievable. Most importantly, create a vision for an improved experience on behalf of your prospect that is easy to imagine and embrace!

9. As you sense an interest, it is appropriate to introduce the elements of Exchange. Yes, this may be costs or pricing, but it may also include timing, work conditions, periodic evaluations or anything else central to designing something into existence where the price relative to quality and impact is appealing.

10. Whether through a formal agreement or casual correspondence (like email or other documentation), specify the obligations of both parties in the intended Exchange *in writing*. Obviously, the greater the commitment and the more sophisticated the

organization, the more fitting it is to ensure review by other authorities and the proper legal parameters. But regardless of whether the situation calls for signatures or handshakes, a similar interpretation of Value Creation and a complete understanding of the respective deliverables is a must.

CHAPTER 10:

Good Buying Makes for Better Selling

Stacking the Odds in Our Favor

Procurement is a term used to describe the acquisition of materials and products for the specific purpose of resale, or the acquisition of assets to, simply, assist a business. As an example of the latter, a law firm will procure furniture for newly leased office space. From the waiting area to the conference room to the desks for the partners, each item purchased will have a role to play and, perhaps, a statement to make . . . But, of course, the furniture for a law firm will not be resold to help ensure the forecasted income for the upcoming quarter.

For traditional merchants, restauranteurs, and others in the retail industry, procurement is viewed altogether differently. It's more like legalized gambling. It is the regularly required (and permitted) wager of hard-earned resources on something expressly chosen to produce a return greater than the acquisition cost and any affiliated expenses. More specifically, the process of procurement resembles table games at casinos, where novices and professionals alike flaunt formulas and strategies, monitor trends, and seek momentum . . . not before leaning into a little bit of superstition and luck.

This analogy is not all innuendo. We are, indeed, making a bet with every purchase order written through our procurement efforts. When boxes of produce become bowls of salad and piles of lumber become custom staircases, it is an oxymoronic gamble when we buy what we sell.

And to be sure, this is the type of "procurement" on which we will focus in this chapter.

All the mortar of soft skills addressed in Section I contributes to our effort to improve our odds with these lawful retail wagers. Research in fact tells us the better our Interaction and Environment (the foundation of our "Experience," per chapter 4), the less likely it even matters what we sell. In results reconfirmed in 2021 by Forbes Books author and entrepreneur Gui Costin, 60 percent of Millennials stated a loyalty to brands alone "if treated well through a customer-centric experience."[1] Furthermore, the inherent power of our Broadcast Towers (see chapter 5) provides additional opportunities for increased sales across all consumer segments, as personal recommendations remain the number one reason why people shop and dine where they shop and dine. In addition, consistent and capable execution of transaction acceleration programming (TAP) and Value Creation (see chapter 9) reliably increase the number of opportunities to present our products to prospective patrons with significant—even bulk—purchasing intent.

But we can do even better. We can reduce the risk associated with procurement even further. We can do what most people never do when playing games of chance in Las Vegas: we can win. In fact, we can run the tables and win big when our world-class service proposition, our ever-improving marketing efforts, and our business development activities are mixed with a proven approach to procurement.

More Money in Our Pocket and Better Guarantees on the Docket

These days for my businesses, the most common intersections for "Yes" and "No" answers are *not* found in hiring decisions or real estate negotiations. Instead, they appear with the new products and updated models presented to our buyers. The manufacturers' representatives want placement in our stores and bigger orders; and we want more sell-thru, faster turns, and higher margins. Said differently, we want "more money in our pocket and better guarantees on the docket."

In the early days of my inaugural retail business, the only easy part of procurement was crafting this silly rhyme as an important reminder; everything else related to purchasing was a soul-sucking, ass-kicking grind. Our purchase orders were predicated on biased guidance, personal taste, and gut reactions. Our lack of experience burst through with every question we *didn't* ask. And even amidst merchandise samples, slickly produced catalogs, sales reports, and enticing volume discounts, our buying exercises led us only to an inconsistency with gross margins and sell-thru.

In short, we got what we deserved. We reaped poorly because we sowed poorly.

Fittingly, our earliest results included too much inventory, the wrong product mix, tardy arrivals, bad choices, and constant challenges with cash flow.

To make matters worse, the channels in which we participated had a long-standing practice of changing the most visible products every six to twelve months. Wholesale programs with varying incentives changed almost as frequently. And whether it was our own buyers or the sales representatives with whom we interacted, predictable changes in personnel only added to a habitual unsteadiness in our procurement efforts.

Nothing we did worked. Not consistently, anyway. But with my tilt toward Uninvolved Optimization, I knew we needed to start over with our approach to procurement. But where to start when starting over, I did not know . . .

A Budget from the Beginning

The premise of an "Open-to-Buy" budget came to me both unobjectionably and at the right time. But it did not arrive innocuously. In fact, every bit of my entrepreneurial pride was sufficiently wounded during the initial exposure. I was at a conference where the keynote speaker presumed the audience knew both the intent and the importance of this planning tool. Not a moment of his time on stage was spent to confirm everyone was cognizant of this tactic and capable of absorbing the next portion of the presentation. I felt like the village idiot. By the end of the session, I assumed I was the only person who had not completed some seemingly unstated prerequisites for attendance.

I've since learned it is unlikely I was alone in the knowledge gap that morning. Even in recent years, my experience is that many retail and service-business professionals are unaware of an Open-to-Buy formula. Others are consciously electing not to consider it . . . This is a mistake. And based on my own unsettling experience in that conference session all those years ago—even though there is now ample material online about "OTB"—I begin every discussion on procurement with the prevailing OTB formula and an instructional overview. I've also implemented a twist on the standard OTB formula that I'll introduce here.

In its original state, an Open-to-Buy budget has four key elements: Planned Sales, Planned Markdowns, Planned End of Month Inventory, and Planned Beginning of Month Inventory. As a calculation, it looks like this:

    Planned Sales
+ Planned Markdowns
+ Planned End of Month Inventory
− Beginning of Month Inventory

    OTB

Let's make this more tangible with an example featuring a fictitious soy wax candle company. We'll presume procurement is being done monthly, with the following figures representing the month of February:

    $27,000.00
+ $3,375.00 (12.5%)
+ 54,000.00
− 50,000.00

= $34,375.00

This calculation shows us that Soy Is Joy Candle Co. estimates mark-downs and discounts will average 12.5 percent for this month. In addition, it appears they wish to draw their beginning inventory total in February down $4,000.00 (~8 percent) by the onset of March. With these estimations, they will need to spend $34,375.00 to have the correct amount of inventory to achieve both the sales and the following month's inventory target. If they think a vendor will announce special (temporary) wholesale pricing for Valentine's Day, they may hold some of this OTB budget back for when the details of the program are shared. To be specific, if they only spent $25,000 on orders before the month started, they would still have $9,475 to spend if a special pricing program was announced the first week in February.

Without question, different industries and categories have different procurement needs and patterns. It is even widely believed staple items in a retail or restaurant environment need a different (and less formulaic) approach to ensure no out-of-stock situations. We've all been frustrated when our favorite donut shop does not have a glazed option available at 8:30 a.m. or the gardening section is out of a fine fescue grass-seed mix in the spring. When this happens, we rightfully ask, "How can that be?!" Ensuring proper inventory in the right place at the right time may not capture headlines like our stellar service proposition does—but availability impacts income levels on a balance sheet just the same. If we do *not* have the desired product, there is no training program or wage rate that can preserve a sale to our customers who know what they want and will settle for nothing else. Whether online or in-store, this revenue opportunity is gone for now . . . and, perhaps, gone forever.

Optimizing inventory is not just about achieving a preset dollar target with a total investment in goods or ingredients for sale, either. The correct *amount* must be paired with the correct *mix*. Even if Soy Is Joy Candle Co. sells only (nothing more than) 14.5 oz. soy candles in a glass container with a tin lid, it is a mutually disappointing encounter with a patron who returns for more Holiday Spruce candles when they have no stock in this scent . . . Despite our likely comments to her to the contrary, this customer will not be equally pleased with Gingerbread Kitchen. It is even worse for the sports retailer who is out of stock of bicycle pumps—but has too many youth-sized helmets available. The sales we *miss* never appear on sales reports . . . Even worse, the money we've tied up on unproductive inventory is not eligible as payment for an operating expense. Instead of your normal remittance, imagine a call to the electric company to let them know you're paying this month's power bill by shipping them seventeen youth bicycle helmets, instead!

Fortunately, the merits of an OTB budget can be applied beyond the total inventory investment. I believe its usefulness compounds when a total investment is comprised of adeptly forethought subtotals in designated subcategories. For example, if we know our December Open-to-Buy budget for Soy Joy is $32,000, it's even more helpful if that figure constitutes wisely made OTB calculations *by scent* suggesting the following:

$11,500.00 for Holiday Spruce
+ $7,500.00 for Gingerbread Kitchen
+ $5,000.00 for Cinnamon Strudel
+ $5,000.00 for Peppermint Stocking
+ $2,500.00 for Twinkle Twinkle
+ $500.00 for Grinch Butt

_____

= $32,000

Regardless of how inventory is subcategorized, we are rewarded when we are strategically granular, and we directly connect the more distinct classifications to the overall OTB budget. To assist this practice, I've instituted a twist on the standardized computation for OTB. This deviation enables me to see the roots of my inventory—and not just the numbers that traditionally sit on top. For example, when I'm only looking at my total investment in Footwear, it may appear we've optimized our assortment. In other words, the total value of inventory in this category might sensibly coincide with our anticipated revenue and margin. However, when we dig deeper into the inventory "soil," we often find the conditions can be healthier. And as we get to the roots, it connects us back to the distinctions italicized previously with both amount *and* mix. Let's start with the formula:

Current Sales
+ <u>Projected Sales Increase</u>
= Projected Sales
× Gross Margin
– <u>Projected Sales</u>
= Cost of Goods Sold (COGS)
+ <u>On-Hand (Existing) Inventory</u>
= OTB (will likely show a deficit, reflecting
the amount that needs to be spent as OTB)

There is rarely a season or product when the amount of on-hand inventory (OH), as a percentage, should greatly outpace its contribution to the overall revenue (as a percentage). In other words, if we imagine hiking boots are 3.75 percent of our Footwear business during the holidays (or throughout the year), there is little reason this subcategory should constitute 8 percent of the total OH in the Footwear category at that time. When this happens, our excessive inventory harms cash flow and is additionally responsible for too little inventory in something else contributing a greater percentage of sales. To continue our example, an analysis of the Footwear category inventory *at the roots* yields that sandals are a specific victim of our excess in inventory with hiking boots, as we'll imagine they are 6.5 percent of sales—but only 2.85 percent of OH. Yes, if you have reliable sources promising the surgeon general is about to announce a newly discovered and debilitating condition brought about by wearing sandals—and successfully remedied by wearing hiking boots—the discrepancy between sales performance and inventory levels is justified. Without such inside information, we must work to bring equilibrium to the percent of sales with the percent of inventory.

What benefits might come if we balanced the inventory of hiking boots and sandals to reflect the current selling trends in each subcategory?

The answer likely includes higher margins (because of less end-of-season discounting on hiking boots), improved cash flow (with less frequent reorders and reduced shipping charges on sandals), fewer missed sales, a larger number of transactions—and more revenue.

It's Art and Science ... But It Is More Science Than Art

Let's face it: many buyers—or persons influencing procurement invest-ments—are hired and given spending authority because they have good "intuition" or "a good sense" of what sells. In these forthcoming statements, please don't get me all wrong: there is some "art" to successful procure-ment, and possessing a proven ability to spot or research trends has its merit. However, to be sure, stellar performance with procurement is mostly conscious reasoning through analytical intellect and mathematical acumen. And it is certainly trained thinking much more than it is "gut feeling."

To bring this sometimes disappointing statement to light, we will return to our previous example with hiking boots. Many retailers, despite the obvious proliferation of markdowns and abundance of seemingly unwanted stock, will first presume, "We chose the wrong styles or brands." From there, the work exclusively focuses on new manufacturers and similar products with nuanced variations. A procurement-tasked search party is dispatched, and new orders are written for mostly "more of the same," with the irrational confidence this subcategory will now earn its keep. In the end, this is an effort to solve the challenge primarily through the "art" of better product selection . . .

Let's try it a different way—and let "science" lead. To do so, we will build out the altered OTB formula referenced above for hiking boots. For appropriate texture, let's assume we sell $10M in Footwear each year. We already know from the commentary above that hiking boots constitute 3.75 percent of the total business—that is, $375,000 in total sales. We will forecast it to grow 5 percent, which, for this example, is consistent with the growth projected for the overall Footwear business. In other words, this subcategory is projected to grow at the same pace the overall category is forecasted to grow.

To ensure comprehensiveness in this example, we'll also suggest gross margin for hiking boots is 45 percent and the current inventory in this subcategory is $104,000. As such, here is our arithmetic, in keeping with the outline above:

$375,000 (Current Sales)

+ $18,750 (Projected Sales Increase of 5%)

$393,750 (Projected Sales)

× 0.45 (Gross Margin)

$177,187.50 (Gross Profit)

− $393,750 (Projected Sales)

− $216,562.50 (COGS)

+ 104,000 (Current OH)

− $112,562.50 (OTB)

In this example, we've strategically aligned our OTB for hiking boots with its current contribution to the total business and its current margin performance. Just as importantly, the existing overstock has nowhere to hide. If you want to spend more in this subcategory, you must either reduce the existing on-hand inventory (OH) or claim confidence in a higher projected sales total. Without either of these inclusions, you are, simply, overbuying . . . and making bad wagers. Start with a budget down to the most appropriate categorical level—and increase the spending only when the volume or prospects for the business suggest it. This approach does not suggest there is no room for new products or brands. In fact, it still encourages being mindful of trends and meetings with suppliers about introductory styles. At the same time, we know both our boundaries and our baselines before being drawn into the allure of the products themselves.

NOTE: I also like the above formula because it highlights both the gross profit and cost of goods sold (COGS). In addition, the negative sum is easy to equate to how much we're "short" with inventory if we are going to hit our sales target. Even so, this formula can be shortcut by multiplying the projected sales by COGS, as a percentage.

$375,000 (Current Sales)

+ <u>$18,750 (Projected Sales Increase of 5%)</u>

$393,750 (Projected Sales)

× <u>0.55 (COGS %)</u>

$216,562.50 (COGS $)

− <u>104,000 (Current OH)</u>

$112,562.50 (OTB)

The positive figure in this calculation is still the OTB budget.

When we discuss gross margin return on inventory investment (GMROI) in chapter 12, this will become additionally relevant as we work to maximize our business with higher margin products and segments.

It's the Mortar:
Involved Maximization Imperatives for Chapter 10

1. Perform an honest assessment of your organization's procurement. Is an Open-to-Buy budget—or any strategically scientific formula—being diligently used? Whether you are acquiring sandwich pickles or poolside furniture for resale, ask Teammates whether they believe product-related decisions are made more by "art" or "science." If the conclusion is sufficient and satisfactory that science is being applied to procurement spending, consider, too, whether the depth of knowledge and effort for such critical behavior has properly penetrated the organization. If this answer is also reassuring, Uninvolved Optimization is evident—and you're already ready to move to the next chapter! Well done!

2. If either the use of scientific formulas or depth of know-how is not seeded deep enough in the organization, start with the standard OTB equation found at the onset of this chapter. With key Team Members, determine the Planned Sales, Planned Markdowns, Planned End of Month Inventory and Planned Beginning of Month Inventory for an upcoming buying season. Even beyond the likely improvements in cash flow and inventory productivity, this routine is a cornerstone for Uninvolved Optimization in a retail or restaurant operation. After all,

no matter how much of a "knack" those currently involved in procurement have for sourcing good (and good levels of) inventory, the tenure of gifted Team Members is never intended to outlast the organization. For procurement, it is only a proven system in an organization—not any special talent attributed to a specific individual—that can be passed along. Move toward a target to complete an OTB budget with Team Members in a manner that suggests eventual mastery of this standardized formula for your organization.

3. As Open-to-Buy budgets become a standard operating procedure, drill deeper into your existing inventory. If you have not done so already, subcategorize your inventory and perform OTB at this level. For whatever period is relevant to the procurement cycles of your respective business (weekly, monthly, etc.), determine if existing subcategory levels of inventory wisely connect with the current and anticipated levels of sell-thru. In those areas where you find dissonance, begin corrective action. Whether overstocked or missing sales, inadequacies with inventory rarely heal themselves.

4. Work toward the eventual achievement of OTB budgets for each subcategory. The variety of inventory and the present usage (or lack thereof) of scientific formulas in your organization will impact the rate at which this can be achieved. Be patient. Most importantly, be sure the tenets of Involved Maximization are evident so that you are readying this new approach to procurement for secession to others.

CHAPTER 11

The Immutable Laws of Inventory Acquisition

Proven and Preventative Measures to Improve Procurement

Alongside regular changes with products and personnel in our early days of wholesale purchasing, there was an even more daunting source of repeated roiling: our Guests. They, too, were dynamic and regularly changing. And our observations aligned with published research on the fickleness of consumers and the always-shifting marketplace trends.

Before the end of my first year as a retail entrepreneur, I realized the procurement landscape was incapable of sheltering my business with any sense of safety. Even with a reseller's authorization from some of the most recognized brands in the world and wholesale access to the most desired products in the industry, I was still capable of mistakes that could altogether capsize the enterprise. In a frighteningly short period, I acquired costly lessons in procurement that doubled as lingering scars on my operating capital. I knew we had to become the "wind" in our purchasing responsibilities—because it was painfully clear we would never persist as the "flag." And as I applied increasingly steep discounts to an increasingly high percentage of suboptimal inventory, it was obvious our business was unprepared for the constant fluctuations around us.

Amidst a dire overstock situation, our inexperienced Leadership Team came together. While also calculating our mistakes, we sought bona fide bedrock to support the evolution of our organization and the predictable transition of Team Members into or out of procurement roles. We hoped the retail formulas with which we began to desperately experiment would serve as figurative lampposts and lighthouses. They needed to shine bright across multiple product categories, as almost every inventory-related aspect of our business was a mess. Our mentors warned this difficult season—should we survive—would not be the last. They suggested finding a touchstone in our procurement procedures that felt just as secure whether headwinds were up ahead or if we had the wind in our . . . sales. Most wisely, they said we needed a philosophy that could withstand the passage of time and the fleeting fancies that would forever be part of a retailer's riddle.

Immutable (im·mu·ta·ble) *adj.*: unchanging over time or unable to be changed

While reading this common definition of *immutable* for the first time, it was immediately obvious to me that its meaning had application to procurement. Like *hospitality*, it helped me view procurement as a forever unchanging responsibility in a retail business. I began to understand that the framework we employed for buying needed to be consistent *because* related demands and shifting preferences would be constant.

From a makeshift meeting space in our stockroom, we traveled to the seemingly forgotten frontlines for procurement: our show floor—that is, where the merchandise is sold. And in place of exhaustive discussion or unbridled brainstorming, it was through three intensive inquiries that our Team discovered the premise for what became our Immutable Laws of Inventory Acquisition:

1. How Guests shopped in our stores, as well as the demonstrated and stated reasons they purchased specific products. We concluded for the sake of customers who do not know exactly what they want, there is much to be learned from those customers who do.

2. How Team Members sold and perceived various brands and products, as well as how these purely personal approaches so tangibly impacted which products were recommended or referenced. In our business, this influence was manifest most in which products always emerged from the stockroom—and those that never did.

3. How product representatives presented their products to us. In the instances we could grasp through discourse how a product would benefit our patrons or a target market, our sell-thru rates were much better than when we simply became enamored by the litany of features described.

For every business, each person hired—and every prop acquired—should have a distinguishable, purposeful role. The same level of stewardship is no less required with inventory for a restaurant or retailer. Brian F. Harris, who coined the term "category management" in the late 1980s, ushered forth the most comprehensive and now legitimized procurement methodologies of our generation. His eight-step approach optimizes both customer satisfaction *and* retailer profitability.* Our Immutable Laws complement his model by incorporating the dynamic human influences that come alongside the inanimate realities associated with merchandise (or product) categories. As both productive and protective guidelines, they are carefully administrated by our buyers—and they are openly shared with our suppliers. They are "laws" because we cannot violate them without a naturally occurring consequence or penalty. Best of all, they are the turbines we need to be the "wind" in our procurement efforts because they have applications everywhere this task is performed for the purpose of profitable resale.

Based on both personal experience and continued study, our Immutable Laws are presented in their order of importance for a full-service, full-price operation:

1. Law of Demand
2. Law of Confidence

---

* To learn more about Harris's approach, he and co-author Dr. Russell J. Zwanka unpack textbook-like teaching in their 2016 book *Category Management Principles.*

3. Law of Relevance
4. Law of Attachment
5. Law of Results

Law of Demand: Obvious Demand for Product by Target Customer

"Thou shalt prioritize products where demand is established."

The notion of "obvious consumer demand" is associated with the easiest Immutable Law of Inventory Acquisition to explain and understand. Mistakes with overstock rarely occur with this principle as it simply relates to authorizing procurement of popular products in your operation and resale in your business. On the other hand, it is common for challenges with margin to occur with these items where there is proven demand. In many instances, these "no-brainers" come with distribution to the point of saturation and high levels of promotional activity from hungry competitors. With ubiquitous availability and nearby competition, a noble service proposition becomes the best advantage to achieve the high turn rate necessary for even a modest gross profit with highly popular products. Whether it is pepperoni pizza or a case of bottled water, any "slam dunk" offering is only verifiably valuable when it contributes favorably to conversion metrics, profitability, and organizational efficiency.

Law of Confidence: Exceptional Staff Confidence in Product

"Thou shalt procure what *our* people want."

Alongside confirming reams of research, here is what we instinctively know: salespersons prefer to discuss, promote, and share stuff (products!) they personally like. I'll make the further assumption this is true for almost all human beings: we like to sell what we like to use and consume ourselves.

We also like to sell what we know *will* sell. It is universally satisfying to assist a patron with a product that recurrently rises up and meets the needs or desires of others. Even if never connected to a sales incentive or promotional activity, sales associates rarely miss an opportunity to present products they believe will please their audience.

No, the Law of Confidence is *not* a veiled suggestion for procurement responsibilities to be turned over to the sales team or the tableside servers. But the plain truth is that there are many worthwhile products and services where "obvious consumer demand" is, simply, not evident. The most effective means to convert these countless items into confirmed sales is our sales force. If we are not doing so currently, we must have a way to ensure feedback and buying suggestions from those who stand in the space between the merchandise that arrives on the warehouse dock and the purchases that exit through the main door.

Here are a few simplified examples:

- If the business development manager for your advertising agency has an affinity for thoughtful graphic design, figure out a way to introduce this offering to your suite of services.
- If the store manager at your tennis shop likes a certain brand of racquets, ensure it is in the featured collection.
- If a few of your best servers are vegetarian, make room on the menu for more of these offerings.

With the Law of Confidence, the eventual results will speak for themselves. Top-selling products that do *not* have either "obvious consumer demand" or substantial discounting almost always have an insider who is also a confident sales influencer.

Law of Relevance: Product Attributes Are *Uniquely* Relevant to a Confirmed Audience

"Thou shalt seek unique product relevance."

Another overused and under-understood word in the corporate lexicon is "relevant." Heck, I have used it regularly and almost unthinkingly throughout this manuscript! But let us not carry on without a collective understanding of this term. Oxford Languages suggests each of the following as a definition:

- Appropriate to what is being done or considered.
- Appropriate to the current time, period or circumstances.
- Of contemporary interest.

Regardless of which parcel in the definition is chosen, the basis is the same: connection. More fully, it is a perceivable connection to a specific time, project or preference. By definition, this is also the premise for the Law of Relevance. Think about it this way: when our product *connects* in a tangible way ("appropriate to what is being done or considered" and/or "appropriate to the current time") to those who derive meaning from such a connection ("of contemporary interest"), we have established an inarguable relevance. Procurement is the bridge we use to *connect* the current state of being with a desired state of being for those in our market and in our care. More concretely, as sellers, marketers, relationship builders, and leaders, it is our responsibility to connect relevant products with a deserving audience. And when we do, it is broadly beneficial! It benefits others with satisfaction, while we advantage ourselves through sales.

The other word that needs to be highlighted with this law is "uniquely." I will drop you into a contrived example to properly pair uniqueness with relevance. Let's pretend you are the proprietor of a local skate park with a pro shop. Your revenue comes from memberships, usage fees, rentals, and retail sales. You are open from 10:00 a.m. to 10:00 p.m. every day, with almost 100 percent of your users and shoppers using skateboards (and not roller skates).

Without question, every four-pack of polyurethane-injected wheels has relevance to the target market making purchases in your pro shop. Nonetheless, any skate park owner will go broke if she elects to procure every option that offers those product specifications. There are just too many wholesale options to procure for resale. On the flip side, if a distributor shows you a product that is the first of its kind with the added feature of Bluetooth-enabled LED lights, this offering is worth trying because it is both relevant and importantly *unique* for a shop that offers a "Night Skate" every evening.

Conversely, if the distributor says, "Lucky for you, I also have the same novel technology for inline skates," it's an easy, "No, thank you." Your lack of interest, of course, is not because the product is not unique in comparison to the lights made for skateboards; rather, you wisely pass on this product because it lacks relevance to your market which is almost entirely skateboarders (and not inline skate users).

Law of Attachment: A Marketing Activity, Stream of Revenue or Asset Deemed Valuable Can Be Acquired through Procurement

"Thou shalt acknowledge procurement as leverage."

Let's be honest: there are tantalizing possibilities and alluring promises of every kind all around us. And despite the known and inherent danger of covetousness, it is monkish to think we are not ever willing to trade what we have for what we do not have . . .

Thankfully, we are not tempted all the time.

Or everywhere.

But enough . . .

And the same is true with procurement, where new programs, special offers, side deals, and bartering are omnipresent.

Fortunately, the Law of Attachment suggests enticements are not always bad or precarious. But they do have to be acutely evaluated. To be clear, this law is not about an aimless negotiation. Instead, the Law of Attachment speaks to an often-unstated truth: an inventory investment can be leveraged to subsidize the price of something else. In fact, I believe our most substantial procurement outlays *should* further serve as a rightful means for other assets, items, wants, whims or needs. Purchase orders present a unique opportunity to obtain something additionally beneficial—but otherwise unattainable. The prospective benefits include cooperative marketing funds, creative employee incentives or rewards, and merchandise samples or promotional items. In essence, our orders become the currency by which we may afford these valuable "attachments." It is prudent pork-barreling for retailers, if you will.

Here are a couple of examples:

- Brand A has just become the "Official Beer" of the only professional sports team in town. We believe *if* we could effectively connote an affiliation with that same team to the marketplace, more customers would visit our restaurant on game weekends. Unfortunately, we cannot afford to forge such an affiliation through our resources. However, the investment we are currently considering with Brand A may initiate a visible connection—or, perhaps, even some direct pass-thru rights—to this potentially advantageous asset now held by Brand A. Even if we only hit the lowest threshold of beer sales with their respective brands, we are entitled to an in-restaurant presence package that includes logoed patio umbrellas, neon signs, and bar coasters.

- Brand B recognizes the importance of sales training. To this end, they have taken an approach beyond a curriculum focusing exclusively on their products. Instead, they have in-house category experts who are familiar with consumer research, products from competitors, and related trends. If we begin to do business with them, we can incorporate an annual on-site staff education requirement to assist with sales of their products *and* other products.

- Brand C has a vice president of national sales who has been known to take his largest customers to any post-season game for which the football team of the local university qualifies. Our owners really like football—and they really despise cold weather. If we order a heavily considered portfolio of prospective products from Brand C, the resulting value of such a purchase order should land our owners on that list of post-season game invitees. Meanwhile, the forecast is that the team is likely going to be very talented this season . . . and Arizona is always nice that time of year 😌.

So long as procurement efforts are strategically grounded in the objectives and operations of the business, the Law of Attachment is smart dealmaking. For me, the law itself was realized in light of a suggested inventory investment from an entirely unproven brand. In short, if I authorized the required quantity and placement of products inside my stores, it gave my business direct access to an unrelated and incremental revenue opportunity. More specifically, recent venture-capital funding enabled this unknown brand to secure prime placement at a significant local tradeshow. While considering whether to feature this brand in my stores, I requested to be their exclusive resale and promotional partner in this upcoming activity. I estimated that the potential revenue from the off-site sales—and the elimination of the fees previously required to participate in this same exposition—would equate to a financial return quadruple the amount of the purchase order for the inventory inside my stores. In this scenario, these orders were essentially a marketing investment. I further reasoned if the inventory did not get traction that a markdown of 50 percent would incent enough marketplace interest to clear the merchandise and recover our initial investment (with the tradeshow revenue already in the bank). Of course, if the inventory and promotional incentives did gain solid footing and, ultimately, grab some notable share, it would be even better . . .*

Law of Results: Terms of Business Associated with the Product Are Unmatched by Similar Products with Similar Sales Results or Potential

"Thou shalt note the finer details."

When evaluating multiple or even abundant options, our Law of Results is the proud default when all considerations are seemingly equal. In other words, demand from the marketplace and stated preference for specific products by Team Members still matter more. So do uniquely relevant features and conveniently associated benefits or opportunities. But there will be occasions when the options all likely satisfy or exceed the expectations of each previous Immutable Law of Inventory Acquisition . . . and yet strategic and sensible procurement mandates that we cannot take it all. To be sure, our Open-to-Buy budget requires restraint.

So what are we to do in these moments when flipping a coin seems as strategic as any other means for a procurement-related choice?

As we consider this important question, it is the ideal time to address the most obvious—and obnoxious—option for making any decision directly

---

* The latter did not happen. Nonetheless, the revenue and profitability associated with the expo more than justified the temporary existence of the associated inventory in our stores.

connected to the outlay of financial resources: purely personal gain. We look no further than the local news (everywhere!) to see the deleterious nature that can spawn from the authority given to those who make purchasing decisions. Stories laced with illegal or questionable kickbacks, unscrupulous favors, and gross misappropriation are entirely disappointing and frustratingly common.

It is my estimation such displeasing behavior is more prevalent when there is *not* a framework (of any kind) connected to procurement responsibilities. And this dangerous freestyle approach seems to become more tolerable when it is otherwise unclear which options will be most beneficial to an organization. Yes, it can sting to consider this as the basis for any organizational decision. But such discomfort does not make such an easy inclination less available or its pervasiveness less true . . . Purpose-filled leaders in the retail industry must be on constant patrol for this menacing methodology. It can be too easily found in our enterprise or department—or even our own behavior. When it is spotted or sensed, it must be sufficiently addressed. Breaking bad habits later is not nearly as rewarding as building good habits at the onset. There is no room for this approach to procurement in any organization that pursues Uninvolved Optimization. As a worthy pursuit that inherently favors systems over individual preferences and the organization beyond the owner or any leader, it must oppose self-fulfillment. Even amid uncertain choices.

Now back to the Law of Results.

Expert procurement always requires scrutiny of the finer details with each viable prospect. It becomes additionally critical when there is a stalemate between various options to serve the constituents of our business. Elements like payment terms (usually related to discounts and dating), shipping costs, manufacturing practices, and other measurable matters are more forcibly nudged into the spotlight with the Law of Results. For many service-oriented leaders, it is not easy to lean into this law and choose an answer that is potentially more quantitative than qualitative. Moreover, the Law of Results always involves tough choices. It does not naturally indicate which detail is most vital or attempt to rank the numerous possibilities in order of importance. Such polling is for you and your Team alone to decide.

But akin to the various ways that exist to settle a tie at the end of a soccer match (depending on the league or level of play), there is always an objective way to choose through the Law of Results. Again, this recommendation usually connects to the terms of business associated with each offering. In most instances, these are the figures, features, and benefits that our customers, clients, guests, and patrons do *not* see. In larger organizations, the sales associates are likely unaware of these details. But without question, these ancillary details matter to the operation and the business. Greatly, perhaps. This is where we identify and develop margin and organizational efficiency; it is when we fashion balance-sheet superheroes. In every difficult decision with procurement, we learn anew that not all options are created equal.

Procurement Is Mortar ... Not Wet Cement

In service-centric businesses, the "real" product is the service and the experience itself. It includes the certified knowledge, the energetic atmosphere, the sermon on Sunday morning, the special touches at the special event, the comfortable store layout, and so much more that builds our reputation, explains our traffic increases, and epitomizes our organizational mission. But make no mistake! It is the assortment of goods found on the shelves, the labor rates listed on the estimate, the donations made online, and the choices for lunch listed on the menu that, ultimately, enable the monetary deposits we make each day. It is these same deposits that ensure our financial well-being and our future possibilities. In the spirit of our ongoing analogy, inventory and offerings are some of our most visible "bricks." They must perform and contribute. Said best, they should profitably complete the retail experience over which we've obsessed.

On the other hand, procurement-related proclamations are mortar—not loose instructions or "wet cement." For successful resellers, they are set in stone. They are essential "cash flow commandments" that monitor behavior and reduce questionable choices. For many service businesses, there are only a few (if any) bigger investments than the acquisition of inventory. And no matter how it is classified on a profit and loss statement, our ability to raise pay for the Executive Team, pursue an acquisition without a pre-approval or even assuredly engage in pillow talk with our spouse about a kitchen renovation is instead usually dependent upon the productivity found in an inventory report. To be considered a worthy expenditure, the acquisitions we make on behalf of our enterprises do *not* need to hold up to all five of the Immutable Laws of Inventory Acquisition. However, each selection *does* need to adhere solidly to *at least* one.

It's the Mortar:
Involved Maximization Imperatives for Chapter 11

1. Whether by yourself (initially) or with your Team, review an inventory report to determine the specific Immutable Law of Inventory Acquisition authorizing each item in your assortment. Not only will this present a clearer picture of each law, but in your scrutiny you will also identify products that have snuck past security. In those instances, liquidate and separate from the poor performers or reengage with its supplier to determine if there is a more permissible arrangement to justify their presence.

2. In the next discussion with a supplier—or your buyer(s)—about new orders or new products, run each prospect through the Immutable Laws. Ensure every option finds alignment with one or more of the laws. In those instances where there is a lack of certainty, ask yourself this admittedly elementary—but frequently unconsidered—question: "Why is [product] on the order?" As you verbalize your answer, you will find your selection properly aligns with one of the laws . . . or you will begin to wonder whether it is worth the investment.

CHAPTER 12

Enemies in the Inventory

And GMROI to the Rescue!

As shoppers, there are items we like, and others we do not. As purchasers, we conclude some products were worth it; some were not. And like consumers everywhere, we have likely preserved a range of marketplace memories spanning great satisfaction to tremendous disappointment . . .

But whether we are casually browsing or actively buying, we rarely have a palpable sense of a formidable opponent. Even with our biggest acquisitions, we have been given no credible reason to feel we must prepare for combat! We are occasionally frustrated, yes. And we regularly have second thoughts. We have even likely experienced "buyer's remorse." But no product or purchase truly unwinds our well-being or gnaws at the core of our intent.

For leaders and procurement professionals in retail, however, there is no such assurance. The alluring assortment bathed in radiant lights on racks, shelves, and hangers can have a dark side. Sinister, really, as the risk goes beyond the inborn uncertainties with inventory that are associated with *amount* and *mix*. When unmonitored or without keen oversight, our inventory becomes a deceptive alibi for a conniving enemy that greatly compromises our time and money.

Dastardly Duplication

Our inventory's antagonist is "duplication." In countless retail environments, the quantity of largely duplicative items is unknown or altogether unconsidered. Even if not visibly contributing to an overstock situation, this redundancy still opposes a maximally productive inventory and a maximized cash flow.

Let's start with examples of questionable duplication to which we can relate as consumers. These are circumstances I've recently noticed without evidence of a strategic basis. In each instance, I've wondered aloud—and even directly to senior leadership—whether such overlap is necessary:

- There are two full shelves of tile cleaners from numerous manufacturers, with most of the selection barely having different ingredients, packaging or suggested pricing.
- On the rack for that popular lunchtime side item, potato chips, there is a national brand option, a regionally made small-batch option, and a kettle-cooked option—and the same flavors of Sea Salt and Mesquite Barbeque are available from all three.
- On the pro shop's slatwall, a white-label alternative for golf socks hangs next to the national brand. There is only a modest price differential . . . and none of the nearby pros or caddies can articulate any performance difference.

Ugghh. In each example, this is seemingly pointless proliferation. It matters not whether the tolerated redundancy came from long-standing procurement practices or a slow, almost imperceptible creep. Duplication is often difficult for organizational insiders to identify—and it can be even more challenging to halt. But make no mistake: perpetual lenience with freeloading inventory—that which has no defendable objective—expends resources without the appropriate accountability and takes direct aim at the otherwise rightful expectation of topmost returns from this investment.

In physical stores, this substandard condition often exists because we feature numerous brands, a larger selection and/or a diverse assortment in a popular—but mostly baseless—approach to meet the desires of our patrons.

In other instances, the malfeasance lies in witlessly appeasing our own organizational powerbrokers. Regardless of its basis, unwarranted duplication opposes progress and waylays potential through

- overstock *and* out-of-stock,
- wasted time, and
- squandered purchasing power.

A Dangerous Duo: Overstock and Out-of-Stock

When we offer an overly generous number of products in a similar or identical category, it is likely unsurprising to find ourselves overstocked in some capacity. Yet this approach can also be known to unexpectedly yield the opposite—that is, we encounter occasions when we are missing a wanted item. We have someone (literally) standing in front of us, asking for a product that is the very reason for their visit. It may even be a product we sold her last time . . . But she cannot find it or seemingly purchase it this time.

Whether on a menu board or in a department store, how is this possible?!

For most buyers and procurement specialists, it is intuitive that housing too many products is responsible for overstock issues. It is less instinctual, however, to perceive the same culprit for out-of-stock challenges. We scan the vastness of our selection, and this result is unimaginable!

But alas, it is the commitment to width over depth with our inventory investment itself that can make this true. To make things worse, when this occurs—with sales revenue hanging in the balance and an AlixPartners 2024 Holiday Survey reporting that "two-thirds of respondents will outright leave an online or brick-and-mortar store and shop elsewhere if an item is out-of-stock"[1]—frustration understandably ensues and many retailers default to survival mode. Said differently, we desperately chase transaction preservation through the recommendation of a similar product. Dastardly Duplication put us in this unfortunate situation . . . and now we hope it can bail us out.

But attempting to convince a patron another product is equally good, if not better, is tough work and dirty business. More accurately, it is our unproductive duplication inflicting double-trouble. After all, our customer arrived seeking something fully acceptable to her previously. Now, as we ask her to consider an alternative, we are simultaneously suggesting *just maybe* she should not have been as excited or as pleased with her last visit as she was . . .

Strange? Insensible? Insensitive?

All of it. The most desired outcome for a retailer with every transaction—to increase confidence and trust—is unquestionably hampered by any redirection away from a requested item or a previous purchase that was otherwise satisfactory. Unfortunately, the other popular remedies to save a sale in an out-of-stock situation are equally unattractive and more immediately costly:

- A whiff on the sale altogether (and the loss of revenue that accompanies the miss)
- A default to more costly measures to retain the sale (back order, special order shipment, transfer from another location, etc.)
- A calculated and considerable risk to suggest an alternative product

A Better Way

When procurement is executed optimally, fewer options are doing the heavy lifting on most sales—and an even smaller number of options are doing any lifting on even lesser sales. We simply dedicate more dollars and units to a tighter number of offerings. With an inventory investment the same as when the assortment was spread necessarily thin, we reduce missed sales by having strategic depth in the products where most purchases (and confidence) reside. Just as when our friend is hiding extended fingers behind his back, our odds of guessing the correct number of fingers extended are even higher when he is using only one hand to conceal the answer.

This approach is validated in most sales reports, as they reflect that top-selling items are also a lofty percentage of overall sales. To reference a popular expression, it is the 80/20 rule—even if the exact percentages are not always that stark. To put it differently, let us consider a realistic example and a common set of circumstances. There are three similar products capturing 70 percent of the sales, and another three similar products capturing the rest. Despite the comparable inventory levels, the bottom trio of options is a known collection of loafers (as they contribute a much smaller percentage of sales). Without any complex arithmetic, we know an assortment exclusive to the products at the top would deepen inventory on the bestsellers without incremental spending. The higher turn rates on popular products—and a reduced number of missed sales on those same products—easily offset the infrequent fumbles on the otherwise bottom performers. Whether a big-box format or a proud specialty purveyor, there is nothing special about hard-to-find inventory that does not objectively earn its keep or justify its availability.

In conclusion, out-of-stock instances are missed sales in both practice *and* on paper. After all, even the most sophisticated point-of-sale system is unable to capture the sales we "could have had" if the right product *was* in the right place at the right time. Consistent with the commentary in chapter 10, Open-to-Buy budgets are increased through additional revenue when the percentages of sales and the percentages of available inventory are closely aligned. Simply put, it is both best *and* "less bad" when stock and investment overages exist exclusively on inventory equated with the top-sellers. Expiration dates notwithstanding, a few cases of the bestselling hot sauce are likely better to have on-hand than a few units of the worst performer.

Lastly, before we get to our recommended formula to refute the traditional practice of an ever-burgeoning number of options, let's make an obligatory tip of the cap to Barry Schwartz's 2004 book *The Paradox of Choice*. His investigation cuts across almost all shopping spectrums, product categories, and purchase classifications as he argues that eliminating consumer choices can also greatly reduce anxiety for shoppers. Although not grounded in any procurement-centric methodologies, the paths paved therein travel to the same destination we should seek for an optimized retail business. Both clinical research and social science repeatedly suggest that "less is, indeed, more."

Have You Met Jim Roy?

For my retail businesses, there is a metric preferred above all others to assist the critical and regular evaluation of inventory proficiency: GMROI—or Gross Margin Return on Inventory. As an abbreviation, it is pronounced, "Jim Roy." Far more importantly, as a calculable formula it is most often deployed for accounting purposes or last-ditch efforts to locate a cash-flow leak due to inventory levels. Better yet, the individual productivity of any specific product or service can be measured by GMROI, regardless of its classification. As we unpack how this mathematical procedure can prove valiant in efforts to optimize inventory, let us first ensure a basic understanding of the calculation itself.

To properly complete this computation, there are three required inputs: annual sales volume, gross margin, and the wholesale value of current inventory. For the lattermost consideration, it is often expressed as an on-hand inventory value (OH).

To get the caution flag off the track quickly, let's acknowledge a familiar mistake with the inputs for the equation we share below: the absence of Sales Volume from a *full* year. It is certainly permissible to use a fiscal year or a rolling twelve-month total (August 1–July 31), but taking a GMROI reading from January 1 to the current date (unless you've just completed December 31) will only yield an inaccurate, and thus misleading, figure.

We must also acknowledge a lack of universal acceptance of a hyper-specific target or scoring range to confirm absolute success with GMROI. For sure, there is a standard that has substantial application across numerous channels in the retail industry. Even more specifically, 3.0–3.5 (where my businesses intentionally reside) is the most customary range of confident acceptability with GMROI. Still, there are industry segments with more unique margin structures where lower targets can be safely assumed or a higher bull's-eye becomes a critical necessity.

Here is the actual formula and an example to showcase the equation itself:

Formula	Example
Annual Revenue	0.2,350,000
× Gross Margin	× 0.425
Gross Profit	1,116,250
÷ OH Inventory	÷ $345,600
GMROI	3.23

We will continuously use the example above as a reference. For practical purposes, let us assume these figures are associated with the overall

GMROI performance of your favorite toy store last year. With our free-dom to be so deeply creative in our examples, we will call this retailer . . . Your Favorite Toy Store. ☺

When considering our GMROI formula, these numbers do *not* tell us if the income totals were better than the previous year, nor do they give us any indi-cation of how the current margin fares versus any comparatives or competition whatsoever. Candidly speaking, those oft-completed exercises are not qualified to serve as true indicators of the competence of our procurement efforts. As the retailer's adage goes, "Any fool can sell more if they have more to sell."

On the flip side, we can conclude from this example that the 3.23 GMROI reading is acceptable in a normal retail context, based on the above-men-tioned conventionally acceptable range. Said more reassuringly, this operator is neither massively overstocked nor likely facing a cash-flow crisis that is due to unproductive inventory. A solid foundation, they've set!

And yet as with everything reflective of the popular Core Value shared in Section I, we can still Make It Better.

So let us do so.

Again, GMROI is most frequently calculated cumulatively—that is, across all product categories. This is not erroneous, as the basis for the formula itself is to support prudent accounting practices for the overall business. Even so, the secret charm of this effort, especially for procurement purposes, lies in its equally useful capability to monitor and evaluate our procurement in bite-sized nuggets. To best illustrate uses often overlooked, let's consider the following figures and applications while assuming they are directly connected to Your Favorite Toy Store and the example above.

A GMROI Case Study: By Brand and Category—And So Much More!

Tom's Toys is a relatively new wholesale (manufacturer) entrant in the market for educational games that Your Favorite Toy Store has featured for the last eighteen months. Even though Tom's Toys does not have a deep heritage in the industry, the regional sales team for Tom's Toys is very aware that sell-thru of their products at Your Favorite Toy Store has eclipsed the $50,000 mark. As a result, Tom's has been aggressively pitching its broader portfolio of products to Your Favorite Toy Store recently, while simultaneously suggesting the current sales volume validates bigger purchase orders. We will use these fictitious entities and this common scenario to illustrate the goodness and sensibilities associated with the use of GMROI.

Rational Rationalization

In demanding situations like that featured in our case study, I often reference the need for "rational rationalization." These twinning terms simply suggest we need "logical justification" for any proposed inventory investment. GMROI is my primary contributor to rational rationalization. In our example with Tom's Toys and Your Favorite Toy Store, both the methodology (GMROI) and terminology (rational rationalization) would be major participants in the decision-making process.

As such, let's complete a more precise GMROI exercise to determine if the suggestion for larger orders by the retailer Your Favorite Toy Store (YFTS) from the supplier Tom's Toys (TT) is warranted. (Note that all of the figures below are fictional to support the example.)

- Total annual sales of Tom's Toys in YFTS: $63,375
- % margin for All Sales of TT (including volume discounts) in YFTS: 49.2
- Current OH of Tom's Toys in YFTS: $25,555

Now, the GMROI calculation derived from the figures:

$$
\begin{array}{r}
\$63,375 \\
\times\ \underline{0.492} \\
\$31,181 \\
\div\ \underline{\$25,555} \\
1.22
\end{array}
$$

As we evaluate this equation, we recollect that total annual sales were $2,350,000 for Your Favorite Toy Store. As 2.7 percent of the total business ($63,375.00 / $2,350,000.00), it might be fairly stated the current sales volume with Tom's Toys is acceptable. And, to be sure, the achieved margin in many retail segments would suggest that Tom's Toys is performing admirably in its delivery of sales profitability to Your Favorite Toy Store (at 49.2). Nonetheless, with this arithmetic *and* the conventional standard GMROI target of 3.0+, we can see the total sales volume and a decent margin mask some valid concerns relating to the levels of existing inventory with Tom's Toys. In fact, with a GMROI score that is registering less than 1.5, nothing short of a very generous inventory swap for the losers in the current stock could reasonably suggest additional goods from this supplier. Specifically, there is no logical justification—no rationale rationalization—demonstrated in support of additional purchase orders for Tom's Toys. And if anyone is curious why a larger bank balance does not exist—or where money could have otherwise been found for compensation increases—the current inventory cost for Tom's Toys is a solid place to start . . .

This example also illustrates the *total* usefulness of GMROI. Again, there are three elements contained in its calculation—annual sales volume, gross margin, and on-hand inventory (OH)—*and* this trio of cash-flow-related metrics gives us all the clues necessary to ascertain whether and where a product is performing capably, mediocrely, or miserably. We can also determine exactly where to go to work and which specific factor(s) we should quickly express concern or enthusiastically celebrate. If it is a bothersome GMROI reading, we begin to instinctively know sales are too sluggish, margin is too low or current inventory levels are too high.

Or all of the above.

Using our previous example with Tom's Toys, we can easily surmise the most likely reasons for the concerning figure of 1.22 are either or both of the following:

- There is already sufficient inventory that has only arrived recently (or is seasonal) and needs time to sell-thru at the same margin currently achieved.
- There is too much unproductive inventory in stock.

Regardless of the specific reason for this stinky statistic with GMROI at Your Favorite Toy Store with products from Tom's Toys, we must pause. Yes, the acquisition of more inventory from this supplier may result in more sales—but there is nothing now revealed that suggests any additional stock of Tom's Toys will equate to a healthier business or a higher balance of retained earnings. Again, it would be tough to attach "logical justification" to any immediate purchase order to Tom's Toys . . .

In fact, submitting such an order might be downright irrational.

Categorical GMROI

To further draw the almost innumerable applications of GMROI to businesses serving multiple categories (through either merchandise or services), let's complete a GMROI for our Educational Toys category at Your Favorite Toy Store (and not just to Tom's Toys as an authorized supplier). Although this example remains fictitious, it further represents the way we can apply the formula to any sub-segment of our business.

- Total annual sales in Educational Toys category: $772,812
- % margin across all sales in Educational Toys category (incl. vol. discounts): 48.6
- Current OH in Educational Toys category: $132,679

$$\begin{array}{r} \$772,812 \\ \times \ \underline{0.486} \\ \$375,587 \\ \div \ \underline{\$132,679} \\ 2.83 \end{array}$$

This additional information allows us to infer so much. Some of our conclusions might include:

- The Educational Toys category is certainly not in a "danger zone" at Your Favorite Toy Store—but it does have room for improvement, as it is both below the 3.0 mark and the pace of the overall GMROI for the store (3.23).

- Not only is Tom's Toys a drag on its own to our favorite toy retailer (with its GMROI score of 1.22), but it must also have competitors in the Educational Toys category that are performing very well to account for the discrepancy between its 1.22 rating and the significantly higher overall rating for the category in which it participates (2.83). In short, Tom's Toys is *not* faring positively versus its most direct competitors in the Educational Toys category with GMROI *and* it is currently an anchor on the overall category GMROI.

- Additional calculations, we'll also imagine, indicate that Tom's Toys is responsible for 8.2 percent of the sales in the Educational Toys category of Your Favorite Toy Store—but it currently absorbs more than twice that percentage (at 19.2) of the total inventory value in that same category. This divergence in the sales-to-stock ratio is significantly challenging efforts to optimize sales, maximize cash flow, and ensure inventory productivity.

With this data and these conclusions now in mind, what does prudent procurement suggest? Outside of strategically planned or fully anticipated exceptions, the percentage of total OH from any supplier in wholesale value ($) should be within three to five points of its percentage of sales volume in the total resale business ($). An insensibility becomes clear when reviewing reports, for example, that suggest a particular vendor partner (like Tom's Toys) or available item (like a dessert offering) accounts for 4 percent of present-day sales—but is a double-digit percentage of the currently absorbed inventory dollars.

Yes, to account for recent arrivals or upcoming promotional periods, seasonality, and advantageous buying programs that are time bound, there will always be some difference between OH percentages and sales percentages for specific vendors, categories or subcategories. However, when the total discrepancy across an operation is more than 15 percent—including both OH discrepancies that are too high *or* too low compared to current sales volume percentages—there are undoubtedly some unproductive gremlins residing on the roster of available items. Equally as disturbing when this imbalance occurs, there are likely some popular products where sales are being missed because inventory levels on those items are not deep enough (see: the dangers of Dastardly Duplication). Either way, it is time to start sleuthing. And GMROI calculations are your trusty investigative sidekick!

In categorical conundrums, deeper drilling can be done with GMROI without much additional effort. The same formula and approach are used when taking a reading across the overall business. For the benefit of both our example and your business, we can do so with every supplier of any category with which Your Favorite Toy Store (or you) has conducted business for at least a year. Better yet, we can perform pinpointed calculations with those Educational Toys targeting adolescents or those specifically intended, as an example, for girls ages 2–5. GMROI can also be completed by season, by size, by location, by price range, and by buyer—and so much more. When we have the three required inputs specific to the investigated item (like Educational Toys targeting adolescents) there really is no end to this GMROI rabbit hole! In my sporting goods business, we would occasionally perform GMROI calculations down to the gender and half-size of specific footwear models. Said differently, our favored formula informed us if, we'll imagine, we were overbought in specific models in size 6.5, while simultaneously indicating we were underbought in 10.0. From there, we knew where to take corrective action to better optimize our assortment.

Nonetheless, we must eventually establish a concluding point for GMROI-related efforts. After all, we are ensuring a proper basis for procurement decisions—and not just needlessly completing computations.

As a final word on GMROI, there are principles to be applied in almost every environment:

- A score of 1.0 equates to selling/generating revenue at the precise cost of your inventory. As every endeavor has other costs (operating expenses) alongside the cost of the resalable goods, this reading (1.0) is unsustainable in the pursuit of profitability, or even feasibility. Such a mark is reserved for an enterprise in the start-up phase or in the midst of a committed and significant turnaround.

- Although the most common concern is a GMROI score that is too low, it is also possible for the formula to return an alarmingly high figure. When such happens, the stock levels are likely skimpy compared to the rate of sell-thru—and sales are being missed because of insufficient inventory to satisfy the demand generated. Additional orders, especially for proven products, are indeed warranted.

Again, keep in mind that a conventional GMROI target for the retail industry is 3.0, while the total deviation between the percent of sales and percent of on-hand inventory should not exceed 15 percent. Of course, be sure to check the application of these standards to your industry and situation.

Wasted Time

As a sworn enemy of astute inventory management, I wish Dastardly Duplication limited its destruction on sell-thru rates and profitability measures. That's bad enough. But let's face it: each item or service we offer or procure also takes some amount of time on its own to manage. Whether it is maintaining product details for our POS system or website, speaking with suppliers and team members about replenishment or managing myriad inquiries from the marketplace, incontrovertible responsibilities cohabitate with every product and service residing behind our gates.

Fortunately, most of these elements are worth the time required and are visibly connected to an obvious purpose for their placement in our organization.

But there are likely exceptions.

And these exceptions are trespassing violations against our time.

In many instances, these trespassers masquerade inconspicuously through the organization as careless overlap—but once we start looking for them, they are usually easy to locate. And the arithmetic is quick and simple to determine why we must act heroically to rescue our priorities from further incursions.

To begin this essential salvage mission for personal and organizational productivity, divide the total number of hours (or minutes) needed each week (or month) to manage this part of the business by the number of products or services in a category or operation. When you finish the computation, the other side of the equals sign includes at least a fractional indication of time that is, simply, frittered away in that time frame. Yes, choices and selection for our audience and patrons have their place—but we must also be sure there is justified logic for the time invested in each approved offering.

As a working example, let's put ourselves in the shoes of a category manager for a regional chain of fuel-and-convenience stores. We'll assume she is responsible for procuring the nonalcoholic beverages for this chain of one-hundred-plus locations scattered throughout the Midwest. Among the assortment found in her stores are soft drinks, bottled waters, energy drinks, sports drinks, coffee-infused beverages, juices, teas, and recent introductions of every kind. And whether she is parceling her efforts by the manufacturer (i.e., Coca-Cola, PepsiCo, Nestle, Pure Leaf) or by subcategory (i.e., soft drink, bottled water, tea), she can easily determine the total quantity of products from each manufacturer that is currently placed in each subcategory.

Next, let's estimate there are thirty-two single-serve tea offerings. Of course, it is fair to surmise the bestsellers are easy to observe in the stores, even easier to notice on sales reports and are more likely to be connected to some level of promotional activity. There are other products relegated to the bottom shelves, noncompetitive pricing, and a general lack of visibility. Given the lopsided composition of sales in almost all retail channels, it is not unreasonable to think that the top five selling flavors of tea produce more than half of the sales volume. In short, the 80/20 rule rises again!

As we commence a fictitious review of various subcategories, there is sales-report-supported demand for sweet, unsweetened, lemon, mint, diet, sugar-free, and ginseng. No wonder the stores next to the fuel pumps are getting bigger and refrigerators are occupying more space! This is just tea and its populous extensions.

And, man, this category manager has an important role to play!

As she highlights the bestsellers, however, she must also take time to survey the bottom performers. In most reports detailing performance in a plethora of offerings, the bottom third notably contributes less than 33 percent of the sales. Said differently, the percent-of-inventory investment is higher than the percent-of-revenue generation. Moreover, a sales report will also reveal which products are not performing solidly in their specific subcategory. These are the offerings that are second or worse in diet or mint or some other deviation from the most proven and popular recipes.

For the Sake of Cash Flow and Calendar

With this information, we now have reasonable grounds to cull some unfruitful time weighing down our calendar (and our cash flow!). I will *not* deny there are likely valid exceptions that suggest grace for a few of the bottom-feeders. Recent production and shipping challenges, subpar visibility or placement, and rookie status, among other factors, can defend against the actions any quarterly sales report might suggest for those with the lowest-performing statistics.

At the same time, we are concentrating most heavily on your time in this exercise—or the time of your most valuable resource: your Team. And let's not forget we are pursuing Uninvolved Optimization! We already know any permission to leave first base requires a ruthless and visible commitment to optimizing our schedule. It is equally imperative this be a shared pursuit by those included in your Involved Maximization plans. As the mathematical formula will show below, there is too high a price to pay when poor performers are allowed to languish in your assortment—*and* on your calendar.

In almost any operation, sales figures already suggest hardly anyone would miss at least the three products with the lowest sales performance. So let's start here. The existence of specific numbers always improves our effort. Even so, the trio ripe for elimination may not always or appropriately be those three items at the absolute bottom of the sales performance roster. Again, there may be a reason for exceptions or exemptions.

Regardless, three—or whatever quantity is selected—must go. From our example with the myriad tea offerings, this figure is less than 10 percent of the total selection (3 of 32). In most cases, it is probable the patrons who account for the measly sales of bottom-dwelling products would make their purchase elsewhere in the assortment. For this example, these at-risk purchases might gravitate to other products in the tea segment—or to another subcategory altogether. Either way, the likelihood that income from the worst of the worst performers is otherwise unattainable is small.

To calculate the prospective time savings, we will draw out our example further. Of course, you can easily substitute specifics for your situation in each place where fictitious figures have been provided.

For this storyline, let us assume our buyer dedicates time on Tuesday afternoons to her oversight of the tea segment. Among other responsibilities, her weekly tasks include reviewing sales reports, considering new products, updating forecasts, performing categorical research, approving suggested orders, and responding to general correspondence with those involved with this subcategory. Given the traditional time frame she employs for this effort, it is a seemingly fair conclusion this work requires no less than four hours per week. Even though it is admittedly unlikely such plays out this neatly, the contention and anticipated realization remain the same through the following equation:

- 4 hours = 240 minutes
- 240 minutes / 32 tea subcategory options = 7 minutes, 30 seconds (average) dedicated to each option per week
- 7:30 x 3 (number of options to be eliminated) = 22:30 minutes saved each week
- 22:30 × 48 (weeks per year, with 4 weeks off) = 18 hours saved annually

Of course, this example is only three items in a single subcategory. Without belaboring the point, we quickly come to understand that purposeless duplication is dreadful for productivity. It is a virus that transmits sickness to our priorities. "Rational rationalization" is needed to ensure the time for any offering is worth it and well spent. And as we recapture and reallocate our precious time in the pursuit of both Involved Maximization and Uninvolved Optimization, we will soon find ourselves trading the question, "Have we gone too far?" for "Have we gone far enough?"

Squandered Purchasing Power

Financial product comparison service SuperMoney reports, "The hallmark of mass-market retailers is affordability. They leverage their bulk purchasing power to offer products at competitive prices, making them accessible to a wide audience."[2] Of course, this is not the only successful element in the channel of mass retail, as this format continues to expand across the globe—but it remains the cornerstone on which the rest of its shopping proposition rests. There are also other retail channels and concepts that tap into this approach, even if not with the same ability to shrink wholesale pricing to a comparable degree. Smaller, independent retailers may wish the playing field was more level, but they cannot deny the inherent sensibility of lower prices for higher quantities.

Although short of omnipresent, tangible benefits associated with higher amounts of volume are common and consistent throughout retail. And the rewards themselves are not exclusive to specific channels or thresholds. Tactical procurement done in a manner to spread ordered quantities across fewer products—and fewer suppliers—is increasingly popular for savvy operators, as profitability through other measures becomes more challenging. In a nutshell, good, old-fashioned "purchasing power" is no longer just a way to lower prices for shoppers; it is also a proven means toward improved balance sheet performance for those enterprises purchasing wholesale products for the purpose of resale. Even businesses that visibly favor remarkable service—with no promises of competitive pricing—are smart to seek valuable perks exclusively connected to elevated order levels.

These perks include volume discounts on invoices, rebates for surpassing financial targets, cooperative marketing investments to increase visibility, and an enhanced perception by key external resources. Purchasing power further increases as procurement efforts become more systematic and streamlined, and as accounts payable become more concentrated. Like many superpowers, the more it is used—and as an increased number of favorable outcomes are achieved—the more it grows and attains the potential to be a uniquely influential asset to improving lives!

As no surprise, the opposite is true, too. When purchase orders and authorization for mostly duplicative products are widely divided among suppliers, this potentially powerful advantage is lost. The purchasing power is squandered.

Don't let this happen.

Here are additional ways purchasing power can meaningfully contribute to an organization.

Product Knowledge and Purchasing Power

Product knowledge held by our Team builds shopper preference in a way that is immune to inflation and other largely uncontrollable factors. This is, in fact, the element in a service operation that can be most aptly parlayed into a truly transformative engagement with clients, patrons, guests, and shoppers. After all, once we obtain product-specific information, sharing it is the easy part!

The product knowledge itself can be most reliably acquired from those closest to the development and manufacturing of the products themselves (manufacturers' representatives, sales agents, etc.). But with finite resources in every sales department, educational efforts and materials can only be most generously dispensed where the most impressive purchase orders are found and where the most sales potential is evident.

For the sake of our Guest Services proposition and the "Experience" we deliver, it is a beneficial achievement to be in that place. To put it simply, size matters when we are buying what we are selling.

Freebies and Purchasing Power

"Freebies." This is a real word. And they are a real thing. These "spoils gratis" are associated with real marketplace practices and can be a real asset to any enterprise! Advantageous items from product manufacturers at zero (or very low) cost for use by Team Members and select patrons are an inarguable asset. From promo sunglasses at an outdoor event to five-figure gifts for Oscar nominees, branded collateral and samples are intended to help us sell more of something. In the end, these are extensions of enthusiasm for merchandise to which we are already connected as authorized resellers and representatives.

The availability of freebies can also be synonymous with "employee perks." Whether your Team includes the friendliest clerk at the local grocery who is the first to try a new flavor from a nationally recognized cereal brand, or is the top-selling associate at an independent bike dealer who is given a new frame to test ride, freebies empower our colleagues, generate enthusiasm, and instill an appreciable sense of worth. Regardless of the value, the accessibility of these freebies to both the front lines and senior management connotes and creates influence. Although access to these intangibles does not get tallied in any compensation review or make the roster of official employee benefits, such freebies most certainly matter when cogently woven into the fabric of most organizations.

Supply Chain Status and Purchasing Power

On the backside of the COVID-19 pandemic, it is arguably tougher than ever before to navigate the choppy headwaters of most supply chains. With ongoing production disruptions and shipping challenges, there is even a bit of mystery with otherwise confirmed purchase orders. Equally noteworthy are headlines reflecting inflation and inventory shortages in the face of marketplace unwillingness to accept alternatives to personal preferences. Most patrons do not sympathize with a restauranteur who cannot currently procure favored pizza toppings or the merchant who is missing key sizes on the most popular products. Other options for these purchases are barely a click or a block away . . . More so than ever before, we must be both nimble and astute in our purchasing of merchandise and promises to the public. Focused procurement that results in any measure of "Purchasing Power" can be overtly obvious or more camouflaged as it relates to our placement on the supply chain. In short, being perceived as a priority by suppliers is a worthy pursuit. To repeat, size matters when we are buying what we are selling . . .

When done expertly, procurement results in purchasing power. And rooting out duplication helps us do this better and more quickly. The pursuit of such is not a hollow arms race against competitors or those entities that capture headlines for the benefits their scale enables. It is, instead, two crucial *and* reciprocal advantages that make us indispensable to our customers, and our best business partners: healthy returns and healthy relationships.

It's the Mortar:
Involved Maximization Imperatives for Chapter 12

The most important formula for consistently adroit inventory management is GMROI. Period. Full stop. Its regular employment takes an understanding of business health beyond sales and sales growth. It greatly assists a cash-flow forecast by enabling the critical pairing of operating expenses *and* inventory costs. It is also an effective exercise to measurably determine the quality of specific inventory for both amount totals and productivity levels. For skilled users, its computation is always done to the deepest level necessary to unearth opportunities and remove problems at the root. As such, it is a nonnegotiable imperative for those who pursue Uninvolved Optimization to ensure immersion and usage of GMROI deep into the organization. Yes, this tool will be most used and cited by those in procurement—but it is also vital for those in store/restaurant/facility management and operations to understand its significance.

Of course, the foundational calculation and some relevant examples of this formula are found earlier in this chapter. However, as a predictable imperative, it is now time for YOU to calculate GMROI for your operation at both an overall and a designated subcategory level. For those who are arriving at this formula for the first time, I'm going to provide a final example. I will use book sales for a self-published author to determine how much inventory she should print to reflect the sales potential and the importance of an appropriate investment in inventory. As she, hypothetically, wants to be cash-flow conservative, we will aim for a GMROI of 4.0 to aid in her Open-to-Buy budget.

- Total sales in the last 12 months: $21,500.00 (1,000 books at an average selling price of $21.50)
- Cost to print each book: $7.30
- COGS: $7,300.00
- Gross Profit: $14,200.00
- Gross Profit %: 66.0
- Current # of books on-hand: 212
- Current value of inventory on-hand: $1,547.60
- Current GMROI: 9.17
- Growth forecast for next 12 months: 10%
- Revenue forecast: $23,650
- Anticipated gross profit %: 66.0
- Anticipated gross profit: $15,609
- Desired GMROI: 4.0
- Total OH for desired GMROI (w/ Growth Forecast): $3,902.25
- Less current value of OH (-$1,547.60): $2,354.65 (this is the Open-to-Buy budget)
- Number of books to print (to maintain GMROI target): 322 ($2,354.65/$7.30)

This example shows us (with the economics and figures provided) that the current suggestion is to print and keep approximately 322 books in inventory when the intent is to sell 1,100 units in the next twelve months (with a desired GMROI of 4.0). Yes, pricing is likely better when the number of books printed is higher—so it is acceptable for these numbers to fluctuate throughout the year. Even so, the author knows where she ultimately needs to be with inventory to obtain the return she seeks *and* ensure cash for other operating expenses.

Now, we transition from theory to practice . . . Even better, the time has arrived to move from our contrived examples to your meaningful enterprise. So whether it is a product, brand, category or any other relevant classification, please use this Involved Maximization Imperative to substitute the numbers above for those specific to your situation. As you begin to do this consistently, make sure to bring others alongside. You will only arrive at Uninvolved Optimization when the practice becomes a permanent, brick-like benefit to any procurement efforts!

CHAPTER 13

Prioritizing Profitability

For the Sake of Purposeful Work and Fulfilling Potential

"Profitability is the sovereign criterion of the enterprise."

Our concluding chapter is not a downhill finish. It cannot be. The quote above from Peter F. Drucker, described by many as "the founder of modern management," minces not the importance of subject matter connected to earning more money than that which is spent. Moreover, the marketplace already knows too many high-quality service providers that failed, under-performed or missed their potential because of an inability to perpetually ensure proper net margins for their offerings. The premise of any business committed to service matters too much for its fate to be dependent upon a specific season or its success to be unwound by a bank statement balance.

As such, I will land this plane on a runway that keenly welcomes those who have built a systematized service proposition to deliver a remarkable experience, are committed to the empowerment of others, and have managed inventory and resources with terrific acumen. Organizations succeeding in these areas are likely enjoying some deserved fruits of their labor. Even better, they are ripe for Uninvolved Optimization (or are already representative of it!) and in a good place to further explore the perimeters of profitability.

In the following content, I will also refer to "landed margin." Simply, this is the total revenue from the sale of our product, less the sum of all costs required to complete the sale of that same product. Some would rightfully say this equates to net profit. To avoid wading into the nuance for now, our homestretch pursuit is singularly focused on the profit margin *per item or service* presented for resale. For sure, we will take our approach beyond the bland terms associated with the operating expenses captured on a profit and loss statement and the sunrise side of activity-based costing.

Common Origins for Pricing

Although many factors contribute, profitability begins with the resale price. For most of us who elect to resell what we've procured or produced, here's how it usually goes:

We breathe a product into existence. It is an impressive product—or, at least, impressive enough to generate a sale. And whether it is a tangible good or a notable service, it becomes income-producing.

Success!

Still, we often do not intimately know the cost of production, acquisition, implementation, and delivery of this newly created product to its end user or eventual destination. Said differently, we finished the heaviest lifting and the hardest work—but we did not ensure the healthiest conditions for its prosperity. After all, it is more expedient to make assumptions.

And so we do.

Or we end up on *Shark Tank* to have the investors tell us what we missed or underestimated.

The most common pricing tactic is to follow the competition. This doesn't necessarily mean an identical price to a similar offering from another purveyor . . . It may be the decision to price our product five dollars less to garner some attention or make our suggested retail price 10 percent higher to connote our premium retail status. Regardless, the price declared is an eventual nod to the understandable influence held by competitors who preceded our arrival. There is an "industry" and/or "localized" standard for prices—and we adopt the norms and fairly assume some sensibility must be associated with such.

For many industries, there is also the traditional guidance of manufacturer suggested retail price (MSRP). It is exactly as it says. The manufacturer has an obvious comprehension of the wholesale pricing *and* a seemingly solid understanding of the operating expenses associated with the successful resale of this item. The provision of an MSRP suggests all parties can live on the financial particulars that accompany any sales at this specified price.

It is appropriate to follow the pricing lead of credible competition and posted MSRPs. In fact, for a new business, doing so is likely necessary to establish a foothold. At the same time, when we are not mindful of "the sovereign criterion," per Peter Drucker, we attach price tags and list labor rates without considerable forethought. We may also adjust rates without the proper consideration of key contributors to net profit. I've seen many instances where pricing changes are instituted for reasons that do not go beyond "it is a new year" or "it has been too long." Even more common is the shortcut that trades the operating specifics of our business for the general metrics associated with reported inflation rates or a recently published Cost of Living Index.

Even in long-standing and well-known industries, pricing habits that are outdated or inexplicable abound. My familiarity with athletic footwear alone points to pricing practices that are increasingly difficult to justify and should serve as a caution flag to more dynamic industries. Even among a herd of known competitors, it is difficult to break free from the pack . . .

In 2002, the most popular MSRP for a pair of technically capable running shoes was $79.99. Whether it was an offering from a purely perceived running brand like Asics or Brooks—or a globally recognized sporting goods brand like Nike or Adidas—this specific price carried the day. For sure, there were other shoes priced slightly differently (usually within $20 of this figure)—but the range was predictable and this specific price of $80 (or $79.99) had more prospects from which to choose than any other retail price . . .

If we fast-forward twenty-plus years, the most popular MSRP was $140 (or $139.99). When considering this increase, please do not be consumed by whether a 75 percent increase in average pricing during this two-decade time frame is the appropriate inflationary rate. This is *not* where the lesson resides. Moreover, we could get further tangled in sneaker-pricing history by knowing not a single increase from any manufacturer came in an increment that was not divisible by $5. Yes, there were occasions when the adjustment for an updated model was $10 or even, if only rarely, $15. But it was never in an amount not divisible by five. Not including the $0.01 shaved by retailers for the sake of appearances, the MSRP for every shoe in this classification ended in a zero (i.e., $140) or five (i.e., $145). There is obvious institutional resistance to MSRPs like $136.50 or $143 (let alone something along the lines of $142.19!). With full-price retailers likely to follow the lead of hyper-visible MSRPs, rubberstamp price increases are an industry shortcoming, void of an explicable connection to operating-cost increases, organizational priorities or gross margin standards. Pricing decisions are unintelligent if they are, simply, arbitrary adjustments or the robotic contin-uation of baseless norms.

Do It Like Don

On a recent trip to Melbourne, Florida, I had lunch at Don's Famous Hoagies. As I surveyed the menu for a vegetarian option to give the ani-mated woman who stood *in front of* the counter to take my order, I could not help but notice the oddball prices. The Italian Stallion was $7.48, while the Reuben was $13.55. The Ham & Provolone was $11.68, while the Harbor City Pleaser was $13.02. It was the best example of self-directed (and likely strategic) pricing I had seen in a long time. At the risk of stacking the line of customers more than I already had, I inquired about the pricing. And as she jotted down my request for a Tuna Melt (for $12.62)—since a nonmeat choice was as absent as any local forecast calling for snow—she simply said something each of us would be wise to remember: "Our prices change all the time because we know our costs change even more often."

While Don's opened decades ago, it still knows a key to continued longevity is the landed margin it captures with each sale.

Again, let's be clear: This chapter is *not* about money management or tackling fiscal responsibility. That is a book—a library, perhaps—in itself. As a bestselling author and the host of the third-largest talk show in the United

States, Dave Ramsey is a resource for individuals and entrepreneurs alike. Through multiple broadcast platforms—and reams of actionable advice from thirty-plus years of publishing relevant information—he is unceasing in his message for wise decisions and good stewardship with our money.

Is he always right? Does everyone like him or find value in his guidance? Probably not. But given his popularity and the assistance he provides to legions of fans, the repeated call for ownership and discipline in his curriculum seems inarguable. It is the same theme and call to action for this section . . . even though the focus is on profitability and landed margin (not money management, revenue, income or sales). This is an effort in which retail businesses must take total control.

Before we unpack how to practically facilitate this requirement, let's start with examples of how landed margin can otherwise evade us through deceptive, yet understandable—if not almost excusable!—ways.

"I Never Thought It Much Mattered"

As my primary retail operation found its stride, we added private-label and store-branded merchandise to our assortment. We did not manufacture goods for this category; instead, we obtained collections from reputable suppliers without an aspiration to establish or build their own brand. In their words (not mine), their objective was to produce and source great products—not build big brands. The lower wholesale prices on this non-branded merchandise provided us the opportunity to embellish those lines with trademarks *we* owned. The cumulative costs for artwork, screen printing, embroidery, and any other customization would be ours to manage alongside the acquisition costs and factored into the retail price. From there, each introduction was strategically subjected to the scrutiny of sell-thru rates, the rigors of performance evaluation, and the predictable comparisons with other similar products we sold—or were sold by our competitors.

Unfortunately, it was not the achievement of a sales target that motivated having our screen printing and embroidery completed "in-house." It was an unending frustration with the timelines associated with the screen printing resources we employed. We had long streaks of agreed-upon deadlines that were missed or adjusted without sufficient notice. For sure, a global pandemic did not help the reliability. The costliest example was the mid-January arrival of a licensed collection specifically commissioned for the recently concluded holiday season. Even the rookie retailer understands how each day missed with seasonal products is a day forever lost in the pursuit of maximal product productivity and total sales.

In exasperation, I initiated keyword searches to find a local screen printing operation that had only favorable reviews. I paired this effort with networking and accompanying research to uncover an enterprise owned and operated by the same individual for over twenty-five years. To add to its very admirable reputation, the address was within a few miles of one of our retail stores. Of added interest, my detective work revealed the entire operation was soon headed to a business brokerage for listing. Without much delay, we visited the facility, met the long-standing proprietor, and tended a letter of intent to purchase the assets. The litany of subsequent correspondence was tediously boilerplate, however fully necessary for our own due diligence. As the prospects of a deal intensified, so did my requests for historical data to better determine synergies with our existing businesses.

From the documents provided, it was easy to see the profitability of the company over the last few years. Equally noteworthy, the seller's discretionary earnings indicated the proprietor had carved out a comfortable lifestyle for herself. But we were not entertaining this acquisition to absorb competition or roll it up for industry scale. If this was going to be an integral and eventually valuable component in our growing Trademark Goods category, it had to contribute to increased profitability on its own.

"How much do you make on the embroidery jobs you do for a client?" I asked the owner.

She responded that "each arrangement is different."

"All right," I followed up. "How about on average?"

"It's hard to say," she said, without hesitation.

I did my best to have my startled expression not reveal my disbelief.

I must have failed. In fact, it was likely my sudden facial contortion that prompted her to continue.

"Because of the way each project uses a different amount of thread and other supplies, you cannot really assign an actual cost to each product or job. We know what our competitors charge, so we just price it similarly or slightly higher. It seems this approach has worked out pretty well, so I never thought it much mattered."

"It Kind of Is What It Is"

As an ambitious teenager, my son started a property management endeavor. This was not just "mowing a few lawns on the side." He purchased and maintained his own equipment, had others who worked with and for him—and corresponded with his clients in ways that would make most business development professionals take notice. He was seemingly born with a bold, entrepreneurial spirit that perpetually leaned toward expansion and revenue growth!

In a season where fuel prices were both steadily increasing and showing no indication of a near-term plateau or reduction, I initiated a predictable conversation for any business owner with gas-powered or petroleum-dependent products.

And, yes, I was also demonstrating some rightful concern as a parent.

"How do you account for the spike in gas prices, buddy? Do you have to raise your prices to keep pace?"

"Dad, do you remember the note I sent to all my clients before the cutting season began?" he responded, as he met my questions with one of his own.

With this query, I did, indeed, recall the communication. To be specific, it was thoughtfully written and smartly timed correspondence to each client from the previous summer. Although his primary purpose was to confirm which clients intended to recommit to his services for forecasting purposes, he was very clear in his missive that pricing for returning clients would remain the same as the previous year. Especially when considering the total value of the business he was proactively confirming—and that would undoubtedly be courted by other service providers—it was a strategically solid incentive. Nonetheless, at the time it was presented, that same incentive did not anticipate the volatility now defining the price-per-gallon problem that had materialized. This pre-season pledge took the most convenient remedy for repairing the profitability declines off the table. Said differently, passing along the cost to the customer was not an option. Even as a young enterpriser amid fuel-price inflation almost 50 percent higher than the previous spring, my son would not consider a price hike for those who had responded to his note and affirmed his services earlier in the year.

I was proud of him.

But my fatherly pride was not going to alter the drastic reduction in profit if something did not change . . . I had to press further.

"So what do you do? Your reliance on gas for all this equipment, as well as all the driving required to get to your clients, is a brutal combination right now. At this rate, your take-home pay will surely be less than it was last year."

To some degree, Campbell had already thought about this challenge. "I pretty much know where on my schedule I can add new clients. I'm going to have to quote any new prospects at somewhat loftier prices than I would otherwise prefer to charge them at the onset. And I guess I'll have to take my chances they'll still come aboard. With my inability to magically change gas pricing, it kind of is what it is."

His replies hit me forcefully. It was obvious he was acutely aware of the forthcoming profitability obstacles due to the increase on a key expense. He was also fully cognizant this fiscal challenge resided alongside his principled inability to alter prices to a key constituent—returning customers. Alongside the weight of these realizations, he must have inherited a misperception I had when I was younger.

Because I, too, used to think most things were beyond my control . . .

Break It Down and Make It Up

On the surface, there is not an obvious convergence of the squeeze on my son's profitability by fuel costs and the lack of substance in the answers from the screen printing proprietor relative to average margins. However, if we look more deeply at these instances—and consider interchangeable scenarios in businesses where net gains are largely unconsidered—we find a prospective cure to the leaky profitability too commonly accepted. In full transparency, it was a discovery made while addressing my own instances of compromised yield.

The key to better understanding or further improving landed margin is to focus on what is known. More pointedly, do *not* get stuck on what is *unknown*. Although this sounds elementary, my experience suggests most conversations or investigations concerning profitability cease when the most desired information is unavailable.

Our instinct with a locked door should not be to just pound on it in frustration. If it matters—and landed margin certainly does—we must instead look around to find other possibilities for access. In most instances, they will be there.

As I began to adopt this mindset and implement complementing methodologies, the resulting work consisted of two distinct actions. I have affectionately, yet accurately, termed them as follows:

1. Break It Down (with relevant data)
2. Make It Up (with proper emphasis)

Break It Down

Regardless of how the income is generated in a service business, there are many elements that impact landed margin. Of course, these encompass the most visible operating expenses and the cost of any goods sold. But they also include more unique costs. Whether labor rates, facility charges, shipping costs or anything that invariably accompanies an ability to generate revenue, they are always present . . .

Even if they are not always evident.

In examples like those we're using, line items like "Thread" and "Fuel" do not provide much of a backstory when only viewing them on a spreadsheet. And those terms are not usually the attention-grabbers on a profit and loss statement. The same is true for terms like "printing supplies" or "mileage reimbursement" when found on quarterly financials. Nonetheless, it is only when we further distill these otherwise mundane expenses that we can draw more useful conclusions about the costs tangibly connected to revenue.

With my son's enterprise, the profitability riddle is more solvable when we seek answers to the following questions:

- How many total miles were traveled for the amount spent on fuel?
- What is the aggregate of accounts payable associated with those total miles traveled?
- Are there specific days or times during the week or month when the most fuel is consumed?

The questions relating to any individual expense could surely be unending; this is an inborn risk with any evaluation. As such, the responsibility is to unwrap an expense that often goes unnoticed or neglected—and Break It Down to find the most relevant data contained therein. Our digging is not to simply put holes in the ground. It is instead to unearth valuable golden nuggets that can lead to meaningful improvement in our landed margin. The questions presented during the screen printing acquisition were hardly verbatim to those connected to the analysis of petroleum-related charges with my son. Each excavation exercise brings information to the surface that best identifies steps toward added prosperity. Data collection should be both explicit and explicable:

- How many spools of thread were purchased in the last twelve months?
- What were the top five colors ordered? And what percentage of the total outlay for thread do those colors constitute?

- Not including the products to be embellished, how many suppliers were used last year for supplies necessary for embroidery?

Before we return to my real-life examples, let me assure you this is not the acquisition of avant-garde insight. Even if my son could not immediately outline a strategy to counter the uncontrollable increase in fuel expenses, it is no surprise Old Dominion Freight Line can crisply articulate the almost finite expenses associated with every mile traveled by their trucks and containers. And when the former screen printing proprietor was struggling to do so, Nike, Inc. was reciting with exactness recently adjusted expenses in its textile businesses on an earnings call. For many service-business leaders, expense deconstruction is simply a yet-to-be-acquired skillset or an unpracticed approach. In the end, the recommendation to Break It Down requires little more than a profitability-minded leader probing with purpose.

Perfectly enough, step 2 is also a straightforward process that rewards an inspired leader for a customized approach.

Make It Up

I have spoken to many leaders in various service businesses about my "Make It Up" suggestion. It is fair to say the encouragement of creative thinking is more generally appreciated than the creative license I've taken for the moniker itself . . . It seems most leaders do not like to "make up" much of anything. ☺

Still, a discernible degree of leeway is necessary to achieve progress with profitability. Bestselling author and leadership authority Seth Godin is known for suggesting that being a leader is to embrace an inherent responsibility to "solve interesting problems." Though many profitability problems can be neatly categorized, accomplished leaders know "the most interesting problems" will likely need customized solutions.

To demonstrate more fully, we will continue to pull from our previous examples. But again, regardless of the circumstances, there is a universal application in our very calculated fabrications. And where a belief resides that an MBA or certified actuary is necessary when drawing from statistics, probability, and financial theory, I would argue in instances where landed margin demands improvement, it can best be improved by those leaders who are already positioned on the field of play. To make admirable progress with any profitability quandary, intelligent questions paired with a smartphone and calculator app is all that is usually necessary . . .

To get started, identify where a tangible profitability difference could be made. In our examples, the questions we asked—and the resulting information we would have acquired—showcase the proposed emphasis. More specifically, our questions visibly postulated that costs for printing supplies and fuel might expose an otherwise hidden path to improved profitability and an enhanced landed margin with each sale.

Next in this exercise, we begin to "make up" a formula that will potentially reveal useful knowledge. Of course, the information to be considered is *not* made-up. But we have raw data points that do not fit together in the absence of an existing formula—and we must determine or properly evaluate profitability. Our Make It Up approach becomes the bridge connecting the information we have to a beneficial answer we do not yet have.

For our screen printing and embroidery acquisition, we used a six-month journal of paid invoices to suppliers who provided any ink, thread or stitching-related product. Alongside a considerable quantity of thread spools, the bobbins, backings, stabilizers, pins, needles, and other accessories were all included. The sum of these payments for the last half-year tallied almost $36,500. Alongside these expenses, sales reports in the Due Diligence packet yielded that the same period produced 21,313 fully completed units requiring embroidery. These same 21,313 finished units netted a total of $218,756 in revenue.

From there, our Acquisition Team "made up" a formulaic determination of how the embroidery-related supplies impacted the final cost of our actual product. It was likely not perfect. But it gave us a starting point—and moved us toward an understanding of landed margin and the previously elusive answer for how much cost was included in each garment embroidered.

And when the figurative dust from our arithmetic settled, we had the insight we desired:

$218,756 (total revenue achieved)

÷ 21,313 (total # of garments embroidered)

$10.26 (average revenue per garment)

Here's another:

$36,500 (costs of embroidery supplies)

÷ 21,313 (total # of garments embroidered)

$1.71 (cost of supplies per garment)

And most importantly, perhaps . . .

$1.71 (costs of supplies per garment)

÷ 10.26 (average revenue per garment)

16.7 (% of per-garment revenue spent on supplies)

By knowing these details, we could much better understand the current level of profitability. We paired this information—including the cost of supplies per garment and percent of revenue per-garment spent on these supplies—with easier-to-discern figures (like the cost of the tees that were embroidered, the annual lease expenses, and payroll). By doing so, we had a better perspective on whether meaningful profitability existed and was sustainable. We also gained markers for where the opportunity to legitimately improve landed margin existed.

To be clear, the significance in this example is *not* our satisfaction with the findings. The significance is found in the Make It Up approach taken to acquire needed information that would have otherwise remained absent and unavailable.

Let's now look at the fuel-focused example with my son. As we wrestled with the soaring cost of petrol in conjunction with the pricing promise that eliminated passing along the increase in operating expenses to returning clients, becoming more efficient with each penny spent on this necessity became paramount. To achieve this efficiency for a seasonal business, an extensive and expedient investigation was necessary—and time was not our ally. With every week of the mowing season that passed, our pasture of profitability would be less bountiful!

Here is the information we decided to gather over the next thirty days:

- A total of all fuel receipts, regardless of whether unleaded, diesel or intended for the two-cycle engines in some of the equipment
- The total number of miles traveled to complete all jobs in the same time frame (thirty days)
- The total revenue from all work completed and invoiced (even if not paid and received) during these thirty days

And here is the information we uncovered:

- Total fuel charges across all uses (transportation and equipment) were $717.42
- Total mileage for all jobs in those thirty days was 1,585 miles (we tracked and backed out those miles driven for personal use from the odometer total at the end of our designated research period)
- Total income generated and invoiced during our timeframe selected was $3,575

Once again, it is the relevant data obtained that enabled us to go to work more easily—and to "make up" the assertions we believed could affirmatively impact our landed margin. In this instance, there was also pertinent information I could find on my own. As a matter of fact, my own research yielded that a 2007 Ford FWD F150 gets approximately fourteen miles per gallon and holds no more than thirty gallons of fuel in a full tank. Most importantly, the price of gas at the station my family used for most fill-ups was $3.69 per gallon at this time.

Of course, it was appropriately assumed at the outset that the only bona fide option to increase the landed margin in this scenario was to reduce the total gas consumption. At the same time, reducing fuel usage on job sites seemed a fool's errand, even though it is proven that a Weed eater is more fuel efficient than a zero-turn riding lawn mower . . . Can you imagine looking across an overgrown expanse of a few acres—and being handed a string trimmer to tackle your task?!

Ugghh.

The most attractive and feasible target for adjustment was undoubtedly the fuel consumption required to get to and from each job. Alongside the new data we would produce for this consideration, we also had to acknowledge the lingering question that would accompany any of our findings: Is it worth it? After all, reordering jobs to save fuel would require numerous clients to potentially give up the day of service to which they had grown accustomed. Even more so, there was a notable number of higher-income-producing clients who had specifically requested a particular day of the week to align with personal preferences (doesn't everyone want their lawn looking its best at the beginning of a weekend?). Demolishing and rebuilding the service calendar would be a task that would undoubtedly fall somewhere between wholly uncomfortable and completely undoable . . . Would the juice be worth the squeeze?

If only as practice, I now leave this question to you for consideration and completion. Please put yourself in my son's position. What arithmetic will you perform? What equation will you construct? I highly encourage you to take a moment to utilize the various results from our research to develop your own conclusion. As you do so, you will build newfound or increased strength in this area! For the sake of comparison, I put our work to this quandary below the Involved Maximization Imperatives in a brief Make It Up section. As you review how we used the information provided, it's possible you devised an even better formula!

For sure, these exercises are strongly reminiscent of the "story problems" assigned in our formative schooling to sharpen skills in mathematics. Today, these exercises generate credible results to our advantage. But unlike when stationed neatly in classroom rows with an instructor who would furnish us with a challenge, we now have the responsibility to both discover the problem *and* settle on a solution. In effect, we now get to directly insert ourselves and our business into a story problem that requires *and* deserves a solution. Even better, when we locate a potentially correct answer to the curious query before us, we get to move our meaningful and mission-minded story ahead to the beautiful places we never envisioned when solving those quandaries in grade school . . .

It's the Mortar:
Involved Maximization Imperatives for Chapter 13

1. Consider the pricing for your best products. This is not a suggestion to redo pricing. It is, instead, a strong recommendation to understand why your products are priced as they are. There should always be a strategically explicable basis for each price presented. If you discover items that seemingly have no coherence in the pricing, an adjustment should be given deeper consideration. And, again, when competition has similar products that are similarly priced—or there is an MSRP provided—we are not obligated to follow those leads. If doing so is the most strategically sound approach for your enterprise, all is well. Those prices have been given due consideration and determined to be strategically sound! On the other hand, if that sense is not achieved, it may be time to break from the pack . . .

    For the sake of Uninvolved Optimization, announce the intention to evaluate current pricing to those *inside* the organization who would be affected by any changes. They will present a valuable perspective on the price-dependent possibilities. Most importantly, have key Team Members complete the exercise with you.

2. Next, if we are going to encourage others to strengthen profitability, we must first build our own muscles in this area. Please return to the unresolved conundrum connected to my son's soaring fuel costs. To help you evaluate your findings—and mine—I've put the work I did with this challenge below. To leave no reader in suspense, the plan became to redo the order of weekly or biweekly service routes and ruthlessly slash the driving miles by 60 percent for the remaining five months of the growing season.

3. Without delay, select a few popular products or services you are currently offering to the marketplace. Deconstruct the various activities and accompanying costs associated with their availability. This scrutiny is strongly advised to determine whether sub-optimized areas are hampering maximal profitability. Yes, we may need to consider a price change—but it may be better to find a way to leave the current price

intact while getting more efficient with the other costs associated with any offering in your assortment.

The "Make It Up" Formula for Improved Fuel Efficiency

In our desire to know whether revising the service order of clients each month would make a meaningful difference to profitability—and what it would take to do so, if it did—here are some of the calculations we did to Break It Down:

$717.42 (total fuel costs)
÷ 1,585 (total miles driven)
$0.4526 (cost per mile driven)

1,585 (total miles driven)
÷ 14 (avg. # of miles covered per gallon of fuel consumed)
113.21 (# of gallons of gas consumed driving)

113.21 (# of gallons of gas consumed driving)
× $3.69 (cost per gallon of gas)
$417.76 (fuel costs for driving)

$417.76 (fuel costs for driving)
÷ $717.42 (total fuel costs)
0.5823 (% of total fuel costs due to driving)

In the end, this exercise demonstrated that fuel for driving—and not powering equipment—contributed to over 50 percent of the total cost of fuel. If we did meaningfully reduce the driving miles, it would seemingly matter enough to make a palpable difference to the profitability. Moreover, by setting a target of 60 percent less driving, we could easily see the "allowance" of miles for any new route of service and the exact improvement in profit. To be specific, we needed to order the lawn care visits in a new way that did not exceed 650 total miles . . . and if we did so, my son would gain an additional $250 in profit (not revenue) each week. With more than twenty weeks left in the season, this additional $5,000+ in net profit—demonstrated by the approach we "made up"—easily suggested it was worth the effort.

Section II Summation

In Section II, we leaned into critical areas where mortar needs to be troweled by the truckload. As a reward for sticking with it, the newly pledged efforts will illuminate exactly where workplace passion can be found. After all, this section was intentionally penned as "Feels Hard." And believe me, "passion" is the appropriate word here. Not as a steamy, romantic attachment, but as the condition linked to the Greek word *pas-cho*. The concise translation is "to suffer"—or, on a more individual level, "a willingness to suffer." Regardless of where you fall on the faith spectrum, this is the context found in director Mel Gibson's 2004 blockbuster movie *The Passion of the Christ*. In essence, it was the "suffering of Jesus." As a more benign example, consider the person who says, "I have a passion for fishing." If that is true, it is not manifest when he is catching his limit on a beautiful day with friends in a chartered boat. Instead, the clues of his passion for fishing emerge in miserable moments standing on the riverbank in pouring rain, holding the bucket for a companion who is miserably seasick or demonstrating bottomless patience while teaching a fundamental casting skill to a distracted seven-year-old angler.

For many of us, we are tangibly suffering for a worthy cause when we commit to the disciplines necessary to properly evaluate revenue streams, build OST Frameworks, systematically create value, perform an honest audit of our landed margin, and submit ourselves to behavior that maximizes resources for the sake of our Mission. Again, this is undoubtedly difficult stuff! The good news is that any knowledge acquisition—and every bit of disciplined implementation—can be easily tracked and will be quantifiably validated. The improvements in revenue, margin, billables and/or expense control will be quantitative—and they will be visible. Yes, the foremost health markers of the business will be increasingly favorable. Best of all, the confidence an organization has in its viability to make consequential contributions to its community will soar!

Friends, the suffering will be worth it—and the claims of "being passionate" about your work will be authenticated. Do not delay!

Some Final Thoughts on a Forever Approach with Your Most Meaningful Pursuits

In his August 1, 2024 *Leadership Podcast* episode titled "The High Cost of Not Letting Go" (released after most of the material for this book was already prepared), author Craig Groeschel powerfully reinforced and perfectly restated a primary message with which you've now become familiar: "If your organization cannot be effective without you, your organization is limited by you. You [as the leader] are the greatest limiting factor. You are the ceiling."

Amen, pastor.

Throughout this manuscript, I've woven two distinct themes into the commentary, the examples, and the suggestions. Uninvolved Optimization and Involved Maximization are paired—and inseparable. It is together they stress the importance of intentionally, consistently, intelligently, and diligently ensuring your efforts simultaneously contribute to organizational progress *and* an ongoing transition of personal knowledge and consequential control. For leaders who aspire to have their most meaningful pursuits outlast their own contributions, there is no other way. This is the practical approach that requires the repetition and the recommended imperatives found herein.

Even beyond that guidance, I know from my own experiences that this philosophy has an equal connection to personal endeavors, interests, and priorities. If you do not engage in IM and UO, there is an unfortunate, potentially dangerous, and unquestionably stifling lid you've placed on important relationships, family imperatives, and enticing opportunities separate from your organizational role: Do not. Let this. Happen. Do not let a natural drift toward doing the work by yourself be your story. Do not let the default outcome of keeping the authority for yourself be your legacy.

Additionally, I hope you've connected with the importance of mortar— even more so than bricks—as a relevant analogy that conveniently connects to a popular industry phrase. The magnitude found in this "bricks and mortar" comparison runs deep, and it begins by knowing that in retail, what is most visible is not what is most crucial. Merchants, restaurants, pop-ups, and family dynasties have all ceased to exist when the "bricks" of the best products, most popular endorsees, and busiest locations did *not* ultimately support the demands of the business. The "mortar" found in the preceding pages are fundamental requirements of a service-centered enterprise, obligating leaders to attentiveness and consistent improvement with practices labeled as both soft and hard skills.

Across our themes, we find a convergence. The "mortar" mixed in each chapter is to be grasped, mastered, and dispensed in an all-out, unrestrained Involved Maximization effort. Along the way, the achievement of Uninvolved Optimization—with even a single task for any priority—solidifies a "brick" (or many of them!) and motivates us toward an expansion and hardening of these conditions. We increasingly seek and institute this approach. As an oddly fortunate benefit, there is no flashbulb moment or visible finish line that signals our arrival . . . It simply does not conclude. Instead, a lasting orientation toward UO is established, and the adaptation occurs. With everything we do, we now begin with an end in mind; it always involves others and continuously moves the main thrust of activity and authority away from us. The possibilities before us align with the potential within us; the priorities we embrace nourish the purpose we embody.

On the backside of our Afterword and Idyllic Musings, you'll find a Retailer's "Ready To Build" checklist. It's a breakdown of the core concepts we've explored and studied together. More importantly, it is a reference tool and progress report for inspired leaders and transformative organizations. I'm not so irresponsible to suggest, "Do this and you can't possibly fail." In his book *Leaders Leap: Transforming Your Company at the Speed of Disruption*, host of the *Remarkable Retail* podcast Steve Dennis tells us retail success may even be harder than we anticipate because "ego defects, blind spots, confirmation biases, defense mechanisms, ardent desires, and [our] deepest fears [all] get in the way of the progress we need to make." *But . . . but, but, but . . .* if these elements and concepts are solidly understood, unabatingly practiced, and faithfully shared, I believe favorable results and suitable rewards will follow. Even better, so will a deserved satisfaction and genuine sense of significance through your service to others!

Your bricks remain ready. And you have the mortar. Apply it thoughtfully and unreservedly. Choose carefully where it is applied and observe how it hardens.

You are building something meant to last for centuries.

"This is the true joy in life, the being used for a purpose recognized by yourself as a mighty one; the being a force of nature instead of a feverish, selfish little clod of ailments and grievances complaining that the world will not devote itself to making you happy. I am of the opinion that my life belongs to the whole community, and as long as I live, it is my privilege to do for it whatever I can. I want to be thoroughly used up when I die, for the harder I work the more I live. I rejoice in life for its own sake. Life is no brief candle for me. It is a sort of splendid torch which I have got hold of for the moment, and I want to make it burn as brightly as possible before handing it on to future generations."

—GEORGE BERNARD SHAW

Afterword

The Payment Is Cash—but the Currency Is Trust

My first entrepreneurial engagement with the retail industry came when I was eighteen. It arrived both honestly and unexpectedly—even though it centered on activities that were both illegal and premeditated. In his bestselling book *To Sell Is Human*, Dan Pink rightfully claims that those who sell properly "leave [us] better off in the end."[1] I'm still not sure my collegiate efforts meet this standard . . .

In 1989, I made my way from Elkhart, Indiana, the "Recreation Vehicle Capital of the World," to Vanderbilt University in Nashville, Tennessee. I was an incoming freshman. Other than a brief visit to campus for a tour the previous year, my only instances of being south of Indianapolis were the popular trips Upper Midwesterners in upper-middle-class families made to Florida during the winter. When I arrived in Music City, I knew nothing about country music, would have considered it a lucky guess that my new city was the state capital, and had little knowledge traditions around college football existed beyond those near my hometown at the University of Notre Dame. Best I knew, fight songs, tailgating, and the tendency to turn four fifteen-minute quarters into a full day's worth of activity were exclusive to South Bend.

Wow. I was so wrong.

But do not allow me to mislead you. Again, I was at Vanderbilt. For those who consider college football a worthy diversion, you already know there are no stable grounds for claiming the football program was a perennial powerhouse. In fact, in the first two years I was a student, the team only managed the same number of wins. By the time I graduated, my alma mater mustered a four-year record of eleven wins and thirty-three losses. And in the meager 25 percent of games when victory somehow overpowered more standard conclusions, it was only a half-dozen times we beat a team in the rightfully storied Southeastern Conference where Vanderbilt is slotted (and where many other National Championship–caliber teams are fashioned).

But my premise is not about football. Or even tradition.

This shallow history lesson in collegiate athletics is simply a set-up for my baptismal efforts to supply goods and services to the public in a very specific and profitable manner.

My inaugural on-campus residential assignment was room 322 in Tolman Hall. Although unconfirmed, my speculation remains this building housed the absolute last group of male applicants to be granted acceptance into the university. I believe such because I've yet to meet a former or current student who did not have a higher SAT score than I did. And I had lots of company in this dorm with other young men who had somewhat admirable grade point averages in high school—but were still notably below the 3.85 median at Vanderbilt.

The building itself consisted entirely of small, one-room dormitories with lots of fresh paint and an even more sizable abundance of outdated fixtures and finishes. No one in the building had a roommate, as the sleeping quarters were too tight to accommodate multiple beds. And none of the rooms had air conditioning. As the T-shirt said, we were "The Hottest Guys on Campus."

In short, we were the lucky ones. This was where all of us wanted to attend college. And we just barely made it. No one was sure how. But we were here.

My initial foray into front-facing customer service came through unanticipated rituals hardwired into the football games played in our home stadium. They produced an enormous amount of discomfort and awkwardness for freshmen (or, perhaps, fresh men) who desired to join a fraternity later in the academic year. To be specific, there were seemingly three very critical ingredients to *proper* attendance at these games for fraternity "rushees": get a date, wear a tie, bring a flask.

Welcome to college football in the South.

For the most trailing element in this troubling tradition-laced trifecta, the flask could not be empty when you arrived at Dudley Field. Not under any circumstances. Moreover, and depending on what time the game started, this same flask doubled as a pregame flip switch to turn on the mimosas or Bloody Marys (for early afternoon games) or the gin and tonics or rum and Cokes (for evening games).

The mixers were provided by the fraternities; the alcohol was not.

To make matters more unsettling for me and my comrades in Tolman Hall, many who were willing dates to the games predictably preferred to go with upperclassmen and current members of fraternities . . .

And who could blame them?

Freshman rushees hardly held an enviable social status—and the institutional veterans had the "Insider's Guide" for any fun that came with the norms and customs of football season. With no easy path to getting a date—and no roommates with whom to share the apprehension—those of us who were "Tolmanites" left our tight, private accommodations and scattered like panicked ants toward Fraternity Row on each of these designated Saturdays. On the way, some of us awkwardly enrolled the companionship of someone we barely knew, while toting along an elixir we were darned lucky to have. Two people having a drink while making nervous small talk—and mostly wishing they were somewhere else (with someone else?)—is not unique to college students. But the young men coming from Tolman Hall had a particularly good corner on it for each varsity football game played at home.

Through the somewhat harrowing stories shared back in our dormitory after the first game, it became obvious I was one of the very few residents who had procured my own liquor to keep the time-honored traditions. Most of my hallmates had been reduced to literal begging, borrowing or stealing to do so. As a result, I soon sensed there was a chore even more daunting to my hallmates than the prospect of finding another date for the second home game.

It was the effort seemingly required to secure another bottle of booze . . .

Fortunately for me, in my senior year in high school—and long before internet sites could almost unabashedly offer falsified identification cards—I secured my own fake ID. A classmate, while standing at the front of the queue in a Department of Motor Vehicles location for the State of Indiana, noticed an absence of personnel at the post where a driver's license was suitably finished with the laminated hologram. This assemblage of heat-applied seals confirming authenticity lay both in plain view and entirely out of sight . . . He hesitated not. He grabbed the entire stack—and immediately left the building, appearing like every other visitor who leaves abruptly, full of impatience and frustration for the lack of progress with such an ostensibly simple errand.

The following week he went to a different DMV location to fulfill his original intent and fully acquire his new license. In the interim, he secured an interesting assortment of items for ulterior purposes:

- An inexpensive shower curtain in a light blue color to replicate the backdrop of an Indiana driver's license for adults twenty-one-plus years of age
- Heavy-duty, off-white corrugated cardboard stock
- Myriad supplies normally suited for classroom art projects at an elementary school, including Elmer's glue, a twelve-inch ruler, and Scotch Tape
- A box of disposable cameras (remember those?!)

When finished, the handmade fakes sold for $100 each. They looked respectably legitimate, mostly because of the pilfered hologram. Each purchaser had to determine how to laminate his or her new card to conjoin the hologram with the newly developed personal photo in front of the creatively fashioned backdrop. For me, a classmate who worked part-time at our local Blockbuster Video (remember those?!) did the trick. Whether laminating a new membership card—or my future ticket to prosperity and popularity—the on-site thermal press at this now-defunct video rental parlor did not distinguish.

Most of my use of the fabricated identification in high school was in Michigan. It was only a short drive . . . and I reasoned that package-store personnel across the state line were less qualified to question its validity. Regardless of whether such added caution was necessary, the card performed flawlessly. In fewer instances, it was equally unchallenged in my home state. By the time I headed to Nashville, my confidence was uncontained, and I presumed the greater distance to Tennessee would make any imposing opposition entirely unlikely.

When my dorm mates became aware that I had a reliable fake ID, requests for my assistance immediately started pouring in. The desperation in the various plans of many fellow Tolman residents for the next football game was both outright and significant . . . As former Speaker of the House and Texas Congressman Sam Rayburn is often attributed as saying, "Opportunity often comes by accident; readiness never does."

As a wholly unconsidered ignition for my first retail-related endeavor, it was time for me to bridge the pigskin canyon between supply and demand.

Retail-industry veterans know there is a distinct difference between purchasing and procurement. In my nascent (and questionable) collegiate venture, I soon bought nothing—but I procured everything. By midweek of the second home game, I had devised and developed an inventory acquisition *system*. For starters, I enlisted a friend who had a car available on campus. For cargo space and a ride to a (no longer existing) party shop/package store in East Nashville—where I anticipated both lower prices and less scrutiny of my identification—I paid him $20 (or gave him two bottles of any of the mid-shelf spirits of his choosing). For everyone else, the cost was the same $20 for their choice of reputable brands that would not tarnish their reputation with the frat crowd or their date for the game. Jack Daniels, Jim Beam, Seagram's 7, Bacardi, Jose Cuervo, Beefeater, Johnny Walker, Malibu, Absolut . . . I priced all of it at $20, for a 750 ml delivered to the front of a designated dorm room door. At the time, I had no idea about the notion of keystone margins (selling something for twice your cost), but I was solidly dominating that still-popular target. I was getting twenty bucks from my "customers," while the sticker price at the store was primarily $8.99 and $9.99 for the brands and flavors I deemed eligible. The scale of my purchase earned me another 15 percent off the receipt total—and I ended up with more complimentary glassware and corporate paraphernalia than my tiny little university residence could accompany.

It's hard to recall how much money I made that season. For a nineteen-year-old who was a full-time student, it was a lot. And I will not deny that I enjoyed the popularity and reveled in the transformation of my study and sleeping space into a walk-in liquor cabinet. Of course, now, as a parent, coach, employer, and the redeemed steward of a moral compass, it is admittedly difficult to fully applaud my enterprising scheme. It would be difficult to purport that an underage procurement specialist securing alcohol for other minors is a noble cause.

As such, I focus on the now decades-long friendships I made and the two most valuable lessons I learned in that season that put me on a lifetime path to being in the service of others.

Lesson one: With intention, I provided more than an alcoholic alleviation to the anxiety that accompanied most freshman football gamegoers. I made deliveries when my customers were in class or away from their rooms. To conform to school guidelines, each bottle was laid at the base of the door, fully concealed by the required paper bag. Inside or alongside the bag, I would leave promo items that featured their purchase. I might also include some freebie "airplane bottles" that I had been given or various accompaniments I picked up at the package store. Other "gifts with purchase" included packs of gum, breath mints, shot glasses or merchandise from the bookstore. For those students I better came to know, I would leave a handwritten note, wishing them luck with the fraternity they most desired or on the date for which they had bona fide enthusiasm. I was customizing the delivery long before upstart e-commerce retailers were highlighting its prospective impact. By the third game, most of my patrons left their dorm rooms unlocked for me. There were no concerns that I would snoop or steal. There was no uneasiness that I would make off with personal belongings or electronics. At a time when I could only tender cash and exact payments, I earned the most precious currency of all: trust.

Lesson two: Even in a retailer's dream-like environment, with confirmed scarcity, unbridled demand, and limited competition, the opportunity to administer what I now highlight as "all that is perceived, understood, and remembered" was worth considerably more. As you may recall, this is our definition of "Experience," as explored in chapter 4. To realize this framework at such an impressionable age is a gift I did not deserve. For sure, it appeared different then . . . but it still feels the same today!

Cheers!

—August 25, 2024 (Oxford, MS)

Idyllic Musings

It is possible any picture—from anyone, at any time—may very well be worth all the words in this book . . . And it is simply true that, for me, the collage below is worth even far more than all the words in all the books ever written.

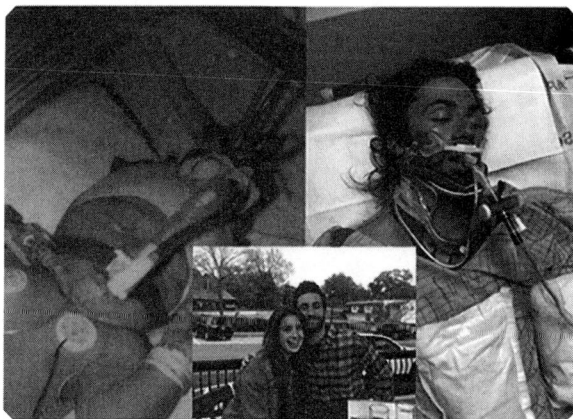

(*left to right*) Monica, February 2005; Monica and Campbell, October 2021; Campbell, January 2021

Uninvolved Optimization Checklist

Foundational Concepts
1. Involved Maximization
2. Uninvolved Optimization

Four Fiercest Foes of Unity
1. Purpose-Driven Delta
2. Disagreement and Disappointment
3. Solved . . . But Unresolved
4. Tolerated Treason

P.A.S.T.E. Service Business Leadership Essentials
1. Powerful Personal Productivity
2. Accountability
3. Service-Centeredness
4. Transparency
5. Enthusiasm

Fundamental Components of a Retail Experience

1. Interaction
2. Environment

Ingredients in the "Cycle of Satisfaction"

1. Attention
2. Time
3. Service
4. Satisfaction

Service Quotient Attributes

1. Friendliness
2. Patience
3. Empathy
4. Willingness
5. Enthusiasm
6. Gratitude

Three Sole Pathways to Increase Sales Revenue

1. Conversion
2. Average Transaction Size
3. Frequency

Elements of Value Creation

1. Investigation
2. Assessment
3. Exchange

Immutable Laws of Inventory and Resource Acquisition

1. Law of Demand
2. Law of Confidence
3. Law of Relevance
4. Law of Attachment
5. Law of Results

Glossary of Terms

(listed alphabetically)

Assessment: The second of three steps in Value Creation; an honest evaluation of whether internal or available resources enable an enterprise to legitimately deliver the value it desires to pledge to an existing or prospective partner.

assortment: The cumulative offering of products or options available for resale in a business, department or category.

attention: The notice taken of someone or something.

average transaction size: As one of the three sole pathways to increase sales revenue, this is the mean from a specified number of sales tickets over a specific period; increases or decreases in sales revenue would be determined by examining this metric in the same environment for a different period.

Broadcast Tower: An analogical reference to a customer who will share his/her experience in a retail environment with others through conversation, social media, testimonials, public review sites, and other means available to detail the engagement.

category management: A retailing and purchasing concept in which the range of products purchased by a business organization or sold by a retailer is broken down into discrete groups of similar or related products; a systematic, disciplined approach to managing a product category as a strategic business unit.

conversion rate: For retail, this metric indicates the success of converting the visitors to a store or website into confirmed Purchasers. It is one of the three sole pathways to increase sales revenue. To acquire the rate itself, divide the number of Purchasers (or transactions) by the total number of visitors.

Exchange: The final of three steps in Value Creation; it is an internal and/or external confirmation of the value to be provided *and* the benefit anticipated as a result. Note that the "exchange" may not be compensatory; it may be a sense of appreciation, an increase in influence or responsibility or an immediate or future opportunity otherwise unavailable.

experience: The totality of cognitions given by perception; all that is perceived, understood, and remembered. As used in this context, it consists of two primary considerations: Interaction and Environment.

frequency: As one of the three sole pathways to increase sales revenue, it is the number of occasions a customer makes a purchase during a specified period. Note that frequency is *not* a metric for the number of *visits*; increases or decreases in frequency are connected solely to *purchase* occasions.

GMROI (Gross Margin Return on Inventory Investment): A metric used to evaluate the profitability of the investment in inventory, as well as illuminate the overall health of a retail business.

immutable: Something unchanging over time or unable to be changed. As used in this context, it is a descriptor for pillars erected to make procurement responsibilities stable, predictable, and profitable.

Investigation: The first of three steps in Value Creation; it is the intentional and deep consideration of what a prospective client, patron or partner deems "of value." It includes research, thoughtful and relevant questions, skilled listening, and diligent note-taking.

Involved Maximization: The conscious decision and concerted effort of a leader to approach a project, department or enterprise in a manner that combines the pursuit of results with a specific intent to transition future iterations of the effort to others.

keystone margin: The gross profit when a sale price is exactly twice the acquisition cost. For example, if a party shop retailer sells a 100-pack of balloons for $14.99, it would be a keystone margin if that retailer was invoiced by the vendor at $7.50 per package.

landed margin: The total revenue from the sale of our product, less the sum of all costs required to complete the sale of that same product.

pace of business: The current performance of a business (department, category, etc.) to which a supplier, product, brand or ancillary business unit must equal to maintain the "pace." This consideration is especially relevant when an entity is performing well or poorly by general standards—but not by that which is the current pace of growth or decline of the measured entity.

Purpose-Driven Delta: The difference in position between two or more entities that have different purposes for doing the same thing *or* elect to do things differently because of their differing purposes. Unless otherwise known and mutually agreed upon, this can be an enemy of Team unity.

share: The portion of a market or business metric occupied by a specific participant in the market or business. It is calculated by comparing a participant's total sales over a specific period to the total sales in the industry or a respective company over the same period.

Tolerated Treason: The violation or disregard of corporate principles by internal constituents allowed or enabled by supervisors and others with positional authority and influence.

Uninvolved Optimization: The condition in which a project, department or enterprise is operating effectively without direct involvement or instruction from a senior leader and/or key predecessor in the effort.

unity: The alignment of all team members toward a shared goal.

Value Creation: The design of quality or impact into existence in a manner that is perceived and confirmed as valuable to another; a three-step process consisting of Investigation, Assessment, and Exchange.

Notes

Preface

1. Brené Brown, "Regret Is a Fair but Tough Teacher," interview with Oprah Winfrey, OWN, October 4, 2015, https://www.oprah.com/own-super-soul-sunday/brene-brown-regret-is-a-fair-but-tough-teacher-video.
2. Anthony de Mello, *The Way to Love* (New York: Image, 1995).

Prologue

1. Dorothy B. Thompson, *An Ancient Shopping Center: The Athenian Agora* (Athens: American School of Classical Studies at Athens, 2012).
2. Kadim Hasson Hnaihen, "The Appearance of Bricks in Ancient Mesopotamia," *Athens Journal of History* (6), no. 1 (January 2020): 73–96, https://www.athensjournals.gr/history/2020-6-1-4-Hnaihen.pdf.
3. Michael Aylwin, "A Brief Journey Through the Ancient Art of Masonry," *Masonry Magazine*, site last updated 2024, https://masonrymagazine.com/Default?pageID=1274.
4. Wikipedia; Wikipedia's "Mortar (masonry)" entry.

Section I: Soft Skills (What Feels Good Is Really Hard)

Section I Introduction

1. Mark Miller, *Talent Magnet* (California: Berrett-Koehler Publishers, 2018).

Chapter 2: Another Analogy … and a Handful of Enemies

1. Paul Adler et al., "Building a Collaborative Enterprise," Organizational Restructuring entry, Harvard Business Review, July–August 2011 edition, https://hbr.org/2011/07/building-a-collaborative-enterprise.
2. Food Research & Action Center, "Hunger and Poverty in America," FRAC, site last updated 2024, https://frac.org/hunger-poverty-america.
3. Simon Sinek, "What IS the Infinite Game?" YouTube, May 18, 2022, video, https://www.youtube.com/watch?v=QFpVVm7AnKI.
4. *Oxford Languages*, s.v. "delta (*n.*)."
5. Amazon Staff, "2016 Letter to Shareholders," About Amazon, April 17, 2017, video excerpt and transcription, https://www.aboutamazon.com/news/company-news/2016-letter-to-shareholders.
6. IHG Hotels & Resorts homepage, "19 hotel brands…," IHG Hotels & Resorts, site last updated 2024, https://www.ihg.com/content/us/en/about/brands; IHG Social Justice & Diversity page, "We Stand Together in the Fight for Justice and Equality," Our Stance entry, https://www.ihg.com/content/us/en/customer-care/ihg-stand-together, https://www.ihg.com/content/us/en/customer-care/ihg-stand-together/advocate.
7. IHG Hotels & Resorts, "How we're creating Room to Belong," IGH 2023 Progress Report, https://www.ihgplc.com/~/media/Files/I/Ihg-Plc/responsible-business/reporting/2024/2023%20Progress%20Report.pdf.

Chapter 3: Stuck in the Middle with Me

1. James Clear, "Your entire life happens…," James Clear (blog), https://jamesclear.com/quotes/your-entire-life-happens-inside-your-body-its-the-one-home-you-will-always-occupy-and-can-never-sell-

but-you-can-renovate-it-if-you-can-only-pick-one-habit-to-build-exercise-might-be-the-one.

2. Eric Artz, "Reductions to Our Workforce," REI Co-Op, Newsroom article, January 25, 2024, https://www.rei.com/newsroom/article/reductions-to-our-workforce.

3. Eric Artz, "Reductions to Our Workforce."

4. SGB Media, "REI Co-op to Lay Off 357 Non-Store Staff; Forecasts Revenue Decline for 2024," SGM Online, January 25, 2024, https://sgbonline.com/rei-co-op-to-lay-off-35-non-store-staff-forecasts-revenue-decline-for-2024/.

5. SGB Media, "REI Co-op to Lay Off 357 Non-Store Staff..."

6. Michael T. Deane, "Top 6 Reasons New Businesses Fail," Investopedia, June 1, 2024, https://www.investopedia.com/financial-edge/1010/top-6-reasons-new-businesses-fail.aspx.

7. Andy Stanley, "How Not To Be Your Own Worst Enemy: Part 1," Your Move with Andy Stanley, YouTube, video, 4:15, January 16, 2021, https://www.youtube.com/watch?v=6JRBeoVsWts.

Chapter 4: Experience Matters

1. Dictionary.com, under "experience," entry 5, https://www.dictionary.com/browse/experience.

2. Antonio Perez, quote by Daniel Burnham, "A Chicago tale: Why we're happy to erase the asterisk from Daniel Burnham's 'Make no little plans*'," comments associated with Burnham's 1909 Plan of Chicago, *Chicago Tribune*, May 31, 2019, https://digitaledition.chicagotribune.com/infinity/article_share.aspx; Adam Selzer, "Burnham's "Make No Little Plans"Quote: Apocryphal No More!", Mysterious Chicago, March 3, 2019, https://mysteriouschicago.com/finding-daniel-burnhams-no-little-plans-quote/.

3. B. Joseph Pine II and James H. Gilmore, *The Experience Economy* (Boston: Harvard Business Review Press, 2011), 44-45.

4. B. Joseph Pine II and James H. Gilmore.

Chapter 5: Empower the Tower!

1. Tao Chen et al., "The Impact of Online Reviews on Consumers' Purchasing Decisions: Evidence From an Eye-Tracking Study," *NIH* (13), no. 865702 (June 2022).

2. National Retail Federation, "2023 Consumer Returns in the Retail Industry," December 2023, https://nrf.com/research/2023-consumer-returns-retail-industry.

3. Slickdeals editors, "Two in Three Americans Believe the Worst Part of Shopping is Returning Unwanted Items, According to Survey Commissioned by Slickdeals," PR Newswire, June 30, 2022, https://www.prnewswire.com/news-releases/two-in-three-americans-believe-the-worst-part-of-shopping-is-returning-unwanted-items-according-to-survey-commissioned-by-slickdeals-301578664.html.

Chapter 6: There Is Nothing Special about Being Exceptional

1. Merriam-Webster, s.v. "culture (*n*.)," accessed September 13, 2024, https://unabridged.merriam-webster.com/unabridged/culture.

2. Wikipedia, s.v. "Empathy," accessed September 14, 2024, https://en.wikipedia.org/wiki/Empathy#:~:text=Empathy%20is%20generally%20described%20as%20the%20ability%20to,affective%29%20empathy%2C%20somatic%20empathy%2C%20and%20spiritual%20empathy.%20.

3. Tracy Brower, "Gratitude Is Good: Why It's Important And How To Cultivate It," *Forbes*, December 10, 2021, https://www.forbes.com/sites/tracybrower/2021/01/03/gratitude-is-good-why-its-important-and-how-to-cultivate-it/.

Section II: Hard Skills (What Feels Hard Is Really Good)
Section II Introduction

1. Jennifer Herrity, "What Are Soft Skills?", Indeed, August 15, 2024, https://www.indeed.com/career-advice/resumes-cover-letters/soft-skills.

Chapter 7: Take It from the Top—After All, It Always Starts with Topline Revenue

1. Jim Collins and Morten T. Hansen, *Great by Choice* (New York: Random House Business, 2011).

Chapter 9: The Creation Story

1. Brad Sugars (@actioncoachceo), "Business is all about relationships," X, June 10, 2015, 2:30 p.m., https://x.com/actioncoachceo/status/608717 906080337920?lang=en.

2. Jerry Weintraub, *When I Stop Talking, You'll Know I'm Dead: Useful Stories from a Persuasive Man* (New York: Twelve, 2010).

Chapter 10: Good Buying Makes for Better Selling

1. Gui Costin, "Millennial Spending Habits and Why They Buy," *Forbes*, December 10, 2021, https://www.forbes.com/sites/forbesbooksauthors/2019/05/01/millennial-spending-habits-and-why-they-buy/.

Chapter 12: Enemies in the Inventory

1. Thomas J. Ryan, "Study: Out-of-Stocks Drive 66 Percent of Consumers to Another Retailer," SGB Media, November 1, 2024, https://sgbonline.com/study-out-of-stocks-drive-66-percent-of-consumers-to-another-retailer/.

2. Silas Bamigbola, "Mass-Market Retailer: What It Is, Characteristics, and Examples," SuperMoney, March 28, 2024, https://www.super-money.com/encyclopedia/mass-market-retailer.

Section II Summation

1. Steve Dennis, *Leaders Leap: Transforming Your Company at the Speed of Disruption* (California: Wonderwell, 2024).

Afterword

1. Dan Pink, *To Sell Is Human* (New York: Riverhead Books, 2012), 38-9.

Acknowledgments

Mom and Dad, even today, I cannot thank you enough. The pictures, the memories—even your shared headstone—are faint indications from the world that you are gone . . . Still, the efforts I put forth each day that yield any favorable impact are my ongoing indications to the world you are not forgotten.

Big Peach Leadership Team, do not be fooled. The author's name listed on the cover may be mine—but we all know darned well that every morsel of experience and improvement documented on these pages was the sustained effort of our collective.

Mom and Dad Campbell, your love, support and encouragement for me with your daughter—and all we hold dear and worthwhile—is a compounding yield that increases with each passing year. It's a wealth I pledge to share with others with a spirit as generous as yours.

Fellow residents of Fannin County, Georgia, your love, care, compassion, and resolve to uphold the families involved in the accident on January 12, 2021, is beautifully unforgettable—and entirely replicable everywhere. We are a city on a hill. Even with all those who come for the scenery, this is our home because of the community.

Northeast Georgia Medical Center and all the hardworking men and women associated with the trauma center and its supporting network, this book would have never materialized without your care and skilled dedication.

Georgia State Patrol, your ability to orchestrate a soulful blend of compassion with a keen sense of what is crucial to save lives on our roadways is truly amazing. It matters so much.

Steve DeMoss, to work with you is a gift and overwhelming privilege . . . Far more importantly, though, is the example you set for me with friendship, empathy, effort, and your perpetual orientation directed toward doing the right thing for others.

Joe Szombathy, any day where I achieve a semblance to you in how I encourage and lead others is a day I rest well in knowing I made a meaningful difference in the lives of those with whom I work.

Sydnie Grace Jones and the Jones family, your impact never lessens . . . and your legacy lives as a beautiful testimony for the boldness with which we should approach each day.

Greg, your brotherly love, counsel, and involvement is the best soil I've experienced for the seed of an (even mediocre) idea. Even more influential on me is the way you sustain and nourish all those who are tilling, tending, and harvesting alongside you!

FDV, no one has provided or intentionally exposed me to more books or more content than you. Through this and more, you've challenged and inspired me to be increasingly better in more ways than you likely know.

Kash Ahmed, you are my living proof that the most valuable of Team Members can also become the dearest of friends. I may sing, "Hold the Line"—but I define "perfect timing" as your arrival in my life.

J-Rock Carson, I am so thankful for my observations of you with people, projects, environments, and possibilities . . . Without fail, you make them all markedly better. Your continued influence is my compounding return.

Milli and the Team at Brown Books, your confidence, enthusiasm and instruction was always on time (even when I wasn't . . .) and served as the linchpin to any good that comes from this endeavor. Ben Davidoff, your insight was exactly what this manuscript needed—and your encouragement was always there when I needed it most.

Marji Ross, your editing acumen brought this together. I've learned from you that feeling deeply inspired and having deep insight are only good enough for this type of effort when they can be legitimately and cogently connected.

Ranee Alison Spina, your arrival, expertise and guidance on this project was right on—and right on time. You do, indeed, "Make magic happen."

Alex and Fe Rodriguez, you are the "Big Peach Power Couple." Your friendship, faith, and fearlessness has become a powerful and celebrated gift in my work and in my life.

Pat O'Hare, from the time in Tolman until this moment in time, your friendship and example is a gift of truly epic proportions. My apologies for all of the times "I don't know what I would do without you" was put to the test.

Jason Pilarski, our adventures are not nearly as frequent as they used to be… but the possibility the next one may be just around the corner helps keep me ready. You likely have no idea how this impacts my routine and favorably impacts all that I do.

Chad Terry, your example as a business partner and as a personal friend is a life lesson in itself. Thank you for bringing me along for the ride! The best is yet to come . . .

Brett Kathey, our long-ago backyard discussions about great ideas—and what is required to bring them forth—have never left me . . . and they continue to inspire anything new I pursue. Your influence on me remains a gift.

Bob Weinhold, you are my role model for relationship-building, friendship-enhancing, and fellowship. The number of times I drew from your example when leading others and penning this manuscript are too many to count . . . Thank you.

Bret Rachlin, the progress myself and others make through your encouragement, thoughtful conversations, and masterful ability to pull people together is more substantial than you likely consider. Thank you for the consistency and beautiful persistence.

1480, what a journey it has been with all of you! Wow. Thank you for demonstrating how lifelong friendships can so positively impact all that is important in life . . .

Chan Mitchell, your spiritual mentorship and your care for my family is a blessing I do not deserve. Thank you for the example and for so skillfully operationalizing a Mission that matters . . . Oh, the good that comes when we pledge continuous improvement with how we Love God, Love People, and Make a Difference!

ABOUT THE AUTHOR

As a former national-class endurance athlete, Mike Cosentino has more recently put his persistence to work in the retail industry and as the founder of multiple service-sector businesses. His Big Peach Running Co. and Big Peach Ride + Run concepts are among some of the sporting goods industry's most awarded and most successful privately held retailers. He has consulted with hundreds of other business leaders in various channels and has been a keynote speaker for numerous organizations, including Cox Enterprises, Nike, Inc., Sports Distributors of Canada, Centers for Disease Control and Prevention, and the National Sporting Goods Association. Before his entrepreneurial ventures, he was employed by The Coca-Cola Company and the Atlanta Braves National League Baseball Club. He and his wife, Inge, live on a poultry and alpaca rescue farm in Blue Ridge, Georgia. They have two adult children, Campbell and Monica, who remain the inspiration for this book and for much they do.